Feed
The Entrepreneur
In You

Practical Steps on how you can satisfy your hunger of becoming an Entrepreneur at any age, with any qualification at any location through Quick Service Restaurant franchise model.

Feed
The Entrepreneur
In You

Practical Steps on how you can satisfy your hunger of becoming an Entrepreneur at any age, with any qualification at any location through Quick Service Restaurant franchise model.

Sameer Kuncoliekar

Copyright © 2018 Sameer Kuncoliekar

ALL RIGHTS RESERVED. No part of this book may be reproduced or transmitted in any form whatsoever, electronic, or mechanical, including photocopying, recording, or by any informational storage or retrieval system without the expressed written, dated and signed permission from the author.

Title: *Feed the entrepreneur in you*
Author: *Sameer Kuncoliekar*

Publisher: Success Gyan Publishing
A division of Success Gyan India Pvt. Ltd.
Old no:30 New no:24, Bhagirathi Ammal St,
T.Nagar, Chennai-600017
www.sgpublication.com

LIMITS OF LIABILITY or DISCLAIMER OF WARRANTY: The author and publisher of this book have used their best efforts in preparing this material. The author and publisher make no representation or warranties with respect to the accuracy, applicability, or completeness of the contents. They disclaim any warranties (expressed or implied), or merchantability for any particular purpose. The author and publisher shall in no event be held liable for any loss or other damages, including but not limited to special, incidental, consequential, or other damages. The information presented in this publication is compiled from sources believed to be accurate; however, the publisher assumes no responsibility for errors or omissions. The information in this publication is not intended to replace or substitute professional advice. The author and publisher specifically disclaim any liability, loss, or risk that is incurred as a consequence, directly or indirectly, of the use and application of any of the contents of this work.

Success Gyan Publishing bears no responsibility for the accuracy of information on any websites cited and/or used by the author in this book. The inclusion of website addresses in this book does not constitute an endorsement by, or associate Success Gyan Publishing with such sites or the content, products, advertising or other materials presented.

Opinions expressed by the author do not necessarily represent the views and opinions of Success Gyan Publishing. The publisher assumes no liability for any content or opinion expressed by, or through the author.

Printed in India

*This book is dedicated to
H.H. Sri Sri Ravi Shankar
For inspiring me to take up the
challenges in life and to spread knowledge*

*To my father,
Late Kanta R.Kuncoliekar*

*Founder of Ambica
For giving me the freedom to learn about financial
literacy and seeding entrepreneurship in me,
you will always remain in our hearts*

TABLE OF CONTENTS

FOREWORD 11

PREFACE 13

ACKNOWLEDGMENTS 15

CHAPTER 1: INTRODUCTION 19
   My Story 19
   Success is a dream away 22
   If not you, who will? 24
   Why are you here – Your purpose 24
      What you will do, so that people remember you? 25
         The Story of Henry Ford 26
   You are designed for success 29
   Procrastination steals your time 30
   You can lead; it's all about your mindset 32

CHAPTER 2: INTRODUCTION TO BUSINESS 37
   Story 37
   The Pyramid of Financial Freedom 40
   The world is a dynamic market place 46
   Time is precious, use it well! 47
   Myths and Truths about business 48
   Business is a vehicle; use it to achieve your dreams 55
   The Seven functions of business 58
   Intrapreneur and Entrepreneur 72
   In business, an army mindset is stronger than the family mindset .. 74
   You can win the world by serving 75
   Effect of you becoming a businessman to the world 75
   National pride – business as a value addition to society 76

CHAPTER 3 : ALL ABOUT THE RESTAURANT INDUSTRY 79
- Why start business in the restaurant industry? 79
- What are the different formats of restaurants that exist today? 80
- Scope of starting a restaurant...82
- Competition in the Restaurant Industry 84
- The Unorganized Businesses 84
- The Role of Technology 85
- The Impact on Economy...86
- Delivery Services in Restaurants 86
- Impact of online food services on the restaurant business in India ..87
- The rising quick service restaurant industry......................................87
- The Future 88

CHAPTER 4: FEAR OF PEOPLE WHO WANT TO START A BUSINESS..93
- List of fears of people who want to start a business 94

CHAPTER 5: MISTAKES THAT MOST ENTREPRENEURS DO.....103
- List of Mistakes that most entrepreneurs do 103

CHAPTER 6: HOW TO START A BUSINESS..................................115
- Story of Sukhiram 115
- K- Knowledge 117
- S – Skill..120
- T – Technology..122
- P– People..123
- I – Infrastructure 124
- Be a businessman not a busy man..125
- Find a mentor 126
- Keep the goal in mind then start your journey 127

CHAPTER 7: BE FUTURE READY 129
- Energy is success...129
- How to be happy always..132
- The Rocket story...136
- Market trends 139
- Take charge of finances 139

CHAPTER 8: FRANCHISEE – THE ULTIMATE BUSINESS MODEL 143
- The commonly used terms in franchising: 146
- Copy first and then innovate 147
- Types of franchising 148
- Models of Franchising 149
- How did the concept of franchising emerge? 151
- Single Unit and Master Franchise 153
- Other People's Money (OPM) and Other People's Experience (OPE) – Pillars of the franchising world 153
- Myths about franchising 155
- Advantages of a franchisee 160
- Disadvantages of a franchisee 163
- Franchising takes a special type of person: 163
- Common mistakes prospective franchisees might make— and how to avoid them 164
- Business simplified 166
- A ready-made success model 167
- Share your challenges –make value addition 168
- Don't always expect everything from the franchisor 168
- Sell more to earn more 169
- Start small and finish big 169
- The future of franchising in India 170

CHAPTER 9: HOW TO CHOOSE THE RIGHT FRANCHISE 175
- Introduction 175
- Evaluating the Franchisor 177
- Make your decision 181

CHAPTER 10: START SMALL, FINISH BIG 185
- Exclusive interviews with successful franchisor & franchisee's 185
- Gaurav Marya (Franchise India) 186
- Shahnaz Husain (The Shahnaz Husain Group) 191
- Pritam Agarwal (Hello Kids) 202
- Atul Tyagi (Wow Kids) 208
- Asha Arondekar (Tatva Salons) 214
- Kush Khaitan (Sunshine Worldwide School) 217
- Lina Ashar (Kangaroo Kids Preschool) 222

Hazel Siromoni (Maple Bear South Asia) 228
Karan Tanna (Yellow Tie Hospitality) 233
Dheeraj Gupta (Jumboking) 240
Venkatesh Iyer (Goli VadaPav) 246
Chandrika Chalasani (Kangaroo Kids Franchisee) 252
Prasad (Hello Kids Franchisee) 255
Shreya Karkhana (Hello Kids Franchisee) 260
Ritu Handa (Maple Bear Franchisee) 264
Hari Babu (Hello Kids Franchisee) 270
Nagamani Rao (Maple Bear Franchisee) 274
Adhly Rasheed (Kangaroo Kids Franchisee) 279
Jaya Prasad (Maple Bear Franchisee) 284
Rajkumar Kamat, (Executive Director, BNI – Goa Region) 289
Karthikeyan R. Naidu (Jumboking Franchisee) 292
A leader can either lead or bleed 297
What money making activity will I do today? 298
Make your business dashboard 299
Invest wisely in what is required 299
Be happy and hungry 300
Try first with one store - taste success and set others 301
Helicopter ride 306
The story of the Chinese bamboo tree 306

SAMEER KUNCOLIEKAR 309
ABOUT OUR VENTURES 311
RESOURCES 313
BONUS PAGE 315
ABOUT SUCCESS GYAN PUBLISHING 317

FOREWORD

"The SECRET of getting ahead is getting STARTED." – Mark Twain

There are two types of people in the world: entrepreneurs and everyone else. Entrepreneurs are a different breed. They take their destiny in their own hands; they follow their dreams and are willing to do whatever it takes. A lot of people think about becoming entrepreneurs but very few jump into it. You may have thought of various business ideas but never brought them to life. The doubts, fears, and limitations would have stopped you from turning your ideas into a reality. Through this book, the author, Sameer Kuncoliekar, will help you take the best decision of your life—the decision of becoming an entrepreneur. He will provide the steps to make that dream a reality.

What makes Sameer an amazing person to learn from is that he is an amazing student himself. Sameer's journey is truly inspiring. He has been a role model entrepreneur himself who has turned his vision into reality by building a successful business. This book is special because Sameer's desire to make a difference and contribute to entrepreneurship is taking shape through the pages you are going to be turning. As you read this book, remember that you are learning from a person who has been there and done that. He is not an armchair author. Sameer is a dreamer and a doer with a desire and drive to make a difference.

His mission is to handhold aspiring entrepreneurs to set up their businesses, and take this movement PAN India by generating enormous business and employment opportunities along the way. He has included interviews of franchisors as well as their franchisees to give the readers an understanding of the franchise business from both ends, which has never been done before. This makes this book one of a kind. It will benefit readers immensely. Through this book, he is carving the path for anyone with an aspiration to become a successful entrepreneur.

Feed the Entrepreneur in You is a practical book sharing decades of experience that Sameer has accumulated from his journey in the food industry. He has been on field, handled two successful companies, interacted with numerous business houses in the franchise industry, and counseled several business owners through his seminars. This book shares tips on how to start a low investment, high return food business in today's economic scenario. As this captivating book takes readers through a journey of exploring one's dreams, overcoming fears, understanding the industry, and learning about the quickly growing franchise business model, aspiring entrepreneurs or any professional who wants to start his or her own business can be confident about the benefit of reading this book. It will be a crucial part in your process of becoming a success.

Rajiv D Talreja
Bestseller Author - Global Speaker - Business Investor

PREFACE

The ultimate goal of life is to attain *Moksha*, or complete liberation. But while you are living in this planet, you are in a constant state of struggle to achieve spiritual, financial, religious, social, and personal well-being. These are various aspect of human life, woven together to provide absolute harmony. Each of these aspects achieves specific goals, together striving for a well-balanced life.

The spiritual well-being provides peace of mind, while financial independence provides freedom to act. The constitution of religion is aimed at providing education while personal well-being takes care of yourself and your family. In today's world, to achieve most of these things, you need money. In the days of yore, when barter system was prevalent, the transactions were simpler. But with the advent of monetary system, the complications began. From release of a birth certificate to filing of a death certificate, money feeds the entire system, making it the fluid running in the social veins for sustenance and growth.

Due to insufficient money we land up to stage where we have to make choices, either this or that, either money or health, either relationship or money. This creates imbalance in life. We live life of mediocrity. We decide either good education for child or vacation for the family, either financial security or freedom. We think that both cannot be possible. We live a life of making choices, either this or that. This way we cannot live life fully nor do we explore our self fully

So as we strive for excellence, financial independence and growth, the doors of entrepreneurship seem to be the most rewarding. Many of us have a silent desire to be a business owner. But either through personal failures, mistakes or fears, we don't take that step that can transform our life. Through this book, I have tried to break some myths and highlight some common fears and mistakes that bind the entrepreneurs together. "You are not alone." When you have this confidence, I am sure you will move forward with the zeal of a true business owner!! Life is not about either this or that; it's about living fully with both. This is possible with entrepreneurship. This book is about the guidelines to live life fully, where you explore ways to take control of all the aspects of life. This book will help you to increase your capacity to handle your financial problems a thousand fold.

This book can be a guiding star for those who are exploring the idea of entrepreneurship, but confused on where to start. It will give you tips and clarify your concepts, giving you suggestions and tools to equip you to be a great entrepreneur. Thank you for choosing this book. Choosing this book indicates your thirst for learning and practicing the tools, methods, and suggestions in this book. The journey of a thousand miles starts with this single step.

This book could be of interest to those who are already entrepreneurs and to those who want to learn more about entrepreneurship and explore new opportunities.

This book also reinforces the POWER OF DREAMS. This amazing power has the capacity to transform lives. A simple sales guy can turn into a millionaire or a tea seller can run the country. I always believe "Aim for the stars and you'll always reach the moon." It is this thought that inspired me to write this book. It is a composition of my experiences and lifelong learning's that can help you recreate my success and bigger.

Like every great entrepreneur this world has seen, this book also teaches you to **Think Big**, achieve bigger goals, and finally give back to the society to whom you eventually owe your success. It teaches you to be grateful and socially responsible. This book will give you insights on how the franchise model has boomed in India, and how it is the best way to start a business today. There is a section in this book, where interviews of some top franchisors and their successful franchisees are included, which is rich in knowledge and gives you a lot of insights about the industry. This book also lays the foundation.

I am inspired by the extraordinary ordinary people who have created remarkable success stories, which form the basic purpose of this book—to share their ideas, experiences, and lives. Through this, I would love to create more entrepreneur stories with you.

This book also lays the foundation of financial education, which is needed by every individual who is looking for financial freedom.

ACKNOWLEDGMENTS

Writing this book has been a remarkable experience. I met so many people from varied backgrounds as we built various chapters, and they have taught me so much. Writing this book has enriched me beyond my expectation. I would like to express my gratitude to the many people who helped me during this journey of writing the book. First and foremost I would like to thank the world spiritual leader H.H. Sri Ravi Shankar for guiding me toward spiritual upliftment, and giving a lot of knowledge on life. I would sincerely thank Coach Rajiv Talreja and his team for helping me organize myself and my business and taking me one step closer toward writing my own book.

I am grateful to be surrounded by such wonderful people in my life, a big thank you to my Art of Living family, for providing me with the many opportunities, support and inspiring me to lead at various fronts. I have to mention my role model Anthony Robbins for the major influence that his book "Awaken the Giant" instilled in me, which changed the course of my life forever. I would also thank another teacher Robert Kiyosaki, for giving me in-depth knowledge of the financial life of an individual, through his Rich Dad, Poor Dad book series. I am grateful to the BNI head of Goa, Mr. Rajkumar Kamat, for his help and teaching about networking. I would like to thank all my masters for imparting precious knowledge. I would also thank all Franchisors and franchisees for spending your valuable time with me and for sharing your valuable experiences in this book. Sincere thanks to Sandeep Maheshwari, who has taught me to contribute to the society.

I would like to acknowledge the team of Success Gyan Publishing for helping me with this book and their guidance throughout the journey. Thank you for guiding me in building this book page by page.

I want to thank my family, specially my wife Supriya who supported me, went through my drafts and encouraged me, and my son Vedhant for being there always. I would like to thank Egina Roncon, for helping me in putting down my thoughts and bringing the words to life in the book. A special thanks to Divya Meena for reaching out to various franchisors and franchisees relentlessly to schedule interviews with them. I would also thank Amey Hegde for always encouraging me in my endeavors and guiding me when required. I would like to thank my team (at Ambica) for the dedication in their work, and the support and participation given in working toward achieving the company's goal; this is what inspires me to be a better leader every day. I take this opportunity to thank all our business associates. We are sure to grow bigger and better as a team.

A thank you to all those who gave their support, talked things over, read, wrote, offered comments, allowed me to quote their remarks, and assisted in editing and proofreading.

learning
schoolin

CHAPTER 1

INTRODUCTION

"Success is measured by you SMILE, and most importantly on how much you can CONTRIBUTE to others."

After graduation, I aspired to enter into the family business, but when I looked at myself I realized that I was not confident about my abilities to do business. I felt that I was lacking something. So I decided to pursue an internship in a Chartered Accounting Firm. It was during this internship that I realized that there exists a huge gap in the current education system versus the practical financial world. This led to the start of my quest to gain the required knowledge.

I would work half a day, while my friend would work for the other half for a stipend of INR300 each which was sufficient to cover our fuel expenses. I interned for 1 ½ years, which laid the foundation for a strong and confident backing in accounting. I was analyzing the financial statements of different types of people, NRIs, landlords, investors, business owners, self-employed, and the working professionals. It was during this time that I realized the direct correlation between financial status and making money.

After about 2 years, equipped with practical knowledge, I finally joined the family business and started marketing poultry products in the Goan market. Success followed within a short time span and my confidence grew. I was well recognized and respected, and people started acknowledging my work and skills. I have always treated my customers as my family members and focused on providing value to them. I have always believed in building lasting relationships with my customers based on mutual trust. This attitude and approach of mine led to business reaching new peaks. I had a very hands-on approach to the business and would work from 7.00a.m. to 8.00p.m., driving the company vehicle (truck) and delivering products to the customers. This also helped me build a personal rapport with my customer base and made me aware of the ground realities and challenges of my business.

But I also realized that these daily transactional operations were consuming a lot of my time and energy. I was not spending enough time and effort to take the business to the next level. I then resolved to focus on expanding the business and decided to purchase a shop. I put my entire emphasis into standardizing the operations, attracting new customers, innovating, and putting systems in place to make the business scalable. I hired people to take care of the daily operations and meet the delivery schedules of customers.

The new shop was generating good money and everything was going smoothly leading me to believe that I am successful now. However, I still had a nagging feeling that something was lacking in my life. Even though I was happy with the money I was making I still wanted to do something for the community. Around this time I joined the spiritual movement by H.H. Sri Sri Ravi Shankar, called the Art of Living. I believed that through this movement I will be able to explore additional areas where I can actively contribute to the society. I started volunteering for the courses and began undertaking leadership roles in community development projects. It is here that I learnt how to lead organizations and effectively get things done from others. It has always been my dream to contribute toward the betterment of the society, and this passion has been my motivation that will remain even after I die. I always believe in solving problems permanently.

I would like to share an incident which happened in my life that made me embark on the journey of community service. I received an SMS mentioning that someone needed blood in a hospital that was very close to my office. The SMS did not mention any contact number so I called my friend Rajeshwar who had also received the message from his friend but did not have the contact number of the originator. I kept on pursuing the contact number by calling multiple people and after five such additional calls I was finally able to get in touch with a lady Ms. Souza, a social activist. The requirement of blood was for a priest known to her who was undergoing an open heart surgery in the hospital and needed an urgent O+ve blood donor. Ms. Souza requested me to visit the hospital immediately to donate blood. I went and promptly donated my blood. Many well-wishers complimented me for the deed but the satisfaction achieved from helping someone was what gave me immense gratification. A few days later, the same lady contacted again seeking help for other people who needed blood. With the help of my friends I began organizing blood donors for many such people as my office was very close to the hospital.

It was 3 months after this incident that something happened that left a long lasting impact on my life. I was called to donate blood in the hospital, where the patient was a nun. As I entered the room, I saw her talking on the phone with a priest. On seeing me, she said "Father, Father one angel has just come." These words had a profound impact on me, and I was touched emotionally and mentally. They gave me a sense of fulfillment and the feeling still gives me goose bumps. I realized the importance of donating blood and touching the lives of others.

Gradually with time my existing database of possible blood donors got exhausted, and it was a challenge to help people in need of blood. I felt helpless and dejected as people were suffering and I was unable to help them. Plenty of people do blood donation, and the blood banks are full but there is still a dearth of fresh blood in case of emergency. Often, blood banks have excess blood which is not utilized and has to be eventually thrown out. The crux of the issue at hand is there is no dearth of patients in need of blood or of donors who are willing to donate their blood. But there is no single efficient communication channel connecting the recipient and the contributor at the right time.

I mulled over this question on what can be done to reduce or eliminate this gap. I was constantly on the lookout for a solution. On 23rd September 2013, while performing a group meditation activity, I had an insight into the answer to the dilemma in my mind. I decided to start a website which could list the possible blood donors in my city Margao. I further thought why limit myself only to my city and why not expand to the state and eventually why not to the entire country. It was with this thought process that the blue print of this social project was firmly embedded in my mind. I confidently stood in front of a group of 80 people and announced that we are going to launch a social website where blood donors and blood recipients would be able to connect. Similarly the website will also allow blood donors to register on the website and donate blood whenever required.

The reason for making a formal pronouncement of the idea before the group was to mitigate the possible hesitation in case I did not take action immediately. The idea would then remain a nonstarter and only in my mind. I received an overwhelming response from the group with everybody praising the initiative. I was still skeptical about my ability to successfully execute this idea. I reached out to one of the associate volunteers and we penned down the idea along with the necessary steps to commence the project. This is how **Save Life India** project was conceived (you can log on to www.savelifeindia.org, or you can give a missed call on 8905 100 200; you can help someone in need by passing this information as well).

There were many hurdles that I faced during the inception of this project. Coming from a nontechnical background, I had little to no knowledge on how websites or databases work. There was scarcity of funds as well as absence of a team, both of which were other major hindrances. I was also unsure of the direction to follow but my heart was filled with positivity about my dream and my passion to contribute toward the well-being of society. **Save Life India** is an initiative that will be remembered long after my lifetime.

Taking the first steps toward bringing this project toward fruition, I started approaching different people. I received varied reactions from these interactions; while many mocked the idea, there was also encouragement from others. Four members from the Art of Living organization expressed interest in actively contributing toward the project. This positive development instilled a new sense of vigor in me. The journey toward the launch of the website was full of difficulties with extensive research and development involved along with gaining knowledge and developing the requisite skills to manage an online portal. The journey finally culminated on 4th June 2014 when we were able to successfully launch the project in India. This pet project of mine which I have truly cherished has become very popular and proved extremely beneficial for a lot of people. Through this project we were able to save lives of thousands of people across India. We received an overwhelming response from people from day one with many joining as donors fascinated by the idea of helping others and making a difference. H.H. Sri Sri Ravi Shankar himself launched this project. He rightly said "This is a very necessary project for today's society."

It has always been my motto that corporates contribute to the community through CSR (Corporate Social Responsibility), but it is also our responsibility as an individual to contribute actively toward the community through PSR (Personal Social Responsibility). I am proud to state that my PSR has been one of the greatest achievements of my life. It is often said that if you like something with all your heart, the whole world works toward fulfilling your desire. Similarly if you pour your heart and passion into your business nobody can stop you from succeeding.

Success is a dream away

"The whole SECRET of a successful life is to find out what is one's DESTINY to do, and then do it." –Henry Ford

---

a. Dreams give you a purpose

Successful and content people recognize the power of dreams, and are always working toward achieving them. Truth be told, a majority of history's greatest accomplishments are fueled by the expressions of individual or collective dreams for something better. The dreams manifest themselves into reality through hard work and dedication but all of this comes to a naught if you don't dream in the first place.

Unless you dream, you will not achieve is the maxim which I have always believed in.

Dreams are the source of energy that propel you toward achieving success, helping you and others lead an improved and happier life. Dreams provide a sense of direction and enable you to create a structure for realizing them. They provide motivation and a sense of purpose in life and inspire you to scale greater heights and keep on growing. Lack of dreams is frequently associated with complacency and stagnation. Like the common saying goes "An empty mind is the devil's workshop."

I strongly believe that dreams promote positivity in your life by boosting your mind, body, and spirit.

So I say, Dream Big! All you need is your thinking, and thinking is free! Think big and dream big!

b. Achieving dreams gives us a sense of accomplishment

I have always got a sense of fulfillment and satisfaction on accomplishing each of my dream or goal. This has also raised my confidence levels significantly. It has also given me the zest to dream bigger, giving life a whole new meaning.

Hard work is the key to this sense of fulfillment and accomplishment. It cannot be invoked by other people's actions or activities. The fruits of one's own hardwork is always sweet! It is also something that is not stimulated by chance encounters.

"If you don't build your DREAM, someone will hire you to build theirs. CHOICE is yours."

---

c. Dreams keep us going

The secret to a successful living is caring and giving. The true sense of living is to chase your dreams for when you achieve them; your success serves as a source of hope and inspiration for others. This positivity then resonates with multiple people, making the society at large a better and happier place. This can be one of the greatest contributions that you can make. Courage of conviction is strengthened when you passionately chase your dream. You tend to forget all the negativity in life and start focusing on the positive things to pursue your dreams. You take the obstacles in your path as a challenge and strive to overcome them to reach your goal. Dreams have the capability of turning you into an unstoppable force.

As they say, *"Some people dream of success, while others get up every morning and make it happen."*

If not you, who will?

"Successful and unsuccessful people do not VARY greatly in their ABILITIES. They vary in their DESIRES to reach their potential." – John Maxwell

---

Life is a choice where you can either choose to become a bystander or a leader. As a leader, you can help create a better world for everybody around us by seizing the opportunity and create something that impacts the life of others. You can offer a beacon of hope to the followers and show them the path.

Great people who have left a successful legacy behind have always been those who have taken the responsibility of their own future. They have always focused on the purpose to understand this beautiful world and how they could contribute toward the growth of self, their families, friends, society, nation, and even the environment. Rather than being a passive observer, they have actively taken the mantle to create opportunities for success. Taking ownership and responsibility for growth nurtures your creative thinking and allows us to look for ways and means of triumph. The hope for a better tomorrow lies on our own shoulders. We have been given the power and ability to be the agents of change for the communities in which we live in. We have the enormous potential of becoming the future leaders and can shape our tomorrow only by proactively acting today.

Why are you here – Your purpose

I believe that in life the following two goals can give us a life of contentment and peace -

1. To gain knowledge
2. To spread love

Use the knowledge as a tool to gain information that will help us upgrade or evolve in our lives as well as the lives of those around us. Learning is a continuous process and a tool that helps us to keep on growing and evolving in life. A true student is always humble with an attitude to learn and grow.

In my opinion, the three key aspects to learning are:

- Start with " I don't know"
- Trust the person who is teaching you
- Have conviction in the tools and techniques used in teaching.

The three key elements in a learning session are the student, the teacher, and the subject of learning. You must teach to pass your knowledge for the gain and benefit of others as the next logical step. This way you strengthen your own capacity for learning and improve your interactions with different people.

As our father of the nation, Gandhiji wisely said, *"An eye for an eye will make the whole world blind."* In today's world, the biggest strength is to have an empathetic, caring attitude toward one another. An ability to forgive and forget and contribute positively to someone's life gives an immense sense of satisfaction. We should always infuse this love and passion into everything that we do, our surroundings, our relationships, our work, our life, and the whole world. This is the only way we will be able to make the world a truly beautiful place to live.

"The good life is one INSPIRED by love and GUIDED by knowledge."
– Bertrand Russell

What you will do, so that people remember you?

I would always love to create a lasting legacy for which people will always remember me. It is my goal to create something of value and present it to the world.

We should always strive to create an inspirational story for others to emulate and make them want to follow in your footsteps. It's been a century since the Industrial Revolution, but Henry Ford will always be remembered as the father of Industrial Revolution. He has built an eternal legacy with his contribution of the development of the mass production line which has revolutionized the automotive industry.

The Story of Henry Ford

Henry Ford profoundly altered the way of living by providing a vehicle that immensely extended people's range of movement within a short span of time. In doing so he laid the foundation of the 20th century. The mass production assembly line became a permanent fixture across industries ranging from photographs to hamburgers. Standardization of the work resulted in the creation of high wage low skilled jobs facilitating the movement of Americans from the farms to the cities. This also resulted in immigration of people across cities and added to the burgeoning of the middle class leading to an improvement in the quality of life for the people and society.

The moving assembly line idea of Henry Ford was a massive breakthrough and a turning stone for the Industrial Age. Henry Ford did not let failure of the previous attempts deter him and at the age of 40 years he had successfully built a powerful, affordable, and reliable mass produced car. With the help of his moving assembly line, this self-taught pioneer with an eighth-grade education was producing more than half the cars in the USA by 1919. The mass production line also resulted in lowering the economic costs of automobiles automatically expanding the available market for business growth.

Ford was born in Michigan on July 30, 1863 in a farming community. There were early signs suggesting an entrepreneurial streak promising a successful, powerful, and famous future. He would gather other boys to build basic water wheels and steam engines. He gained knowledge about steam engines by befriending the people who ran these steam engines. He taught himself to fix watches to gain knowledge on the intricacies of machine design. He demonstrated a great mechanical aptitude and leadership skills. He was a hands-on learner and would keep on learning through a trial and error approach. These qualities laid the foundation stones of his success story.

In 1879 he left the farm to become an apprentice at the Michigan Car Company, a manufacturer of railroad cars in Detroit. Over the next two and a half years he kept moving between jobs seizing every opportunity to learn and gain knowledge. He returned home in 1882, but his heart was not interested in doing farming. He was always driven by the desire to work on his own rather than work for somebody else. Ford was married in 1888 and moved to Detroit to join Edison Electric Illuminating Company as a night engineer. It was here that he learned a great deal about electricity even though he had no background and through sheer determination and hard work rose to the position of a Chief engineer by 1896. His curiosity and interests pushed him to work in barns and small shops to build horseless carriages. Aptly aided by a team of friends, he was able to build the first self-propelled vehicle in 1896 called the Quadricycle. It was characterized by four wire wheels similar to big bicycle wheels and was steered with a tiller similar to the one used in a boat. The vehicle also had only two forward speeds and no option of reverse.

Ford's innovative ability and the ability to convince other people to complete his vision resulted in the creation of a second car in 1898. He had an innate knack of persuading people to buy into his idea which would truly become a game changer for the world. He used this ability to convince a group of businessmen to provide financial assistance in setting up a company to make and sell horseless carriages. As they say the greater the risk, the greater is the reward. Ford had no prior experience of running a business and his philosophy of learning by trial and error was bound to fail. His first venture as a businessman failed as did his second venture into the business world. Undeterred by failure Ford took it up as a challenge and began building and driving racing cars. This venture caught the attention of financial backers and on June 16, 1903 he incorporated his third automotive venture, Ford Motor Company.

Ford knew that the success of the company was dependent on the team that he built. He hired a core of young and able men who believed in his vision and shared his passion to make Ford Motor Company as one of the world's largest industrial enterprises. The company's first car was called Model A which was subsequently followed by a variety of other models with an improvement in performance each time. In 1907 Ford's four-cylinder Model N, which was sold at $600 became the best-selling car in the country and pushed the company's name to the forefront of everybody's mind. Ford's innovative mind would not allow him to rest on his laurels, and he wanted to achieve an even greater vision of providing a better and cheaper car for the masses. The determination to achieve his vision gave birth to Model T, introduced on October 1, 1908.

Model T was highlighted by its ability to handle rough roads and ease of maintenance. It turned out to be a game changer and achieved stupendous success. This in turn presented a fresh set of challenge for Ford. The demand for the model was so high that it was becoming difficult to satisfy it with the limited production capacity available in the plant. While most people would be happy with selling all they could make, Ford wanted to make all that he could sell. This required investment into a bigger factory and augmented capacity which the company did by moving into a bigger plant in Highland Park in 1910. Bigger plant inevitably meant increased costs, but Henry wanted to increase production while lowering costs. He decided to adapt concepts from a variety of industries from watch makers, gun makers, and bicycle makers to meat packers. He and his team customized those ideas with a mixture of their own ideas to develop the moving assembly line for the plant. This was a game changer for the company and modernized the automotive industry.

It is important to learn from this story that Henry Ford neither invented the automobile nor did he invent the assembly line. His genius lies in the fact that he was able to adapt the assembly line concept to mass production of automobiles to manufacture cars at significantly lower prices than the competition. In doing so he went a step ahead of his competition and at the same time opened a whole new customer base of people who could earlier not afford the high price cars. Ford's contribution in streamlining the assembly line for cars is a picture-perfect example of just how powerfully an assembly line can be utilized for mass producing products. He was single handedly responsible for converting the automobile from a utility of the rich into a car that would be affordable and available to the multitude of the masses. In doing so he has positively impacted the industry in the 20th century which continues to affect our lives till this very day.

Henry's main contribution over the next decade was to make automobile manufacturing more efficient and less costly. Some of the methods employed by him to achieve that included adding an automated conveyor belt and training each worker to perform a single task. Ensuring that the workers were trained in a single task, he ensured repeatability of tasks thereby improving worker efficiency and work quality. With this he was able to unleash the power of mass production.

Henry was a person with a dream and vision. He excelled in utilizing new ideas sometimes his own and at other times someone else's. He believed in promoting those ideas till they became a part of the accepted reality of our everyday lives. This particular ability requires the person to be willing to take risks and have immense confidence in his own ability. Henry Ford had all these ingrained qualities but it took him many years to realize their full potential.

What made Henry Ford tick can be best summarized by a small incident that happened when he was 13 years old. He had received a pocket watch for his birthday. While most boys of that age would be busy enjoying their birthday present, he proceeded to take apart the pocket watch in order to learn how the watch functioned. He was not only interested in how things worked but also more importantly interested in learning why things did not work. He was curious of everything around him and opportunities at every corner. He was a businessman in the truest sense. He explored innovative forms of education, took inspiration from the past, saw opportunities for the future, and believed in technology as an enabler for improving people's lives. He did not envision technology as just a source of profits but rather viewed it as a tool to harness fresh ideas and, ultimately make a difference to his community.

"If you do not want to be forgotten as soon as you are dead, either write something WORTH READING or do something WORTH WRITING."
– Benjamin Franklin

You are designed for success

Success is no fluke and cannot be achieved by chance. Success is a result of hard work, perseverance, learning, sacrifice and above all a passion for what you are doing. If you do not have your heart in the work that you are doing, you are never going to taste success. You must have an inherent desire to lead a better, happier, and healthier life. Success means creating something that empowers customers, employees, and community as a whole. We pride ourselves on our ability to mold and transform as human beings. It is this very quality of ours that enables us to convert ourselves into someone who is capable to achieve success. Blind luck plays no part in it.

Success is within every person's grasp. All that is required is to reach out with both hands and grab the opportunities that come your way. If opportunities are not available, you need to create them. You need to embark on the journey that will help you achieve your dreams and goals. The only obstacle standing between you and success is to move out of your comfort zone and put in the efforts to achieve your objectives. Most people, however, are handicapped because they will always choose security over growth. They are unwilling to trade the existing comfort and stability for the pain and uncertainty that success demands.

> *"Either you will step FORWARD into growth and achieve success, or you will step back into SAFETY and be a failure."*

Remaining successful means mastering the art of constantly pushing yourself to become a better version of yourself. It often involves complete transformation of all aspects of your life including relationships, finances, health, and personal habits. The constant need to evolve and be better is what distinguishes a successful person. Unless you are willing to adopt change you will not be able to achieve greatness in life.

> *"Success is an ATTITUDE, not just a PHENOMENON."*

Once your mindset is ready for success you are in the advantageous position of grabbing growth opportunities with both hands whenever they arise. You develop a sort of sixth sense for development situations and are better placed to exploit the opportunities presented to you. People do not succeed in life, if they are not ready to embrace change and are not ready to put in the hard work and sweat to achieve the goals.

Procrastination steals your time

Time is an extremely cherished commodity primarily because time lost can never be recovered. Be it a peon, prime minister or president, everybody has only 24 hours in a day. What sets successful people apart is in how they utilize the time available with them. A normal sleep time of 8 hours and day to day activity of 8 hours leaves with 8 hours at our disposal to invest in and take the next big leap of growth. There are plenty of distractions in our life and how effectively we are able to utilize these 8 hours essentially determines how successful we are going to be.

Due to the limitation of time, prioritization becomes of paramount importance. If we spend all our time on daily activities instead of focusing on the important ones we will only end up procrastinating our dreams. Whenever we put our mind and focus on something it naturally grows. So too is true of our dreams. If you are willing to put the time and effort for your dreams, rest assured you will be able to realize them. Don't expect perfection in action. Progress is key.

Procrastination kills your dreams, desires, and motivations in a slow but steady manner. Putting off important tasks will result in lost time of minutes, hours, and eventually days. One fine day you wake up and wonder where has the time gone? When you ask yourself this question procrastination has won the battle.

Procrastinating is one of the easiest ways to destroy your dreams and inspirations completely. It also allows complacency to set in and you become lethargic and comfortable in your current situation. The drive to succeed slowly starts fading into oblivion. Every individual has dreams and goals that he would like to accomplish. Dreams are not realized instantaneously but ask for persistence and resolve. Every small step that you have taken in the process toward your dream is another step closer to fulfilling it. The situation for taking the step toward your dream may never be ideally right but remember the journey of 1000 steps always begins with the first step. Step up and get moving toward accomplishing your target.

People tend to procrastinate because they do not want to move out of their comfort zones. It makes you believe that you have all the time in the world and there is really no need to rush. This is a falsifying state of affairs that your mind is coerced into by procrastination. Hour by hour, day by day, it slowly steals your time without your knowledge. By the time realization of lost time dawns upon you it could already be too late. Someone once said, *"Lost money can be recovered, mistakes can be rectified, but time gone is lost eternally."Think about your past. How so many years have already passed. We have only few more years to live. We are temporary here, may be for the next 10, 20, or 50 years. Then we have to leave this world.*

"You can live a life of a VICTIM or a life of freedom, CHOICE is yours."

You can lead; it's all about your mindset

A mindset is defined by the attitudes, beliefs, and expectations that you hold. These forms the basis of who you are. Your mindset determines your approach to problems and your ability to interpret situations and affects the decisions and actions. Our aim in life should be to identify and create a productive mindset that results in Leadership. The foundation of leadership is a determined by a commitment to lead, perform, and succeed. It involves taking total accountability and willingness to make a difference.

Always remember *"Nothing is impossible. The word itself says I'm possible."*

So what are the defining characteristics of a true leadership mindset?

1. **Visionary**

One of the most critical tasks associated with being a leader is setting a clear and precise vision for the team. This involves helping them understand and accept the future state of the organization. An effective leader will inspire the employees to perform their duties by explaining the vision and the importance of their roles in influencing the outcome. This makes the team work dedicatedly toward the vision, due to the confidence and trust in the leader. A leader should have long-term vision and short-term execution plan, but we tend to do the opposite. As we feel comfortable in achieving short-term goals.

"Motivation is SHORT LIVED, as it comes from an outside source, INSPIRATION is more effective and is long lasting because it comes from WITHIN."

---

2. **Awareness in every activity**

A mark of a good leader is someone who can always see the larger picture and greater good. The ability and willingness to foresee every small detail to understand the working behind it, eventually defines what you become in the future. This ability helps you recognize opportunities that others may often overlook and makes you standout in a crowd.

3. **Inspiring and contributing to others**

Being a leader means you should have the ability to motivate and inspire your team to collaborate. You should be able to grasp the needs of your team, the problems that they are facing and find solutions to make a difference in their life. This will ensure their total commitment and dedication to your leadership. The morale of the team is lifted and they work cohesively toward a common goal. Leaders also have to ensure each member is pulling their weight and ensure adequate training and guidance is provided whenever required. Equipping them with the right tools and knowledge will ensure they perform their tasks to the fullest extent. They will be willing to walk the extra mile for you.

"A leader is CAPABLE of putting himself in others shoes and SEEING their point of view."

---

4. Take more roles

It is said that leaders always lead from the front. A good way to demonstrate your leadership skills is to take on additional responsibility. Stepping out of your comfort zone is the only way to ensure you learn something new. It will help you get noticed and earn your team's trust.

5. Discipline

Discipline is important to succeed in life. Developing and maintaining discipline in your life is of critical importance in order to be an effective leader as well as be an inspirational role model for others. People will always judge your capacity to lead by the amount of discipline you display in all your activities. Start from implementing good habits at home, like waking up early, getting daily exercise, and work your way up from there.

6. Keep learning

The best path to becoming a good leader is to maintain your thirst for knowledge. It keeps your mind sharp and your skills fresh. It helps you prepare for new challenges that may come your way. Learning to give and receive feedback is critically important quality which a good leader must possess. The defining characteristic of a worthy leader is his ability to facilitate, not preach.

7. Create more leaders

Great leaders do not believe in creating mere followers, but in creating more leaders and providing them the freedom and authority to grow into leadership roles. This approach helps many others find and create their own destinies. Good leaders revel in mentoring, coaching, and supporting their team. A leader inspires challenges and always expects the best from his team.

Negative leaders on the other hand focus on creating followers who have no scope for growth and can never achieve success. This type of leaders sees their team as a threat for their leadership. Successful organizations are those in which the owner creates other leaders, in the form of the heads of departments to truly make the teams truly effective.

8. Lead by example

"A leader leads by EXAMPLE, he does not just order. He does it first so that others can EMULATE."

People always try and emulate their leaders. It is important that you set the right example for your team. You need to follow the values that you expect from your team. Employees pick up positive cues from their leaders and when they see you doing things the way you want others to do, they will be willing to follow you whole heartedly. You will thus have a better shot at enforcing the right attitude at the workplace. A good leader should always "Walk the Talk." Leaders guide the team by pointing them in the right direction, but it is the team that shoulders the load. A leader can earn credibility only by working collaboratively with the team and sharing the credit for any success.

"Leadership can be measured only when there is CHAOS. If everything is going smoothly, a leader has NOTHING to do, no role to play."

Now let me take you through an interesting journey that gives you a glimpse in the world of business. In the forthcoming chapters, we will speak on various aspects of running a business, the fears, mistakes, success stories, and failures. It's going to be breathtaking!

Scan this QR code to get the FREE Declarations that are a powerful self-talk. The most successful people in life have an empowering way to communicate with themselves. With these declarations you can practice positive self-talk throughout your day, and you will begin to realize more favorable rewards in life.

Or visit www.sameerindia.com/declarations

CHAPTER 2

INTRODUCTION TO BUSINESS

After completing a business seminar for group of entrepreneurs, the very next morning, I decided to visit a very serene and beautiful remote beach in my home state of Goa. It was a beautiful and sunny day. The goal was to begin the exciting journey of writing my book surrounded by the calm and breathtaking view. Cola beach is one of the many unexplored beaches in Goa with its exotic beauty and tranquility sure to blow your mind away. The cool breeze and beauty of the coconut trees will rejuvenate you with energy. A distinctive feature of this beach is the pure blue lagoon, formed by the union of the river and the Arabian Sea.

It was a typical work day for my business, but I was unperturbed as I knew I had created a leadership team who will ensure the business functions are running smoothly in my absence. A sense of satisfaction engulfs me, for I have been able to set up an efficient system to facilitate smooth running of my business.

I had booked a cottage overlooking the sea and spent time admiring the creativity of Mother Nature. I was totally immersed in observing every element present in my surrounding, trying to understand the working behind it all. After a lot of thinking and meditation, I began to pen down my thoughts accompanied by soft sound of waves, a cool breeze, and the magnificent sea ahead of me.

As I was engrossed in observing the sea and the lagoon an important realization dawned upon me. There is a vast difference between working at a job and running a business. An analogy of the same was right in front of my eyes with the job being represented by the river and the business by the sea. If you observe the river closely you will notice it flows at an even pace. You get a sense of satisfaction when you see a calm river but it does not fill your heart with excitement as the smooth flow becomes monotonous after a while. The sea on the other hand with its war breeze, soft sounds of waves, and the movement of the waves provides you with a thrill of exhilaration. The sea brings out the adventurer in you calling you to explore the vast depths and enjoy the bigger waves. You feel an adrenaline rush as you delve deeper into the sea with the sense of unknown bringing out the explorer in you.

As a sea is characterized by a high tide and low tide, a similar resemblance is applicable to the business as well. In a business there are always highs and lows, the rise and fall of demand, rise in competition, and the impact of economic factors. The key factor for success is to be proactive and not reactive. This is where knowledge plays a crucial role. A river on the other hand does not experience high or low tide but goes through periods of droughts and floods. Similarly in a job employees are laid off in case of no work and overburdened in case of excess work. While a job is inherently insecure by nature, a business will never run out of opportunities akin to a sea never running out of water.

Rivers are easily polluted as they are typically closer to factories, farms, civilization and so on, but the sea on the other hand does not get polluted very easily. It pushes back the pollutants to the shore especially during high tide. In a similar way, the risks and problems in jobs are plenty where one can easily lose his job if something goes wrong. Businesses on the other hand are much more resilient to issues and problems. A lot of times it is seen that people like to visit the sea but are hesitant to wade into the water. Correspondingly people are excited to start a business but don't follow up on their ideas due to hesitance and fear. It is important to have determination and faith in your dreams to achieve success. While success may not be instantaneous, once you embark on the journey with commitment you will definitely be successful.

The sea is characterized by high waves only in the initial stages. Once you wade into the deeper part of the sea, there are no waves but only calm water. Similarly once you cross the initial hurdles of the business by attaining a level of stability, knowledge and a good team, you will experience only calmness. You have truly begun your journey toward financial freedom. As an entrepreneur you are expected to play the below three roles abbreviated as GOD.

G (Generator) – the early stage where you are creating or generating the business

O (Operator) – the middle stage where you are essentially managing the business

D (Destroyer) – the last stage where you are transitioning from one level to a higher level or evolving to the next level.

As a business man you should be in possession of all three qualities. In Hinduism, they say Brahma, Vishnu, and Mahesh are the three Gods. Lord Brahma is the creator, Lord Vishnu is the manager and protector, while Lord Shiva is the destroyer who transforms the world to the next level. You become what you study: education will teach you to become a better engineer, doctor, attorney, accountant, etc. They never teach you to manage your own finances. We need to take responsibility, to take financial education to manage our own finances. The problem is people do not focus on their own financial wealth creation. We think making more money will solve problems, and we end up working more and more. Financial education is must for each individual. We have seen many examples where people who won lottery or jackpot becoming bankrupt in less than ten years. We have also seen doctors and engineers earning lakhs of rupees and still struggling every month. Financial education teaches you financial discipline. You might end up spending your entire life working as an employee for someone else's business making him rich. The rich stays rich by becoming business owners rather than employees. How many times have you encountered the phrases: I wish I had more money? I wish I would get a promotion. On first sight these might sound as sensible ideas but they are missing the important aspect of looking at income generating avenues like running a business.

The middle class in our country is still risk averse and hence cling to a job and a regular monthly paycheck. What they fail to realize is when you work for someone you will always be an employee and never the owner. My inspiration behind writing this book is to encourage people to explore various financial options available. Once the foundation is strong, there are millions of ways to generate wealth and achieve your goal. You can achieve them by using simple tools which I want the readers to be aware of.

1. The Pyramid of Financial Freedom

Our lifestyle is essentially determined by the amount of cash we earn. We spend our whole life trying to make money; we fail to tap into the vast avenues available for generating wealth. If you want to achieve your financial goals you need to be aware about the different types of incomes and be mindful of the pros and cons of each approach. Unfortunately our education system does not emphasize these facts. This is the reason why majority of the people lack financial knowledge which is extremely relevant to life. This is the tool we can equip our children to make their lives prosperous and bright. Let us take a quick peek into the Pyramid of Financial Freedom.

The Pyramid of Financial Freedom

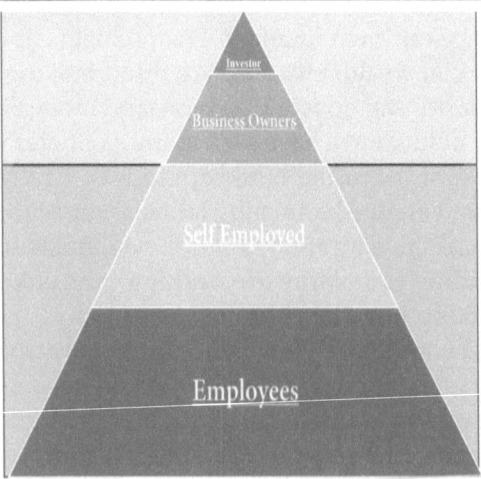

As indicated by the graph of the financial freedom pyramid, there are four levels into which people fall into: Employees, Self-Employed, Business Owners, and Investors.

Employee– This is the person who earns money by working in a job for someone else. He has almost no leverage and the earning is limited. The working hours are restricted and hence the income which is dependent on the working hours is naturally inadequate. The job is without security, and stability is reliant on external uncontrollable circumstances. You are essentially living month to month, and the only option to earn more money is to work longer hours or work for another company that pays better. You do not generate any passive income in this scenario. Employee is a part of the system.

Self-employed (you own a job) – Self-employed category involves professionals or small business owners whose income is directly proportional to their effort. Typical examples of this section include professionals like lawyers, doctors, architects, etc. Small business owners fall in this category as well, for e.g. shopkeepers and so on. They have flexibility in their work hours and income rises and falls as the efforts put in rise and fall. The moment they stop working the income stops. They think that they are the owner of the business but in reality the business owns them. They have more freedom than employees but almost no free time. These people are mostly had seen firefighting. Most entrepreneurs who start businesses end up in the trap of being self-employed. They are a system.

Business owner (you own a system and people work for you) – These are smart and intelligent people who leverage the system and strategies by building business and hiring employees. A large portion of their time is spent in building and organizing the business to bring it as a self-sustaining system. The income generation in this case is dependent on the efforts put by your employees. There is no limit to what you can achieve. You have put in place systems and processes and have competent and committed employees working for you. You are not selling your time for income generation but rather selling a product or service. You own a business which is self-propelling. They own a system; they are the people who can retire financially free.

Investor (money works for you) – These are the ultra-smart ones who make their money work for them. The income generation is passive in nature. Income generation is not through time investment but rather through capital. They enjoy the ultimate financial freedom in terms of time and money. They invest in business and ventures which are expected to generate huge profits. They also invest in other avenues like stocks, bonds, real estate, etc. to generate annual cash flows. Other investments which they venture into include trademarks, copyrights, and royalties. Being an investor should be your ultimate goal to achieve complete financial freedom. They invest in a system

The pyramid is segregated into two zones; employees and self-employed form the bottom half which is the hard work zone, and business owners and investors round up the top half, known as the smart work zone.

Important facts about the pyramid of financial freedom

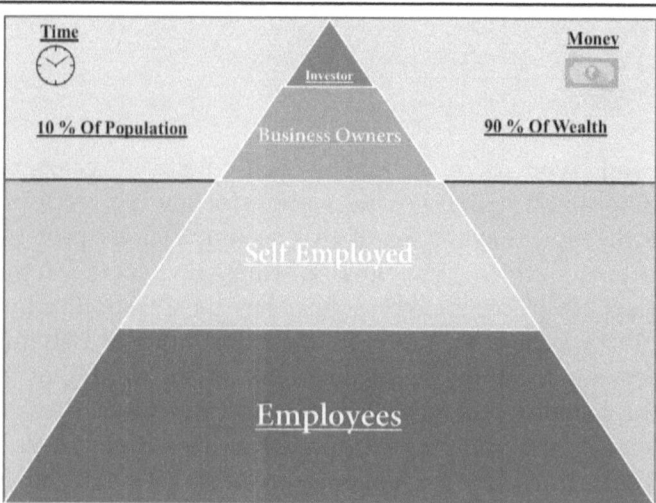

- 90 percent of the population falls in the bottom half or the hard work zone, and 10 percent of the population falls in the top half or the smart work zone.

Introduction to Business 43

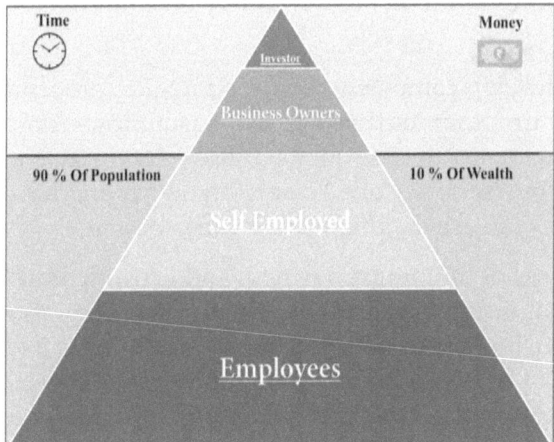

- The top half owns 90 percent of the wealth while the bottom half owns merely 10 percent of the wealth.

To reach the pinnacle of financial freedom, one has to traverse the journey from the bottom half of the pyramid to the top half. People who own a business or are investors are the ones who accomplish their dreams. This in no way means they stop working. It only implies they enjoy what they do and have a choice of both time and money.

Which zone would you like to be a part of?

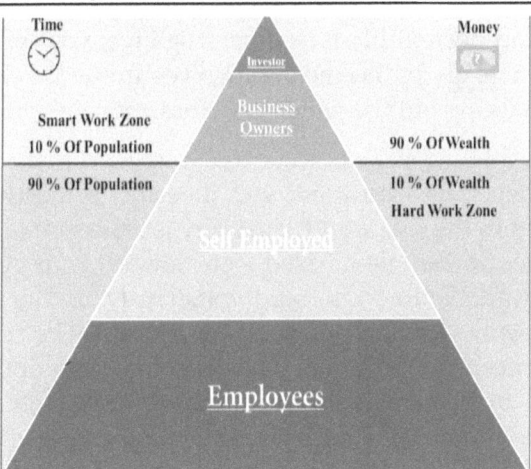

The hard work zone?
- You have absolutely no security and are involved in a daily rat race. You become complacent and compromise your dreams. You are at the mercy of external uncontrollable factors and are trading

your time for money. You must always work to earn money and will never be an owner but merely an employee.

The smart work zone?
- You develop competent teams, strategies, processes, and systems to ensure your business is self-sustaining. You are living your dream, enjoying life to its fullest, learning continuously, and contributing to society. You are an owner and have power in your hands. You are making money work for you.

The attractiveness of building a business and learning how to invest lies in the very fact that is a passive income. The income generation is continuous and once the business is established, it practically runs itself. You are also creating a tool to be passed on to your future generations. It makes sense to work hard to build a business which will provide you with financial freedom for life.

Conventional thinking encourages you to focus on becoming either an Employee (E) or a high-paid Self-Employed (S) individual such as a doctor, lawyer, or accountant. While there is nothing wrong in this idea, it falters when your goal is to attain financial freedom. These two stages seldom result in attainment of financial independence. Finance and freedom go hand in hand. Financial freedom allows you to live a fuller and more enjoyable life.

Your journey from the bottom half of the pyramid to the top half will involve a fundamental shift in your core values and will result in a life-changing experience for you. You need to move out of job security and your comfort zone. If safety and normal life is your prerogative, you will never achieve financial freedom. This by no means involves immediately quitting your job but rather chalking out the journey of your movement toward financial freedom.

The skill associated with business and investor is mostly not taught in school but gained in the real world. Curiosity is an essential character along with perseverance and single-minded focus toward your goal. They absorb all knowledge available to them, read voraciously, and are always on the lookout for opportunities and prospects for growth. The rules of the game vary in each level of the pyramid. They are complete opposite sides of a coin requiring a fundamental shift in mindset, tools, and ideas. Financial education will help you row your boat ashore to the financial freedom.

You have to make a choice of the right track toward the journey of generating income and the choice is contingent on the lifestyle you want to maintain. As the popular saying goes work smart not hard. In case you choose to pursue a profession like doctor or engineer, you still have the option of creating a business around it. For example a doctor can build a hospital, employ other doctors, and create a sustaining business model. You will then have the financial ability to do charity and work toward upliftment of society as well. All you got to do is make the right choice to move toward the smart work zone.

You can learn tricks of the trade from experts and learn fiscal discipline. Learn to build a business and once the business grows and you have gained sufficient money you can step into the shoes of the investor and invest in other businesses. Your income will ultimately be dependent on the efforts of your team who should comprise professionals and experts. Should your choice be the hard work zone, you can still traverse into the smart work zone using the tips and techniques from the book. I have written this book with the primary aim of making you understand that age no bar; you can always achieve financial security. The path will be filled with obstacles but the end result will be sweeter than honey.

A great example of hard working versus smart working is the example of a Japanese soap manufacturer. Once a soap manufacturing company in Japan received a complaint from a customer that they received a soap cover without any soap from the company. The company was highly apologetic and in order to improve the process, involved the company's engineering department. The department through their inherent hard working thinking implemented an X-ray machine manned with people and 100 percent inspection to ensure no soap cover was empty. The same company's employee when posed the question simply suggested using an industrial grade fan focusing on the stage after the soap was assembled into the soap cover. Due to the air from the fan the soap cover which was empty simple fell down from the assembly line into the bin. This example highlights the importance of looking at relevant solution which may be simplistic in appearance but are highly cost effective as well as extremely efficient. This is how smart work always triumphs hard work.

Poor people focus on money only while a smart person focuses on providing solutions. Money is result for value provided to others.

An insight into financial freedom

Financial freedom means you have the ability to take life decisions without constantly being burdened by the thought of its financial impact. This is because you are controlling the finance rather than the other way around. It is critical to note that financial freedom does not imply getting rich by quick methods. It is about creating a business or other asset which will generate revenue for you continuously. Time is a luxury that you can ill afford to lose. You need to begin your journey toward financial security at the earliest. Wise men may say money isn't everything. It is an indispensable part of life though as it controls almost all things in life.

Once you have achieved financial freedom, you can pursue your dreams. You can pursue your passion like travel the world, spend time with people you love, or take up any other activity you desire. Maintaining fiscal discipline though should be your mantra. Sky is the limit for you and you have moved into the HNI (high net worth individual) zone. Money will never be a botheration and you have the option of leaving behind a legacy which people will cherish. You can do plenty of charitable work and help alleviate the problems of others. Once you have achieved financial freedom, the very purpose of my writing this book would have been fulfilled. Take the plunge and begin your journey.

The world is a dynamic market place

The beginning of a market place can be traced back to the early days of civilization. In the early days, the cave man produced only the goods that were required. Subsequently, he realized that he could not produce everything himself and he should utilize others for producing other commodities. This led to the creation of the "barter system" which resulted in the origin of the marketplace that is still in operation to this day.

Subsequent to the passage of time, human wants kept on increasing. The new consumer expects a multitude of things in order to lead a comfortable life. Commodities which earlier were luxurious have become the necessities of today. The demand for goods and services is constantly rising and varying paving the path for continuous transactions of business throughout the globe. This varying need presents a golden opportunity for businesses to cater to the changing needs and wants of the consumers. The world has become a true global marketplace with opportunities for business omnipresent.

Customers are intrinsically unpredictable, irrational, emotional, curious, and dynamic all at the same time. Their focus varies from product, quality, value, or price. They get excited and attracted to different styles, different offerings, and different ways to purchase things. The current consumer is also well read and demanding. Assortments of options are available to him to shop at different places like stores, online, etc. The shift in wants has become more pronounced with the consumer opting for quality and variety. An important thing to note is that every time the customer priority shifts an excellent opportunity for business gets generated.

Time is precious, use it well!

It is said that Time is Eternal. However it is also something which once lost can never be gotten back. The average life expectancy for a person today is between 60 and 70 years. Every single minute of our life is unique and with each passing moment our time on this earth is reducing. Most people don't realize the value of time until it is very late. Time is a precious and priceless commodity and we cannot afford to waste it as time will never stop for anyone or can it be regained. The everlasting truth is that there is time for everything but it is our inability to effectively utilize it that creates a problem. Success stories of great personalities highlight the efficient use of time to master the required skills and determination to become successful. It is critical that we identify the non-value add activities in our business and work toward eliminating them.

Two powerful letters "NO"

One of the most difficult things to say in this world is NO. Humans by nature are social and emotional and it is our innate desire to say yes to everything. It is important that we do not feel guilty or scared to say no to things that won't help us grow, learn, or create opportunities. We should place an emphasis on the things that will help us take better and informed decisions. Today's world presents a plethora of opportunities whilst at the same time presents multiple distractions. Every time you perform a particular activity it is important to ask yourself whether that activity is adding value to your life. If you realize that it is essentially a nonvalue add, it is important to say NO in unequivocal terms.

Tip: Whenever you want to take a decision pause for a couple of seconds, take a couple of deep breaths and then decide. Most of the decision we make are emotional, with the heart taking the decision not the brain.

Commit yourself to success

Commitment is the mantra to success. It is important to dedicate the time to travel on the path of your dreams once you have decided that is the path you want to pursue. Time management assumes critical significance, and prioritization will help you achieve more things in the limited amount of time that you have. Determination and hard work have no substitutes and you will need to use your time wisely to achieve multiple things. However, an important thing to remember is all work and no play makes Jack a dull boy. It is important to find the right work-life balance so that you are also rejuvenated and focused. Breaking a complex goal into simple small tasks along with daily monitoring will ensure you stay faithful to the path and the goal.

4. Myths and Truths about business

Myth 1– You have to innovate first to be successful in business
Truth – You have to satisfy needs and solve problems of your customer to be successful in business

Innovation is not always essential for success. The key is effective execution of ideas and strategies whether your own or others. Remember it is not important to do different things as it is to do things differently. Delight the customer by understanding his needs and solving his problems.

You should commence your journey where other people's innovation has stopped. This way you do not spend time reinventing the wheel. The wiser thing to do is focus on distinguishing yourself from the competition by focusing on customer satisfaction. Henry Ford's story is a classic example of this. He did not invent the automobile or the assembly line for which he became world famous. His genius lay in the fact that he was able to adapt and apply existing products and processes to improvise them and make them perfect. He was thus able to enhance customer satisfaction and create a loyal customer base by providing an automobile at a cost affordable to the masses. He is, therefore, aptly credited with revolutionizing the automobile industry.

Similarly, look for ways and means where you can truly provide glee to the customer by focusing on solving his problems and offering differentiating solutions. Build a team which can complement your creative thinking. You will bolster your business innovation and creativity and deliver better product or service which will tip the market in your favor. This will lead to strategic growth and exponential success.

Myth 2– Entrepreneurs are high risk takers
Truth – Entrepreneurs are calculated risk takers.

They are always on the lookout for opportunities to earn more money and minimize risks

Entrepreneurs always look for prospects where they can gain financial benefits. Different avenues are explored and exploited to maximize the gains.

Did you know the idea of Jio originated from the mind of Mukesh Ambani's daughter, Isha, in 2011? She was pursuing her studies in Yale (in the USA) and was visiting for the holidays. She had to submit some coursework and she said, "Dad, the Internet at our house sucks," recalls Mukesh Ambani. Isha's twin brother, Akash, remarked then that in the old world, telecom was voice dominated and people made money on calls. The world has evolved since he quipped with the emphasis on digital everywhere.

Isha and Akash portrayed the younger, more creative, more ambitious and far more impatient rising India whose dream was to be the best in the world. They had transcended the national barriers and wanted to leave a mark on the world. This convinced me says Mukesh that in this fast-changing technological world, broadband internet is the gateway and India cannot be left behind. India during that time suffered from poor connectivity, poor network infrastructure, and scarcity of digital resource data. The data prices were also unaffordable for the common man and this was killing the demand for data. It was a vicious cycle with high prices keeping the market small and because of low penetration the prices remained high.

It was then that I decided that I would start Jio which will revolutionize the telecom industry by making data easily available and affordable to the vast majority of Indians in every nook and corner of the country. It took the incumbent telecom operators 25 years to build a pan-India 2G network presence. Jio turned the industry upside down by building the 4G LTE network in a short span of 3 years. The Jio network was far more advanced and larger than the existing network and is one step ahead of the competition by being 5G ready as well.

Reliance Jio was founded based on Mukesh Ambani's dream that mobile internet is the revolutionary technology trend of this century. It will undergo several iteration and transformations, but the core technology will remain the same. This was the belief that laid the foundation of his plan to launch Jio and strive to make it the market leader.

Fuelled by an investment of Rs 1.5 lakh crores and ably supported by partnerships with eight global carriers—British Telecom, Deutsche Telecom, Millicom, MTS, Orange, Rogers, Telia Sonera and Tim—Jio has magnificently built the largest only 4G and LTE networks not only in India, but the whole world. A 2.5 lakh kilometer route of fiber optic cables combined with 90,000 eco-friendly 4G towers provide unmatchable 4G coverage in all of India's 22 telecom circles (call zones which differentiate between local and STD calls).

Reliance Jio introduced to the India population what they sorely lacked and deeply desired: high-speed mobile internet at affordable prices. In doing so it created a market expansion for the telecom industry and created a disruption for the entire industry. Existing competitors were forced to play catch up providing Jio with the early bird advantage. It should be noted that before the launch of Jio less than 15 percent of India's population had experienced 4G connectivity.

Successful entrepreneurs are those who know the pulse of the market and identify niche areas which solve customers' desires and needs. In doing so they open up a whole new market for themselves and are almost always rewarded with success and fame. Some of the parameters through which entrepreneurs disrupt the market and dislodge existing players are through offering of new products or services at lower costs and improved quality. This offers them the opportunity to charge a premium for their innovations which in turn allows them to reap the benefit of big rewards.

Myth 3- Entrepreneurs are born
Truth -Entrepreneurs are built.

Entrepreneurship is not an ingrained quality that you acquire at birth. Rather it is one that is cultivated through learning and experience.

Myth 4- You need to be smart to start a business
Truth -You need to hire smart people to start a business

You should be astute to hire team members who are specialized in that particular business function, to get the wheels of the business rolling. It is always advisable to hire people who can focus on the core functions and are result oriented and passionate about growth and success as you. These people are the foundation pillars of your business.

Myth 5- You should always have lots of money to start a business
Truth -You have to be creative to start a business

Nothing could be farther from the truth than this myth. There are countless examples of businesses started with few thousand rupees and have become made million dollar ventures. Start small and finish big should be your motto as a businessman.

Do you know the story of Kailash Katkar, Chairman and CEO of Quick Heal technologies, a leading anti-virus software company in India? Kailash had no big degrees to his name and had barely completed his matriculation when he took up a job at a radio and calculator repair shop to support his family financially. He ventured into the business world by starting his business of calculator repair with a mere 15,000 rupees and eventually started CAT computer services. He asked his younger brother Sanjay to develop a basic version of anti-virus software. He initially sold the software for a meager fee of INR 700. Today his venture has an annual turnover of over 350 crores with offices worldwide and a 30 percent market share in India. The company employs more than 1200 employees and is a source of inspiration for many a young people who want to make a name in the business world.

While it's true that having a ton of money will give you an advantage it holds true only if you have a sound and proven business model. This will ensure that you generate a profit but business by its very nature is unpredictable. Hence it is advisable to start small and then scale up. Test your business model for its validity by investing a small amount, streamlining your systems and processes, and then reinvesting your profits to grow your business. A multitude of examples of starting business from scratch on a small scale and then building an empire are readily available.

A prime example is Subway which is an American fast food restaurant franchise primarily selling submarine sandwiches (subs) and salads. Subway is one of the fastest-growing franchises in the world with approximately 45,000 stores located in more than 112 countries as of June 2017. It is the largest single-brand restaurant chain in the world. Its story began more than 50 years ago when Dr. Peter Buck, a nuclear physicist, changed the life of a college student with a few simple words, "Let's open a submarine sandwich shop."

Peter Buck gave college freshman Fred DeLuca the idea to open a submarine sandwich shop in order to pay his tuition. He also provided an initial investment of USD 1000. Thus a business relationship was forged that changed the landscape of the fast food industry. The partners opened their first restaurant in Bridgeport, Connecticut, where they offered fresh, affordable, make to order sandwiches. The popularity of the sandwiches and the brand grew manifold over the decades but what remained constant were the core values and principles:

a) Exceptional service to the customers
b) Highest quality menu items at affordable prices
c) Low operating costs and efficient systems with focus on continuous improvement.

These early principles still serve as the foundation for Subway restaurants across the world. By 1974, the duo owned and operated 16 submarine sandwich shops throughout Connecticut. Realizing they would not achieve their goal of 32 stores in time, they commenced franchising. The SUBWAY® brand experience remarkable growth with this action which continues to this very day. The success of any business depends on the right strategy and not capital.

Myth 6– Only money minded people start business
Truth –Only responsible people start business

Business occurs when you take the responsibility to solve the problems of others, and money is the by-product of providing the solution.

Myth 7– I need to influence or have contacts to start business
Truth – I need to understand customers need and problem, and also select a target customer to start business

People do not buy from you because they know you, but rather because your product or service is solving their needs and desires and solves their problem

Myth 8– You need to be from a business family in order to start business
Truth – You need to have a business mindset to start business

All that is needed to start a business is the right knowledge and correct team, systems, and strategies.

Myth 9 – I need to have a great product to start a business
Truth – I need to have the right intention to start a business

Your product or service needs to fulfill the needs and solve the problems of your customers. Once you achieve this, you will have developed a customer base and a market for your offerings.

Myth 10 – You need to start at the right time
Truth – You need to start right now

You have to build business today so that you can get ready to serve customers and make profits. Business is all about making things happen rather than waiting for things to happen. Don't wait for all the signals to be green.

The best time to start a business is now. You need to be willing to devote your time and energy to the business. This is not to say that you cannot start a part-time business or while you are still working at a job. As a matter of fact numerous entrepreneurs have started their businesses at the worst possible times in history or their personal lives. Microsoft was founded in 1975 near the end of a recession and later incorporated in 1981, just as the recession of the 1980s kicked off. These were two horrible times to start a business, but it has not stopped Microsoft's success juggernaut.

Whenever you gain the right knowledge and have a right business model that is the apt time to start the business. Just as Rome was not built in a day, so too is a business empire. You can always start small and grow over a period of time with customer's feedback and R&D increasing your sales and the business.

Myth 11 – You have to be young and restless to start a business
Truth – You have to be passionate to start a business

Success does not have an age expiry limit. Truth be told you can start your business whenever you have the passion, perseverance, and right business model. In fact restlessness many a times causes problems.

It is often said that you should start a business when you cannot stop yourself from starting it.

Sanders, born in 1890 in Henryville, IN was 6 years old when his father passed away. Left with the responsibility to cook and care for his siblings he dropped out of school in seventh grade to work as a farmhand. At a tender age of 16, he faked his age to enlist in the United States army. After being honorably discharged a year later, he got hired by the railway as a laborer. He was fired for getting into a fight with a coworker.

He then studied law before ruining his legal career by getting into another fight. Sanders was forced to move back in with his mom and get a job selling life insurance. And guess what? He got fired for insubordination. However, he never gave up. In 1920, he founded a ferry boat company. He tried cashing in his ferry boat business to create a lamp manufacturing company only to find out the competition was already selling a better version of his lamp.

It wasn't until 40 that he began selling chicken dishes in a service station. As he began to advertise his food, an argument with a competitor resulted in a deadly shootout. Four years later, he bought a motel which burned to the ground along with his restaurant. These adversities did not deter Sanders, who rebuilt and ran a new motel until World War II forced him to close down. He then tried to franchise his restaurant. His recipe was rejected 1,009 times before finding acceptance. His "secret recipe" was coined "Kentucky Fried Chicken," and quickly became a burgeoning hit. His booming restaurant was crippled when an interstate opened nearby and he decided to sell it and pursued his dream of spreading KFC franchises and hiring KFC workers all across the country.

After years of failures and misfortunes, Sanders finally hit it big. KFC expanded internationally and he finally sold the company for two million dollars (USD 15.3 million today). This truly proves that age is no bar to start a business. Whether you are 16 or you are 60, it is never too early or too late to start it. You just need to have the right business model in place, the passion, and the drive to succeed and the sky is the limit.

Myth 12 – Business requires luck to be a success
Truth – Business requires understanding the science behind to be a success.

Business is science. The success of a business is attributable to developing a right team, systems, and strategies.

It is not luck but the smart work and science that drive business success.

Myth 13 – I do not have the money, time, and team to start a business
Truth –I will not have the money, time, and team if I don't start a business.

Excuses do not make winners. You need to come up with a way to arrange for the money, prioritize your time, and build the right team in the initial phase.

There are no free lunches. Results cannot be achieved without efforts. Money can be arranged through different avenues such as bank loans, asking your family, from your savings, etc. You can make a start with a small amount by introducing a product or service. Once that sells you can plug in the profits into your business to grow. If you are working in a job, business will generate an additional income source.

> *"Successful people find the TIME to do the RIGHT thing, whereas others are busy doing things right."*

5. Business is a vehicle; use it to achieve your dreams

It is essential that as a business owner you need to look at the larger picture from a bird's eye view. Once you have established the business and reached to the stability stage, you cannot get bogged down with day-to-day operations. Your time is better spent focusing on creating teams and systems which will be self-propelling. The optimum use of your time will involve concentrating on the overall growth and vision of the business. One of the major problems faced by entrepreneurs is being caught in mundane day-to-day functions that creativity takes a backseat. Being busy does not necessarily imply being productive.

As a business owner you are expected to juggle numerous responsibilities. Most businesses are dependent solely on the owner who performs several roles and is in a constant firefighting mode. This approach might work in the initial phase of your business when the volume is still small. However, the main aim of starting a business is to progress and expand. This requires hiring of right competent people and thus begins your transformation into the role of a manager. As the operations continue to expand and you recruit additional people you also recruit a manager or promote existing team members as managers.

However, the ability of doing things which others can do easily by yourself makes you feel good. Unfortunately this is a trap as the business becomes excessively dependent on the owner and eats up much of his productive time and you are trapped in firefighting. The secret is to focus on major tasks and delegate the minor tasks. As a thumb rule, a simple task which technology can do should not be done by your staff. Similarly a minor task that can be done by your team shouldn't be done by you.

One of the primary reasons why this situation arises is because we are not effectively utilizing people. Managing is all about motivating and delegating and making your team responsible and accountable. Many a time owners only delegate those responsibilities which they don't like whilst retaining certain roles. It is important to note that if you do not delegate and provide authority to your team to take decisions, you will end up spending your precious time approving every small decision for your team.

Dhaniram owned a departmental store in the heart of the city. He was a kind man with good business skills. He knew how to talk to his customers and would always advise them on their purchases. Everyone liked going to Dhaniram's store and soon the business started booming. Because of Dhaniram's pleasant disposition, everyone wanted to deal with him only and soon he started getting overwhelmed. In his efforts to please all his customers, he soon ignored his health and family and was working all the time.

One day, a friend visited him from out of town. Dhaniram was very happy to see his friend, but before he could even say a word, a customer came to ask for some products. As his friend patiently waited, watching Dhaniram, he noticed that there was not a single employee in his store who could take his place. The efficiency and knowledge that Dhaniram had was par excellence and no other employee could fit in his shoes in his absence.

Finally, Dhaniram managed to take some time to speak to his friend, when his friend asked— "Do you want to go for some tea and have a nice chat." Dhaniram reluctantly refused saying he couldn't leave his store unattended.

His friend quipped—"Do Birla and Tata sit in their store all the time?"

Dhaniram was confused. His friend finally explained that he needed to develop a next line of command, with his trusted employees who can easily manage his business without a regular intervention from Dhaniram. This way, he can focus on core issues and manage the business only from a high level, to ensure that the growth targets are achieved.

Dhaniram agreed. Motivated to make a change, he took a tea break for the first time!

A flip side to this is also overdoing the authorization responsibility where your staff might feel overburdened and leave. It is important to find the right balance and the right people for the smooth functioning of your business.

So what is the solution here?

Building a team

One does not enter the business world with the intention of creating a job for himself. A business foundation is laid to fulfill your dreams and almost always looking at the broader growth picture in mind. Once you have invested the effort into starting a business it is essential to identify activities which are not adding value or which can be delegated easily.

For example if you excel in marketing it might make sense to delegate accounting or human resource to somebody else. It is pertinent for you to focus on tasks which are the most important for your business.

Setting Systems

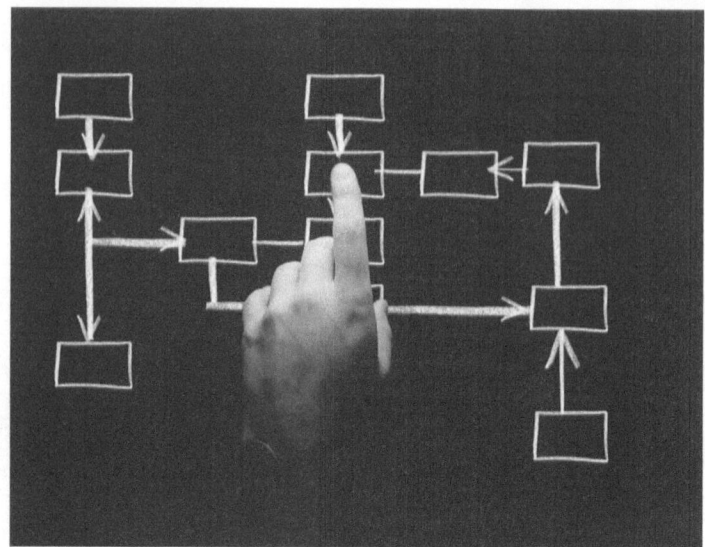

Systems work, people don't. Business owners are sometimes caught in a quandary on how to effectively delegate yet remain in overall control. What is of importance in this situation is to efficiently devise a system which is simple and sustainable resulting in a standardization of doing things. The more the level of standardization you have in your system the easier it is to train somebody new and the transition becomes smooth. The system will allow you to free yourself from daily transactional operations of your business and move into a role that would focus on business development and strategy.

Process mapping can play an important role in recording and improving your system. It also helps in bringing a level of fine tuning to your system so that it functions effectively. Standard operating procedures help you to do the same thing the exact same way every time and eliminate the people dependency on the process. It also ensures that the quality of your work is consistent irrespective of the person performing the work. When you are able to achieve this you can truly say you have perfected your system. One of the principal reasons why business owners don't put systems in place is they feel it takes too much time. This initial investment is of prime importance as it will smoothen the business operation in the long run.

6. The Seven functions of business

As humans we perform better, when we have all parts and organs of the body functioning in harmony. If any body part or organ is missing, it affects the daily functioning of the body. Every part of body has different functions, like eyes help us see, ears help us hear, legs help us stand and walk, and the nose helps us smell. Similarly each organ has different function like kidney filters blood, liver detoxifies impurities, and heart pumps blood and provides oxygen in the blood to every cell of the body. Any body part or organ missing or not functioning, causes imbalance in the body and a major dysfunction including death.

The functioning of a successful business is very similar to a human body, which comprise different departments working in synergy so that business can run smoothly and generate profit. Many a businesses fail due to absence of functions or nonperformance of these functions. So what are the important functions in a business?

There are seven major functions in any business; with the success and good fortune of the company lying in the proper functioning and coordination of these functions. If you plan to build a business which can efficiently work in your absence, it is absolutely critical that the functions work smoothly. All the functions are interdependent like the rings of a chain. Always remember a chain is only as strong as its weakest link.

Multinationals and corporates are aware about the criticality of the seven business functions and that is the reason why those functions are clearly etched out and efficient. An organized business is like a six-wheeler truck, where Marketing, Sales, Operations are front tires and the support functions Human Resource, Accounts and Research, and Development are the back tires. The driver of course is the management on the 7th Wheel.

The truck has a big windshield in the front, through which the driver looks ahead (into the future), akin to having a vision. It has a dashboard to know the current status of the truck, comparable to knowing the current status of the business. It has the rear mirror to see what's happening behind, similar to the business learning from the past to move forward. Truck requires diesel to run, while business requires working capital.

If any of the tires is missing, or the driver is missing the truck will not be able to move.

The business splits into number of different departments, each assigned a specific job or task. The main functional areas of a business are outlined briefly as below:

1. Marketing
2. Sales
3. Operations
4. Human Resource (HR)
5. Accounts
6. Research & Development (R&D)
7. Management

1. **Marketing**

The simplest definition of marketing

Philip Kotler defines marketing as "the science and art of exploring, creating, and delivering value to satisfy the needs of a target market at a profit." Marketing recognizes unfulfilled needs and desires. It defines the measures and quantifies the size of the identified market and the profit potential. It pinpoints segments which the company can serve best and drives designs and promotes the appropriate products and services.

"Good products SELL, but they rarely sell THEMSELVES."

Marketing is creating an impulse in the mind of the customer to buy a product or a service.

The functional goal of marketing is lead generation. A lead is a potential contact, an individual, or an organization that expresses an interest in your goods or services. Lead generation can be described as the process of stimulating and capturing interest in a product or service for the purpose of developing sales pipeline. The more the leads, the more are the chances of making a sale.

Marketing is basically: "The identification of target customers and satisfying their needs or desires which is competitive and profitable for the company or organization; through market analysis, planning, and implementation of different marketing strategies, and controlling the progress and achievements of those strategies."

Main activities constitute:
- Market research
- Creating and implementing marketing strategies
- Developing and delivering of promotional campaigns
- Setting and monitoring prices
- Ensuring suitable distribution
- Obtaining and analyzing customer feedback.

In the marketing department, decisions regarding 4 Ps are taken:
- Product (decisions about new product development, packaging, branding, etc.);
- Physical distribution (decisions about marketing channels, policies and procedures relating to warehousing, transportation, etc.)
- Promotion (involving advertising, sales promotion, and publicity)
- Pricing (policies and procedures relating to the setting up of profitable prices).

Developing a marketing strategy that attracts potential customers is vital for any business, and is the primary responsibility of the marketing department. Failing this, your efforts to attract customers will be unsuccessful and inefficient. The focus of your strategy should be making sure that your products and services meet customer needs continuously. The strategy should respond to changes in customer perceptions and demand. The purpose of your marketing strategy should be to identify and then communicate the benefits of your business offerings to your target market.

Branding strategy and target market will help you position your business in the market. It also entails how you will keep customers interested in your business. It is a way of informing consumers about the product which will address their pain areas. A successful marketing strategy understands that your target customers will fall into particular groups or segments, characterized by their "needs, problems, and desires." Identifying these groups through market research, and then addressing them more successfully than your competitors, should be the focus of your strategy. There is no common template. The key is to find the relevant ones to your business.

Once this has been completed, decide on the best marketing activity that will ensure your target market knows about the products or services you offer. This could be achieved through various forms of advertising like exhibitions, public relations initiatives, print media, and Internet activity. This effectively creates a "point of sale" strategy.

Limit your activities to those methods you think will work best, avoiding stretching your budget thin with too many things. Once you have created and implemented your strategy, monitor its effectiveness and make any adjustments to maintain its success. This control not only helps you see the effectiveness of the strategy in practice, but also helps you devise your future marketing strategy. Once you have decided on the marketing strategy, chalk up a marketing plan. Decide how to execute and evaluate the success of that strategy. The plan should be reviewed constantly so that you respond quickly to changes in customer needs and attitudes in your industry.

Measuring the effectiveness of the marketing strategies is very important to understand. You can follow the below chart to measure the marketing activities efficacy.

MARKETING EFFICACY									
Name of the Activity:									
Description of the Activity:									
Month	Date of Campaign	Marketing Expenditure	Week Before		Week after		Hike in Revenue	Comments	
			Revenue	Tickets	Revenue	Tickets			
January									
February									
March									
April									
May									
June									
July									
August									
September									
October									
November									
December									

Prepared by:
Comments:

Brand building

Brand by definition can be categorized as a name, term, design, symbols, or any other features that distinguishes an organization or products from its rivals in the eyes of customer. Brand is a trust used in business, marketing and advertising, and branding is a set of marketing and communication methods aimed at creating a lasting impression in the minds of customers.

Having a successful brand is an important asset of your business. Brand building just might be the most important activity in the overall business development. It creates customer loyalty and creates awareness in the market. If you are a business owner and plan to build a business brand without a marketing team, you need to be aware that brand building will keep you busy all the time. You need to sacrifice your energy, time, and resources for brand building.

Brand building definition

It is the communication and creation of customer value. It includes all those ingredients that a customer feels and experiences when interacting with your business. In other words, it has a positive impact on brand equity using different promotional strategies and campaigns.

A key element of marketing strategy planning should involve the development of your brand and how you would like to be perceived. When designing a brand strategy, this is the first question you should ask. Example: Are youngsters aware of the brand?

What is your unique selling proposition?

The key to business success is identification of what makes your business unique and attractive to the consumer. If these factors lead to a competitive advantage then you have discovered your unique selling points, or USPs. These USPs are major contributory factors driving business success. This should form the central theme of your brand strategy. Most brands concentrate on several of the most powerful and easily communicated proposition benefits in order to create a clearly understood brand message.

Brand values

USP is why customers are currently buying products and form the basis of any company's "brand values." However, brand values have to evolve with time to suit changing market conditions and should also reflect future business strategy. With these in place it is important to ensure that your customer experience reflects these values in every aspect of the business. This means tailoring every element of the marketing mix to project brand values—from the staff you use, the products you produce, the messages on your advertising, and even the way you handle complaints. Building a respected brand can take a lot of hard work and you'll need the commitment from your employees and stakeholders to make it happen.

Why is brand building important?

Brand building helps create brand identity for your products and services and differentiates you from your competitors. Being a visual voice of your company you should be consistent on every media platform. It should convey a strong brand image in the mind of consumers.

Remember, a brand exists in the mind of the consumer. It is the intangible sum of thoughts and feelings about a particular company, service, or product. A company can steer how a brand is perceived but never has full control. "A brand exists in the mind of the consumer."

A brand is tangibly represented by branding, allowing the customer to easily identify a product using an identity which is sometimes formalized in a corporate identity document. Successful branding focuses on the company brand values.

Benefits of a strong brand:

- Adds value to a company
- Requires less persuasion for consumers to use other products from the same brand
- Ensures a lasting customer relationship due to trust
- Aids recognition in a cluttered marketplace
- Has the ability to command a premium
- Allows differentiation between very similar products, for example mineral water
- Can attract merchandising contracts
- Leads to the perception of quality.

There are two core elements to a strong brand—emotional value and practical value.

Your brand logo, font size, style, color, styling, and packaging are important elements to differentiate your brand and build a competitive advantage in the minds of the consumer. Once you are in the position to offer a unique value proposition, you can position your brand appropriately. A compelling brand strategy always enhances your brand positioning attracting consumers. A brand positioning statement must be based on reality and must fulfill brand promise. When you are converting your positioning statement into a message it should appeal to the target audience.

For any small business or large corporation, brand monitoring and evaluation is critical for its brand building. It helps to assess the brand success in the market whether it has remained the same, strengthened, or degraded the minds of consumers. Business environment changes rapidly, and this allows you exploit new opportunities or face challenges. Brand evaluation is not a one-time process. Even your growth means more expectation and more responsibilities. Regular evaluation keeps your brand moving in the right direction.

2. **Sales**

Whatever leads are generated through marketing have to be converted into sales. Sales is the most important function in business.

Definition of sales

Selling is to identify and uncover a need and then satisfy it with a right product and service for a mutual benefit.

Let's break this definition to understand it further:

First—identify the right person, who is capable of decision making (What is the criterion for finding the right person)

MAN -A person who has **the Money** to buy your product or service

- A person who has **the Authority** to decide
- A person who has **the Need** for product or service

Second—uncover a need or desire and problem. Customers by nature buy products or service which can fulfill their need or desire or solve their problem, e.g.: we buy daily bread and groceries to cook food, it is our need, on the other hand we buy mosquito repellent to get rid of mosquito bites which solves our problem.

You need to ask the right question to know the customers' requirements, needs, desires and problems, know who decision maker is, and know what factors are considered while buying and what the buying process is. But most of us do one common mistake: we never ask and listen, we only talk.

Third—show value. In this step you need to show or tell how your product or service can benefit the customer in satisfying their need, what additional benefits can you product give that they will desire or what problems of the customer can be solved.

The functional goal of sales is revenue generation.

Some Common Sales Myths:

Myth 1- Customer is king
Truth –Customer is a professional friend

Many times we treat customers as king, and we become the slave. This makes us feel that we are a level below the customers, and it becomes a blockage for us to communicate effectively. Selling is more about building lasting relationships and satisfying the needs, desires, and solving problems. Once we start treating ourselves as slaves, how can we do justice in selling? This is the main reason where we fail in sales. You should treat your customers as a professional friend and build a relationship based on trust, mutual respect, and mutual benefit.

Myth 2– Best price wins the deal
Truth –The value proposition wins the deal

Being price competitive is important, but adapting the offerings to customer's unique needs and providing more value for the customer wins the deal. Buyers greatly value salespeople who can be trusted advisers. Salespeople who help buyers think through their needs and reduce those risks stand out. In sales, it is important that you are able to listen to someone, to their needs. A great salesperson will talk only 20 percent of the time and listen 80 percent. It's very important to know the motives of your customer, "What does he really want? Any question your customer asks, about product specifications, or how the product is used, is a signal to a good salesperson to steer the conversation in the right direction. Ask questions that allow your customer to better understand his own wishes and your product will sell itself.

Myth 3 – I need to be a born sales person
Truth –I need to learn and master skill of sales person

Anyone can sell. It is within our grasp and the basic truth is hard work always trumps talent. Nobody is a born salesperson, the same way as no one is born as a doctor or engineer or teacher. We should treat sales the same way you treat any other profession. Take seminars, read up on selling, or even apprentice yourself to an experienced sale professional. The one who attempts to do more sales will keep improving overtime and become great at selling.

Myth4–Sales requires a talent called "Lying"
Truth –Sales require a talent called showing value

Selling is more about building long-term relationships, so that you can sell your product on a regular basis. But if you lie, you can make sales initially, but rest assured in the long run you will end up losing trust and future sales. It is like winning the fight, but losing the war. Never lie, instead work on showing benefits and solving customer problems using your product and services.

3. **Operations**

Delivering the promises done by sales is the responsibility of operations.

Definition

Production is the creation of goods and services with the help of certain processes. The production of goods depends essentially on the organization of men, money, materials, and facilities. It organizes the transformation process that turns inputs (e.g., materials, people) in finished goods and services.

The functional goal of operations is to:

- Create impact on customers
- Deliver customer happiness.

Main activities:

- **Production or processing**
- **Storage**
- **Dispatch or delivery**

Operations create an impact on customer and create customer happiness. They fulfill the promises done by the sales people to create happiness quotient. Operation elements include timely delivery, deliver right quality and quantity, create happiness, fulfill desires, solve problems, promise to do every time, and build relationships. This is the reason that the customer faith in the company increases when the operations head is in contact with the customer.

4. **Human Resource**

To operate, sell, market, and perform any other business activity, people are needed. We may be able to automate most of the activities, but we still need manpower to operate the machines. More competent the manpower the better we can serve the customers. This results in generation of huge profit for business. Employees are assets of the company. Recruiting the right candidate at the right time for the various departments is the important function of HR. Once hired, providing the right training and increasing competency is equally important.

This function is responsible for all aspects of managing the people who work in a business. An efficiently run human resources department can provide your organization with structure and the ability to meet business needs through managing your company's most valuable resources, its employees.

It is instrumental in providing labor law compliance, record keeping, hiring and training, compensation, relational assistance, and handling specific performance issues. These functions are critical because without those functions being completed, your company would not be able to meet the essential needs of management and staff.

Main activities include:

- Hire employees (recruitment)
- Set up and manage employment rules
- Employee training and appraisal
- Monitor the working conditions for employees
- Manage communication with staff
- Ensure business complies with employment-related legislation.

The HR function deals with the human side of business. It is concerned with increasing the effectiveness of human performance in any organization. Specifically stated, the HR function aims at obtaining and maintaining a capable and effective workforce, motivating the employees individually and in groups to contribute their maximum toward fulfillment of organizational goals.

5. **Accounts**

This function involves managing the financial resources of the business and reporting on the financial position and performance. The accounting department is responsible for recording and reporting the cash flows of a company. The department's accountants review the records of each department to determine the company's financial position to run the organization cost-effectively.

The functional goal of accounts is:
- Accuracy in number
- Compliance
- Monitor numbers.

While the specific roles may vary from business to business, one thing is certain: if your accounting department does not perform these key functions effectively and efficiently, you could be headed for some serious trouble.

By developing an accounting department, a company can help ensure full transparency in its financial transactions, while also providing specialized, centralized support to other teams and managers. Quality financial management can help ensure the ongoing health of a business. The accounts department has to closely work with the management.

6. **Research and Development (R&D)**

In the world of innovations and competitiveness, expenditure on research and development is a productive investment and R&D itself is an aid for survival and growth of the firm. Unless there is a constant attempt for improvement and sophistication of an existing product and introduction of newer varieties, the firm is bound to be gradually out marketed and out of existence by competition. R&D plays a very important role in the success of a business contributing to sustainability of business. Many companies do not understand the importance of R&D until it is too late. It is the R&D function that provides a platform for creativity and innovation to flourish in an organization.

The functional goal of R&D is:
- New product and services which can be launched
- To sell more to happy and satisfied customers.

Innovative breakthroughs happen because of the painstaking efforts of the R&D function. Perseverant efforts are needed. Every failure increases the pressure to perform. R&D helps business build a competitive edge over its competitors. It is the R&D function that develops plans much ahead of other functions. The R&D function needs to have a clear foresight about future problems that need solutions. R&D (in its development role) can act as a catalyst for speeding up the growth of organization by way of introducing breakthrough products in the market.

R&D is very relevant in today's competitive scenario when customers are hankering after new products and new technologies. The firm that successfully leverages its R&D efforts by translating their efforts in building new products will find be ahead of the curve. Expenses on R&D are investment and not expenditure. The ROI on R&D takes time to materialize. But once success is achieved, the financial returns can be quite high. Pharmaceutical companies, chemical companies, automotive companies, lubricant companies invest massive amounts of capital expenditure and revenue expenditure for this reason. These companies strive to be ahead of others in their learning curve. Some companies are technology leaders, while others are followers.

Let us take the case of mobile phones. Today there are different types of models that are being launched in market as a result of intensive R&D efforts. Apple, Sony, 3M are the companies that are known for their breakthrough technologies—some of these technologies are disruptive because they make the existing technologies redundant.

Many firms have converted problems into opportunities only through R&D efforts. These companies eventually became technology leaders creating a huge churn in the market. All the modern inventions—laptops, palmtops, music players, iPods, mp3players, automatic washing machines, dishwashers, water filters are examples of R&D efforts that had a successful outcome. Who would have thought that mosquitoes would provide an opportunity for new product development in the form of mosquito mats, repellent creams, vaporizers, etc.

Sometimes R&D efforts are also necessitated to meet the regulatory norms, e.g., green technologies that reduce pollution. Hybrid cars, electric cars, catalytic converters in cars are examples of successful R&D efforts to meet regulatory requirements.

The true test of R&D function lies in time to market. Business exists for the sake of making a profit. So, the role of R&D in shortening the time to market becomes extremely important. Unless the R&D efforts cannot be scaled up within a reasonable time frame, little can be expected in terms of the functional credit to be assigned to R&D.

R&D makes an organization future ready, and equips the business with the wherewithal required for commercialization of lab efforts through large-scale production. R&D function can reasonably predict future technology trends.

Companies tend to focus more on "development" and less on "research" mainly to meet short- term operational goals. It must be understood clearly that R&D has a strategic orientation and using the R&D function to meet short-term operational goals is anything but a wise more.

7. Management

Management is also known as the brain of business. The management team of a company controls decision making that affects everyone from the president down to entry-level employees. Those decisions, along with the way the management members treat the staff, affect the success of the company. Understanding those effects helps the management team make necessary changes to improve the performance of the company. The management is responsible for controlling and overseeing the entire organization. They develop goals, strategic plans, company policies, and make decisions on the direction of the business.

The management is accountable to the shareholders for the performance of the organization. There are several functions performed by the management; some of the most important ones are listed below:

- **Determination of objectives**

It is the management which determines the broad objectives of the enterprise. Within the framework of the Memorandum of the company, the Board must determine the goals of the enterprise. The objectives may be either general or specific.

- **Formulation of policies**

For realizing the cherished goals of the company, the management must also formulate the policies. The objectives and policies must guide the activities of the company; the selection of policies is also included.

- **Long-term planning and strategy**

As long-term plans and strategies are major decisions, they are also rested in the hands of the management. If the planning proves faulty, the company shall find itself in serious financial difficulties.

- **Co-ordination and controlling**

Although the management is primarily concerned with the future, it must maintain guiding influence on the current activities. It must guide in the execution of plans through the organization with the resources assembled. This calls for co-coordinating and controlling the operation.

"An important part of management is creativity. CREATIVITY can only come from silence. Maintaining just a few minutes of silence each day can open up NEW DIMENSION of life."

Each function requires certain set of skills and competences to function properly, and for a businessman to build a successful business that runs without his involvement, these seven functions need to be functioning by themselves, with a second line of leaders taking charge of the functions, and replacing the businessman in decision making in each of the functions.

Once you establish these functions that work optimally on their own, without your direct interference that is the time you have achieved financial freedom.

7. Intrapreneur and Entrepreneur

A relatively newer term intrapreneur has emerged recently and is frequently used for individuals who think like an entrepreneur and take complete ownership of the job assigned, and is capable to lead others but are essentially employees within an organization. It is imperative to tap the potential of these individuals who can generate ideas that can alter your decision making and business path in a big way. Their creativity can be fueled by involving them in the changes planned for the organization and assigning them the responsibility of those changes. An intrapreneur is a huge asset to the business and equipped with the right resources can contribute to the business growth in an extensive manner. Business owners must identify and encourage such employees.

It is crucial to remember the difference between intrapreneurs and entrepreneurs. An entrepreneur must focus on all aspects of the business while the intrapreneur is armed with a much clear vision and information. As they focus on specific areas of the business they are in a better position to take responsibilities and risks in their role which can have long lasting impacts on the business. An entrepreneur on the other hand has much more at stake as he has raised the capital for the business and also bears the entire risk associated with the business. A clear differentiation between an entrepreneur and an intrapreneur is that entrepreneur is the generator of novel ideas or concepts while the intrapreneur is the one who effectively drives innovations in a selected area of the business. Intrapreneurs need to be selected to help the business realize their dream at a much faster rate.

Intrapreneurs should eventually be transitioned to company leaders thereby freeing the owners from daily activities. The benefit of this is twofold. One is that the intrapreneurs are motivated to give their fullest potential as they are suitably rewarded for their hard work. Secondly their growth serves as an incentive for other employees to move into an intrapreneurial role, thus building a strong foundation of rapid growth for the business.

Why is it imperative for a business to have intrapreneurs?

A. For business growth

The foremost reason for starting a business is to grow and expand while significantly increasing your profits. As the popular saying goes a chain is only as strong as its weakest link, so too is the case for the business. Business growth accelerates with the contribution of each and every member of the organization. Intrapreneurs contribute substantially to the profit of the business through their creativity and leadership mentality. These qualities help them to adapt to the rapidly changing scenarios that every business frequently goes through and in turn help bring the change culture in the organization. Organizations that have acknowledged the importance of intrapreneurship have realized greater financial returns, enhanced productivity, additional innovation, and higher levels of employee engagement.

B. Leadership

Intrapreneurs have an ingrained quality of leadership. Other qualities that set them apart are passion, knowledge, and ability to make decisions and risk taking capability. They have the skill set to work individually as well as with their fellow members. Changing and challenging scenarios are relished by them and such situations bring out the best of their abilities. It is this precise feature that sets them apart from the crowd. This talent needs to be nurtured and cherished to create new leaders for your organization. This is one of the best ways to acquire and retain the best talent in the business.

C. Strategy and planning

Intrapreneurs with an entrepreneurial mindset are effective users of the strategy of the business to further rapid growth for the organization. They have the knack of knowing which idea is effective and what will work in different situation. An eye for detail and a broad situation approach simultaneously from these individuals help the company plan for long-term growth. Involving them in the strategy and long-term plans help the business chalk out the right approaches for a profitable development.

D. Innovation

Intrapreneurs have innovation in their blood and are excited about trying and implementing new ideas for the successful functioning of the organization. Innovation is the tool for the organization to get a brand new perspective on things with a 360 degree view. Existing processes and products undergo improvisation which in turn attracts investors and shareholders to your business. This can lead to exponential growth for the organization. It is the business owner's responsibility to create the right environment to foster the growth and nurture of the intrapreneurs in your organization. This has been the key differentiating factor of success for multiple organizations.

E. They are professionals

Intrapreneurs excel in issues within the business domain as their skills are specific to the task or job at hand making them specialists in those subject areas. This allows them to bring the element of professionalism in the organization. Their ability to do things differently, come up with fresh ideas, and take bold decisions help them as well as the business to excel. Stagnant growth is a bane for any organization and can be combated by identifying and encouraging intrapreneurs in the organization. It is not only vital to work hard but more prominently work smart. An employee with the right positive and inventive outlook can help change the fortunes of the business and help the organization outshine the competition. This particular value of these individuals has led to the development of a niche profession for those who possess this skill set.

8. In business, an army mindset is stronger than the family mindset

I have asked multiple people the question during my seminars, what type of working culture is required in an organization? The foremost answer that comes back instantaneously is a "like a family."

I, however, have a different line of thinking. In order for a business to be successful, it is given that a competent team needs to be built. In my opinion the team should have the characteristics of the Army. Like the army, the team should be result oriented, focused, unbiased, and rational. There should be a strong bond between team members borne of respect and a willingness to sacrifice oneself for the better of the team. The team should be like a cohesive unit working toward the final goal of excellence. Responsibility and accountability should be ingrained irrespective of position and seniority. The vision and the march toward the goal should be unwavering. This work culture breeds success in the organization.

In a family setup one typically tends to pick up the slack if someone is not performing in order to maintain the relationship as well as keep a positive atmosphere. This is an incorrect way of approaching things as this not only hampers the growth of the individual but also diminishes the benefits for the company in the long run. If your team is, however, thoroughly professional like the army, each team member is accountable and nonperforming members are pushed to improve and develop. This may cause some tension and heartburn in the short run, but the fruit of these actions is always rewarding in the long-term scheme of things.

However, our first preference is to run the organization like a family where we care for and respect one another. This leads to strengthening of the bond between the team members. However, what we tend to forget that a family can also function effectively only in the presence of tough love and reprimand in case a family member is doing something wrong. While the family setup makes for a pleasing and comfortable working environment, it certainly negates the element of accountability from your organization. Decision making inadvertently tends to become emotional rather than rational. It is important to note that running a successful business requires keeping the interests of the business as the topmost priority followed by the interest of the team and lastly the interest of the individuals. Successful businesses thrive due to a practical approach not an emotive one. In business you should use your head (intelligence) and not heart.

9. You can win the world by serving

Human nature is to expand; we always want to expand, craving for expansion. Craving for expansion has been ever present in humans as the dawn of time. This expansion resulted in violence in the olden days. And the person with more territories ruled or conquered was called a powerful king. This won't work in modern times, how it is possible to fulfill ultimate desire of expansion and ruling others? It is only possible by serving others.

This craving for advancements has been historically present in human from the very early days when kings and emperors constantly wanted to expand their kingdoms. This expansion was intrinsically driven by violence and war in the olden days. The modern day growth story, however, is focused on acquiring and maintaining a large loyal customer base which will propagate the growth engine for your organization.

You can rule the whole world by serving and spreading love. A business allows you that ultimate opportunity to serve the customers and scale up to be present all over the world. A global footprint is now made possible with the advent of technology.

10. Effect of you becoming a businessman to the world

Intelligent businesses understand the need of collaborations to generate success. Humans by nature are social and this cordial relationships nurtured by the business owners along with their customers, suppliers, employees, and other business owners are the key drivers for expansion. Business growth has a ripple effect and affects the surrounding environment through creation of opportunities for employees, suppliers, retailers, storage facilities, courier services and other support services.

Successful business owners not only create opportunities at the national level but also at the international level. Business also creates wealth for the entrepreneur as well as for the employees. It also helps generate taxation revenue for the government which is then used for social development. A wealth of prospects is opened for various stakeholders on an ongoing basis resulting in societal upliftment.

Businesses also generate happiness and satisfaction for the employees by paying them a good salary and benefits to help them live a better life. They help suppliers and service providers by disbursing timely and prompt payments to the supplier. Customers are benefited through acquisition of a value product and service for the price paid which satisfies their needs and resolves their problems. Business leaders pave the way for competition to enhance their product and services as well while also providing opportunities for new entrants to enter the market. Knowledge and information flow freely, standard of living is raised, and massive wealth creation can take place. As the owner of the successful business you have the chance to become a mentor and share your success story. Your experience inspires other to follow suit and launch more pioneering ideas which in turn creates more growth prospects.

11. National pride – business as a value addition to society

The proficiency to create value profit for the organization is the basic prerequisite for any business. The business, however, also lays down the foundation for prosperity in society. Only profitable companies are sustainable in the long term and capable of creating goods, services, processes, return on capital, work opportunities, and a tax base. A company's basic commercial operations are the principal benefits that have an impact on society.

Corporate social responsibility (CSR) has become a key issue for today's business with informed and educated consumers expecting organizations to contribute toward the society. Social awareness is increasing amongst the population with people recognizing the need to work toward the upliftment of the less fortunate. It is but natural that they also look at organizations to do their fair share as well. Consumers also place a heavy emphasis on buying products and services produced ethically. A CSR contribution by your business shows your willingness to tackle larger social issues rather than focusing solely on profit. This helps attract more customers to your product or service and drives a perpetual growth cycle. Employees also pride themselves in being part of a CSR organization and it will help your business attract the best talent.

> *"Someone's sitting in the shade TODAY, because someone planted a tree a LONG TIME AGO."*

Every company, whether big or small can contribute their own meaningful bit to society. CSR activities can range from donation money or resources, setting up social or environmental projects or campaigning on and supporting a certain issues that are affecting people and the environment. Another important aspect that business owners should consider is Personal

Social Responsibility wherein the owners allocate their time, resources, and efforts toward a cause of their interest. This helps you leverage your good fortunes for a noble and passionate cause.

Scan this QR code to get the FREE Daily Planner that will help you to focus on the most important activities, keep track of them and avoid running out of time because of poor task prioritizing.

Or visit www.sameerindia.com/dailyplanner

CHAPTER 3

ALL ABOUT THE RESTAURANT INDUSTRY

Starting a business is a great decision. But equally challenging is identifying the line of business. If you turn your passion into your source of livelihood, life can't be rosier. A person spends 75 percent of his life at his workplace. So to make this life worthwhile, that 75 percent of the time should be fun, pleasant, and a learning experience.

From childhood, I have closely seen the poultry business, as it was our family business and I am personally very charmed by the ways of the restaurant industry. So let's go over the niceties of this industry, which is the source of livelihood of millions.

Why start business in the restaurant industry?

The owner of Amway Corporation (leader in Network Marketing) on being asked why does Amway sell soaps and detergents, gave a simple reply. He said the primary reason was everyone buys it and it is a basic necessity for each and every person. The same analogy holds true for food as well. Maslow's basic need theory lists food, clothing, and shelter as the basic requirements for all individuals in order to survive. Food not only serves a biological function of human body sustenance but also has a key social function.

The restaurant industry today is in great demand and can never be dispensed off as it serves the rudimentary need for human beings. Initiating a business in the restaurant industry offers distinct advantages over other businesses in the sense that everyone needs to eat. Unique taste and desires of individuals open up a vast avenue for different food products. Businesses can tap into this booming potential market and succeed by distinguishing themselves from the competition. It is well known that an average person eats three times a day; namely breakfast, lunch, and dinner. This is in addition to the snacks and other food products we consume throughout the day.

The transaction cycle in the restaurant industry is fast with the consumption of food happening on the same day. Similarly the price for the food purchased is also paid the same day resulting in a rich cash flow for the business. With the ever-changing demographic trend made up of people with high disposable incomes and frequent eating out at restaurants especially among the younger generation, this industry offers limitless upside. The frequent jaunts at eating places represent a combination of celebration, spending quality time with friends and family, relaxing, socializing, and entertainment.

What distinguishes the restaurant business today from yesteryears is the consumer today is looking at eating outside as a total experience of food, quality, service as well as ambience. The entire cycle from the hired employees, preparation of food, thought process behind the recipes, the way the product is served to the customer, and the little innovations to create a niche by the business showcase that the food business is here to stay. Restaurant businesses are making the experience much more personal for the customer with the relationship between the owner and consumers being redefined. This approach has helped the industry achieve marked success and also expand their customer base. The restaurant industry has become the mother hen that keeps on laying golden eggs. The industry has also vastly benefited with the integration of technology in the business.

What are the different formats of restaurants that exist today?

The restaurant industry offers a bevy of options for the business owner. Everything from a fast food joint to a full service restaurant with all their associated benefits is available as choices for the customer to select from. There are various formats of restaurants that exist today:

- Full service restaurants
- Coffee shops
- Cafés
- Snack bars
- Quick service restaurants (QSRs)
- Food courts
- Take out stands
- Street stalls
- Kiosks

Main four categories

I have classified the formats of restaurants into four main categories:

1. **Cafe**

Cafes are a huge hit amongst the younger generation which they frequent to have a hot and cold beverage, predominantly coffee. The current technological advancements and office on the go have also made this destination favorite amongst the business class. People also frequent cafes to have business meeting with clients. Cafes are principally associated with a place where people go to relax, rejuvenate, socialize, and chit chat.

2. **Casual dining**

Casual dining refers to a food business serving moderately priced food in a comfortable setting. This type of business is characterized by an intermediate setup between fine dining and QSRs. This is a place where conventional business meetings can happen in a more formal venue. These restaurants will typically have a buffet or an ala carte option. Some of the place can also house a bar along with a limited wine menu.

3. **Fine dining**

Fine dining refers to the pinnacle of food production, service, and hospitality and is pronounced by its excellent ambience setting. The price that the place commands differentiates it from casual dining. The high price tag is justified by providing top class food, impeccable service, delectable variety, and a classy surrounding. The staff is fittingly trained, extremely courteous, and in a formal attire.

4. **Quick service restaurant**

Quick service restaurant as the name implies speed of execution of orders at a price which is light on the pocket. The churning of customers is at a high pace and minimum table service is provided at this place. The food preparation time is very short and limited menu options are available. The place also has minimal use of cutlery, and the emphasis is on rapid fulfillment of orders to increase customer footfalls.

Scope of starting a restaurant

a. The business is flexible

Business owners can choose from an assortment of options for starting a restaurant. The initial setup can be a simple no frill setup and can evolve over time according to suggestions, improvements, and exposure. A wide variety of choices in flavor, size, ingredients, presentation, customer likes and wants provides the business owners with a multitude of options along with the requisite flexibility. The business can also expand in size as per requirement and capacity of the business owner. What is needed to succeed is to remain in sync with the desires and choices of your customer. After all *"A satisfied customer is the best business strategy after all."* There can be no better marketing message than coming from a satisfied customer.

b. The demand is high

Food being a necessity for human sustenance will always be in demand. Also with the ever increasing population as well as changes in the spending habits of the newer generations this demand will keep on increasing with time. Food is the basic nourishment for the human body and everything from fine dining to street food will always find an audience. The world is changing today from a joint family to a nuclear family with both husband and wife working. This has led to a rise in outside eating and combined with the diverse culinary options available eating outdoor has become the new norm. With a population of over 1.2 billion and 65 percent of the population falling in the less than 35 years category, India provides a huge potential for exponential growth of the food industry. It is also expected that the middle class population of India is expected to touch 550 million by 2025 and will be the key driver for demand of the food and beverage industry. It is important to distinguish yourself from the competition as *"Variety's the very spice of life in food."*

c. Favorable trends and lifestyle changes

The world is constantly evolving with travel barriers no longer applicable. People travel to far off place experiencing the delicacies of that particular place and developing taste buds for variety food. Places of eating and the type of food eaten have come to be identified as statement of status and class. As the old adage goes, you are what you eat has now been redefined to you are what you eat as well as where you eat. Globalization has altered the food industry landscape with people demanding variety and quality. Dining out has become an experience people want to relish as well as a platform for socializing. It has become the ideal place for friends, family, and colleagues to get together, have fun, and have a pleasant experience. Restaurants which have provided a unique and novel experience to customer have excelled in the business as they have succeeded in creating memories for the customer. For example the Sahib Sindh Sultan provides you the unique experience of dining in an 1853 era atmosphere train.

Consumers are more aware than ever and expect the food industry to conduct its business in an ethical and fair manner. Customers also identify with restaurants that provide a difference in the existing crowded market place. For example some restaurants provide a traditional ethnic experience showcasing our cultural heritage providing us the opportunity to relive our history thereby making the dining experience unforgettable. With the percentage of women in the workforce increasing and a nuclear family concept emerging, a demand for convenience is being created which the food business can accomplish. The customer is constantly on the lookout for bold and innovativeness in the food that he eats and exposure to knowledge and social media have revolutionized food eating from sustenance to enjoyment.

Geographically, the prime opportunities are in the urban centers, where higher wages are attracting more Indians. By 2020, it's estimated that 36 percent of India's population will be urban dwellers, up from 32 percent currently.

d. Customer habits play an important role

As the paradigm of food trends shifts, people tend to change their preferences accordingly. Needs get converted to desires, and new needs emerge which create a huge opportunity for growth. Food has moved on from survival to a state of mind. For example some people will eat food for leisure and relaxation while some people will eat during stress. The eat to live saying has morphed into live to eat. It is important that food industry owners realize this shifting pattern and use it to fuel growth for their business.

Competition in the Restaurant Industry

While the market for restaurants is vast, there is also stiff competition that exists in the industry. The huge market keeps on attracting newer entrants into the business thereby raising the level of competition for the existing players in the market. Also compared to a majority of industries the food industry has the ability to encompass everybody due to the volatile nature of the customer base and huge scope.

We normally associate competition as a hindrance when starting a new business, but we should rather view competition positively as it creates an avenue to foster creativity in your organization. It raises the standard of the industry making innovation a need not a novelty. Competition also ensures that the customer get better value for their money. It also provides you an opportunity to become an early bird or trendsetter by providing unique offerings. This increases the loyalty among your customer base and provides free word of mouth publicity.

A business should always be asking what the wants of my customer are and how best can I satisfy them. What are the hindrances in achieving complete customer satisfaction and how can I stand out from my competition. A business that can successfully follow this approach and find solutions to customer desires is bound to succeed.

The Unorganized Businesses

The booming market for the food industry has resulted in ease of doing business and allowing anybody to enter the industry and set shop. Lax government rules and regulations in the past have resulted in the unorganized sector getting a foothold in the industry with no proper oversight and control. Rising consumer awareness on hygiene, safety, ethics, and quality have forced the industry to tighten the norms and adhere to rules and regulations regarding food safety. The rising trend of usage of technology and stringent government regulations for improvement of food safety standards has started stemming the flow of the unorganized sector in the market. Social media penetration has ensured that any unhygienic act by a restaurant becomes viral instantaneously resulting in loss of reputation, customer, and closure of the food business.

In India, full-service restaurants command the largest market share, at 57 percent of sales. The next biggest category is QSRs, at about 16 percent. Considering the country's giant patchwork of cultures and cuisines, it's probably not surprising that about two-thirds of the restaurant units are loosely structured, small, independent eateries—referred to as "unorganized"—that often double as retail food stores. Only about 2 percent of the total inventory of restaurants is branded—less than a tenth of what's seen in other countries with a more established foodservice industry.

The Role of Technology

Technology has revolutionized the way food industry conducts its business. Technological advancements have helped lower the cost of food, made the process more efficient and streamlined. Labor requirements have been lowered, process standardization has taken place, and quality and consistency have improved tremendously. Transportation of goods is quick and effective which has bolstered creativity and variety in food preparation. Mass production has provided economies of scale and driven down costs and increased profitability for the business. App-based food ordering and delivery platforms have completely transformed the industry providing a much wider audience for the business. Improved packaging and storage methods have ensured the food always remains fresh and tasty. Technology has also helped in inventory control for the industry in turn freeing up cash flow for the business. Another area of food industry that is thriving is the convenient food segment with ready to fry, precooked, dried food, and semi-cooked food finding flavor with the younger generation.

The Impact on Economy

In the olden days people used to grow their own food which resulted in limited variety choices available for the customer. This resulted in the good trading practice commonly known as the barter system where you would trade for goods which you could not produce. This led to a niche specialization where people would concentrate on what they did best, and received other goods and service through trade. This led to the creation of the so-called global market and a huge business opportunity for entrepreneurs worldwide.

Delivery Services in Restaurants

Restaurants are maximizing their business potential by offering door delivery services thus satisfying the convenience need of the customer. All restaurants big or small offer this facility as a larger customer base can be serviced through this route. Customer loyalty is also regained and retained through this approach. With real estate being a premium, there is limited capacity of seats in the restaurant which can be offered to the consumers. Promoting takeout helps create a much larger revenue stream and works beautifully not only for fast food joints but also for restaurants. It is in human nature to want to relax at home and enjoy a serene setting eating outside food.

The development of online ordering, phone apps, and other restaurant technologies has resulted in a large-scale increase in the sales of delivery items. Delivery and take out segments are among the fastest growing in the hospitality industry. Smart phone penetration, ease of access to Internet, and low cost data availability have powered the growth of the delivery and take out division of the business. E-Tailing, which means having a sound presence online, is a must for all delivery-based QSR. Compared to the revenues generated from the typical brick-and-mortar format this segment offers exponential growth.

The original delivery model where restaurants used to perform their own delivery is being upended by third-party delivery services. Third-party delivery services are cropping up everywhere locally as well as nationally to take advantage of this trend. If as a business owner you are not tapping into this delivery market either through in-house service or third-party delivery service you are missing out on a major chunk of the revenue pie whilst risking customer dissatisfaction at the same time.

A multitude of global players have their very own websites from where you can not only browse the menu but also eat restaurant food sitting in the comfortable confines of your home. Businesses that don't want to do delivery using in-house services can opt for websites like Foodpanda, Swiggy, and Zomato to foray into this rapidly expanding market. Zomato is probably the most popular along the lot which also provide the customer with an option of leaving a review and feedback rating. An exclusive phone number is also accessible to make reservation at the restaurants. The feedback and rating of customer help restaurants streamline and improve their processes.

Impact of online food services on the restaurant business in India

The home delivery or the takeaway options have gained a lot of traction in locations such as malls, offices, and big-party orders for residential complexes. Everybody seems to favor the online food order and delivery option predominantly for the convenience of food at their location. The fast food business in India is only about two decades old, and is still largely unorganized. Given the rate of growth of the organized sector, it is only a matter of time and a large chunk of global investments that will have a lasting effect on the ongoing restaurant business.

The ever growing population combined with the pain, time, and effort of driving to a restaurant in crowded metro cities has propelled the need to ready to eat and doorstep delivery services. Companies aware of this prospective opportunity will hit the ground running. The stiff completion, however, will ensure that the fittest of the lot will survive. Businesses that maximize their value proposition and keep their brand active in consumer's minds will be successful. Online delivery platforms tend to personalize the ordering experience for the customer through the storage of relevant customer data. It has been largely observed that once a customer signs up with one platform they rarely ever leave for another platform. This creates a loyal customer base where the portals who can sign up customer at a rapid rate are rewarded. Time is of critical essence and delivery wait time can never exceed 60 minutes.

The rising quick service restaurant industry

The traditional Indian consumer who has culturally believed in the idea of eating home food has slowly been warming up to the idea of Eating Out. The restaurant industry in India is mainly being driven by the so-called youth generation typically aged between 14 and 40 years. With a growing population of 1.2 billion comprising mainly of young people the prospects for the QSR industry is enormous. This is exactly what the foreign fast food chains have enchased upon as can be comprehended from the fact that the fast food industry grows 20 percent annually. The QSR chains have also customized their menus to the Indian taste buds tweaking their products and processes to suit India-specific requirements. This has also played a role in shifting the eating out patterns as the younger generation is more experimental in their food choices and more likely to visit the fast food joints compared to the older generation.

The QSRs have both a range of food cuisines and minimal table services to cater to the fast pace need of youngsters and working professionals. The speed of execution is the differentiating factor of these restaurants and this coupled with express deliveries by most of them have provided an additional bonus.

Quick Service Restaurants have been a vital segment for the Indian Food Services market and have grown multifold in the recent years thanks to their emphasis on affordable and competitive pricing clubbed with catering to growing consumer needs such as convenience, increased appetite, and craving for international food. This segment is expected to witness significant growth and entry by several players. The concept of QSRs has gained prominence in India due to the introduction of affordable eating and enabled the indulgence of customers with smaller pockets. This market segment is, however, ultra-competitive in nature with the continuous entry of international brands.

As international, national, and regional players move into the market the momentum is shifting toward more chain-affiliated and standardized operations. A value-seeking mentality, marketing, greater mobility, and social media will all fuel more demand for QSRs.

The Future

India's quick service restaurant (QSR) and casual dining restaurant (CDR) industry experienced a number of policy changes in late 2016 and through 2017; including, demonetization and its lasting effects; a temporary ban on liquor sales at restaurants and establishments near national highways; and, the introduction of a goods and services tax (GST). Smaller outlets, more food innovation, and greater focus on same-store sales growth are driving growth in the face of these policy changes.

The National Restaurant Association of India (NRAI) reported that the restaurant sector was valued in 2017 at U.S. USD 52 billion (INR 337,500 crore) and is projected to grow to U.S. USD 85 billion (INR 552,000 crore) by 2022. It employs 6 million people directly and another 8 million indirectly. Analysts forecast the sectors will contribute 2.1 percent to Indian GDP by 2021. The

QSR and CDR encompass the organized and unorganized markets including pubs, bars, and cafes as well as street vendors. Standalone restaurants are emerging and competing in this segment against several chain and group-owned QSRs and CDRs.

Multiple industry sources recognize India as one of the world's top ten largest economies and expect the country to grow in importance and overtake numerous others in the coming years.

India's urban youth population is vibrant, enthusiastic, innovative, and self-motivated. They have extensive social media presence and use various platforms to convey their emotions incessantly. Dining at QSRs and CDRs is no longer perceived as a sparing luxury. Millennials (people born in or after 2000) who enjoy traveling are the primary customer audience for QSRs and CDRs. These consumers are more disposed toward the idea of experimenting with food.

Many fine dining restaurants have adopted the QSR model by opening kiosk size outlets in food courts of major shopping malls. Their food dishes in this format are priced at a lower rate with reduced portions. Young professionals and college-aged students are seen often at QSRs as they want a quick meal that is also hygienic and of superior food quality at a friendly price point.

QSRs are the most preferred destination, followed CDRs when it comes to eating out. They form 45 percent and 32 percent of the overall market, respectively (*Source*: India Food Services report 2016).

Conclusion

The restaurant industry has rapidly evolved according to time with dining out becoming a major portion of the population lifestyle. A combination of factors including higher disposable incomes, nuclear families, working spouses, and exposure to world cuisine has driven the current generation to experiment with variety food. This in turn has opened up vast avenues for the food business to tap into. Customer satisfaction and service have become paramount for survival along with innovation and adaptation of technology. Customers are looking for an all-round experience like ambience, food quality, variety, and service quality and the one who fulfills this requirement stands to gain customer acceptance and rapid growth.

So there is a huge scope for those who want to make a mark into the culinary world, however, with a caveat. This is a crowded market. So product and service differentiation is the key. So before taking the leap, identify your core competencies, sharpen your USPs, do a market study to identify your niche market segment, and then have a whale of a time in this thriving business, without FEAR.

Did that word just catch your eye? I know it is this emotion that has stopped many from getting onto the road of entrepreneurship. Be it a fear to fail or a fear to sail, prospective business owners feel weak in their knees. So I have tried to address some of these in the upcoming chapter and what you can do to overcome these fears and face the entrepreneurship world with courage and fortitude.

"I learned that courage was not the ABSENCE of fear, but the TRIUMPH over it. The brave man is not he who does not feel afraid, but he who conquers that fear." - Nelson Mandela

---

Scan this QR code to get the FREE additional bonus chapter on How to Lead Silently

Or visit www.sameerindia.com/leadsilently

CHAPTER 4

FEAR OF PEOPLE WHO WANT TO START A BUSINESS

The best part of my profession is that I get to meet a lot of enterprising, motivated, and enthusiastic people all the time. I feel inspired by their commitment. But at the same time, I also sense their hesitation in taking that crucial step that can change their life forever!

Over the past few months, I have been doing the Masters in Financial Freedom seminar. As I interact with people from different professional backgrounds who either want to start their own business or want to expand their current one, I realize that there is one factor that holds them back from taking their entrepreneurial foot forward. That is FEAR.

Let's find out why fear dictates us.

We have hand and legs, we call these parts as my legs or my hands. We never say I am the hand or I am the leg. Am I right? The same way we have something called as the mind. We say it's our mind. The same way mind is not me.

It's very important to separate the mind, from oneself. What is basic function of the mind? It is to protect the body. So it always gives us thoughts and directions to keep the body in a comfort zone.

Whenever we try to take action that is outside our comfort zone, the mind will give a precautionary thought of not taking the action; this is biggest problem we face. Few people know this as they understand the nature of their mind and they take action anyways. Actions give result and they become successful. Whereas there are others who listen to their minds and never take action. This leads to them staying in the comfort zone. But in the long term its leads to failure, which makes them uncomfortable ultimately.

So what is right way? It is to be uncomfortable and take the right action consistently and you will eventually become successful. Once you become successful you will then be comfortable. Practicing consistently, to become uncomfortable increases the boundaries of your comfort zone.

Whenever mind gives negative thoughts one must say **"Thanks for sharing"**. This is magical tool to keep mind peaceful and take action in right direction. People who are unsuccessful are mostly the victims of their own mind. Mind works like an antivirus to protect the body which is the operating system, but many times it tries to dominate operating system itself. Be aware of this. Never allow the antivirus to dominate your operating system. You are not your mind. You are a thousand times bigger and stronger than you mind.

It is FEAR that dictates many of our actions and decisions in life and makes us risk averse. Becoming risk averse can be a gifted or acquired skill for business owners. In these last few years, I have learnt it best. I have mastered my fears and the journey has been memorable!

When I look closely, there is a definite pattern in the way fear dominates these budding entrepreneurs. They have a common set of concerns, which I have tried to address and alleviate in this chapter

List of fears of people who want to start a business

1. I will fail

I see that the most important fear that keeps aspiring entrepreneurs from taking the next big leap is the FEAR TO FAIL. The possibility of losing everything that is invested—time, money, and hard work—is a major stumbling block. While fear teaches you many things, as a human tendency, it is not easy to face it!

Do you know that the success of a venture is directly related to the business owner's attitude? If you run the business to avoid losses you will cloud your decision making with fear and limit the growth of the business, while if you run it to ADD VALUE, it can help you design a scalable business model which will help reap big profits.

Do you know about the Sanskrit concept of "Sankalp" and "Vikalp"? Let me tell you.

Sankalp is the first thought that comes to take an action; it is then followed by multiple thoughts which say that you should not take the action, this is known as Vikalp. We need to understand the nature of our mind; we are designed like this. Nature of mind is to protect this body that is reason most of time it gives thought to keep us in comfort zone. Be aware about nature of this mind and take action to achieve your purpose.

Take the right step, be prepared to not fail. Start by asking yourself, what will make you fail? Then work on each answer to be prepared to not fail.

> *"Whether you gain or you lose, BEHIND every loss there is some gain and behind every gain, there is some loss. DON'T WORRY about winning or losing. Just do your duty."*

Even after you fail you are learning, take it as a lesson and move on.

Henry Ford, who started the Industrial Revolution by changing the entire manufacturing industry scene, has rightly said, *"Failure is an opportunity to begin again more intelligently."*

With my years of experience, one thing I can assure you—starting and running your own business is one of the most enriching experiences of your life. So don't be risk averse and gear up for the challenge! As they say, "life is a gamble," but with due diligence, this risk is lowered increasing your chances of success and greater confidence.

2. I don't know where to start

The information technology exposes us to so much information and choices that getting confused is obvious. We have seen cases where prospective entrepreneurs spend years in just analyzing the opportunities without taking any steps. As it is said, "too much analysis leads to paralyses."

So then HOW DO YOU START RIGHT?

I say—WRITING DOWN YOUR DREAMS. I still do it! And it works!

Journey of 1000 miles starts with a single step. So pen it down and announce it out loud. Read it every day as it will push you closer toward your aim. And my secret mantra—"Zero Procrastination." So get up and get moving! Don't wait for the right time.

Understand that the only person, who can steal your dream away is YOU. When I started with my new venture, the first thing I did was a critical validation of my business idea with my peers and mentors. If your idea has been tried and tested by someone else successfully, a research of the person, his business model, and success story is a tremendous help. If you're lucky, you may even get an opportunity to connect with him for advice. And even if you're not so fortunate, just knowing that the idea has been successfully vetted by someone should give you enough confidence to take the next step. Geared with a right attitude and positive frame of mind, move ahead and the path will automatically unfold.

3. I am not from a business background

This is one more belief that keeps us from exploring business opportunity. Did you know Steve Jobs and Bill Gates were first generation entrepreneurs? Did you know Mark Zuckerberg also did not come from a business family? Of course, having a business background may have its own advantages, but it is also a double edged sword. Without capacity building and continuous improvement, the business empire can stagnate and eventually set for doom. So a first generation entrepreneur who starts from "I need to learn" attitude begins learning quickly embarking himself on a path of successful entrepreneurship.

A man is known by the company he keeps. The company of fellow entrepreneurs and access to mentors offer a huge knowledge and experience bank, providing the opportunity for continuous learning. This real-life experience sharing is better than any university textbook. What more? In a shoe-string budget of a startup, this is a pool for free advice!

4. I am not a business type

There are many rationales people offer for shying away from joining the entrepreneurship bandwagon. From negative perception toward starting a business to finding it overwhelming, the reasons are plenty. But all this stems from lack of adequate information needed to take a logical decision.

"I am not a business type" was a reason my best friend gave me when I was trying to coax him into starting a new business. A little stronger persuasion and a lot of brain washing later, today, he is one of the leading real estate brokers in the state. Till date, he remembers our "mentoring" sessions. "It's actually your success," he told me once. All I did was took a leap of faith in his abilities. The hard work and perseverance was purely his!

Know that you can achieve big dreams in life through successful business. And it is the power of your dreams that fuels the passion behind running the business. If you're ready for change and learning, there is nothing that can hold you back. Strive for excellence through continuous improvement and sky is the only limit.

5. I don't have the required capital

Of all the fears people talk of, I find this the most relevant. But I have helped my students overcome this fear with a positive attitude and power of their minds.

Capital investment is probably the single largest fear factor dissuading entrepreneurs from putting their best foot forward. With scanty funds to bootstrap, entrepreneurs make wrong business choices thereby limiting their growth. On the other hand, successful entrepreneurs base their business decisions on key parameters like ideas yielding high returns and long-term benefits, scalability of business models, etc.

When entrepreneurs ask me about their fiscal challenges and shoe string budgets for business, I recommend them to critically evaluate the prospective business idea, a thorough competitor analysis and financial analysis to forecast the total financial requirement. This analysis can mitigate the risk of undercapitalization or overcapitalization.

One more important practice I advise is "ploughing back of profits" or reinvesting a part of company's net profits into the business for growth and diversification. This method of self-financing gives the confidence to a corporation by reducing dependency on external financial sources. This financial independence ensures long-term growth as unnecessary expenses are indirectly curtailed. In a realistic business world, finding investors is not so easy. So reinvesting in business is a slow and steady process of building a business empire with strong roots.

6. I don't have the right product or customer

So let's break this issue in two parts—customer acquisition and product acceptance. Both these challenges are intertwined.

First, let me speak about product acceptance. So you can have a fantastic business idea, but if there are no takers for your product or service, the business is doomed for failure. So understanding who is your customer and packaging your offerings correctly is of paramount importance. An efficient customer support and a focused marketing approach are required to keep your customer engaged with your product instead of competition. Many a times, it is not important to reinvent the wheel. In a trading business model, reselling products or services of the manufacturer differently can also give you an edge over competition.

Now, customer acquisition—an efficient use of social media platforms like Facebook, Instagram; joining social business groups like BNI, Rotary, Lions Club, Toastmasters, etc. can help you reach out to your target audience of customer more easily than ever. While having a good, old network of business connects can facilitate the process, these platforms and networks today play a very important role in reaching out to the larger audience beyond geographical boundaries. Connecting with mentors, lead magnets who have influence over a large group of your audience can also help build large networks for business.

In an offline market place, where a customer needs to visit your store to make the purchase, location plays a key role. Popular research suggests that a customer's ease of accessing the store location is directly proportional to increased turnover and success of the enterprise.

To identify an ideal location, we can ask questions like:

    a) Where is my target customer?
    b) How easy is it for my target customer to reach me?
    c) Which location can help improve my sale of my products or services?

Being mindful of these aspects will make the process of customer acquisition much more comfortable.

7. I can't see a good scope—the market is saturated

I know that the markets today are more complex than ever. The ever-evolving technology, effectual strategic marketing strategies, access to funds, increased purchasing power of the urban customers due to high disposable incomes have amplified competition. This has also proliferated the customers' demand for various goods and services.

So in such markets, the key to making a niche for yourself is to strive for excellence and differentiation—*How can I provide more value in the same or more competitive price? How can I do the same thing differently?*—answers to these questions will help you create a market for your offering.

Sometimes, differentiation is not just a product, but also the service. Neeraj Gupta, Founder of Meru Cabs, in his journey from INR 0 to INR 850 crores has shown us just that. Before Meru, he owned a garage called "Elite Class" in Andheri, a crowded business suburb of Mumbai, with a competition of 50 other garages in the vicinity on the same road. Offering perks, free services, and a great user experience to the customer while in their garage, they not only captured the market, but grew their business exponentially.

So the challenge is to create a differentiated offering from the crowd.

8. I can't fail my family

Remember, work and life are the two sides of the coin that defines you as a person. Most successful entrepreneurs have started small and slow and gradually scaled up. Neeraj Gupta is a classic example. And strong familial ties have made that journey worthwhile. Did you know Mr. Gupta actually borrowed INR 50,000 from his wife, Farhat, to start this garage business?

It is ironical that while we work hard for the wellbeing and comfort of our family, the same work keeps us away from them. A new startup with shoestring budgets rarely has surplus cash flows. This is a cause of grave stress to an entrepreneur with liabilities. But this can also be a journey that you travel together with your family, thereby growing the emotional and personal bonds and making them stronger.

As I am closely associated with many business families, I have seen that involving the family so they see your passion and dream is very important. An open channel of communication where you share your struggles, concerns, and dreams together can only go a long way in bringing everyone closer and strengthen your support system.

Once you cross the initial days of the business building phase, there will be more time for family. Many family businesses enjoy being with each other and working together for betterment and growth of the business venture. If you are a first generation entrepreneur, then the family and the society look at you like a role model.

9. I am afraid to enter unchartered waters

As I always say, "Business is all about leadership, its moving from the masses to the classes." As a leader it is very important to move out of your comfort zone, and stretch your limits. In order to get comfortable with being uncomfortable, you need to step out of your comfort zone regularly and try new things. Eventually this will become a habit, and taking up newer challenges become a hobby.

Start slow and keep a finite goal to overcome this fear and build courage.

"Whenever you see a SUCCESSFUL business, someone once made a COURAGEOUS decision."

---

10. I am very overwhelmed with business demands

Some 80 percent startups fail in the first year. But not all fail due to lack of business. Some fail due to lack of adequate management capabilities. Success and failure are two sides of the same coin. While struggling to succeed has its own challenges, overnight success is also not easy to digest.

When we interviewed some business owners, it was interesting to see a fear of sudden spikes in business, as they feel incapacitated in handling the demands and stress of a growing business.

In any case, not being able to handle all the customers is a good challenge to deal with than not having enough business.

11. I am afraid of the unknown

In a job, there's certainty. The job, the salary, and the expectations are clearly defined. On the contrary, entrepreneurship is a leap of faith. As a business owner, you need to find comfort in uncertainty and develop trust in yourself. Unlike an employee, you are more in control of your destiny as he may lose his job or his company may shut down. So, while it can be scary at times, it is also incredibly rewarding and exciting.

Uncertainties are a part of life, like any other life experiences. So don't fear it. Understand what drives success in your business by carrying out a deep assessment of your business model. This can put you in the driver's seat with more control.

For example, if you're in a franchise model, follow the systems in place, and reach out to successful franchisees to see what you can do to replicate their success. If you're starting a business on your own, try to find a mentor who has been successful in a similar industry. And success will be yours.

Conclusion

As Thomas Roosevelt wisely said, *"It is hard to fail, but it is worse never to have tried to succeed."* And this has been my motto in everything I have chosen to do in my life. I feel spending a life with regret is worse than trying and failing. A failure can teach many valuable lessons. It is not important where you are on your path, so long as you are on a path toward your goal. The direction is more important. Starting a business is not for the weak and standing up for this challenge takes immense courage and fortitude.

Be proud! You have already taken the first step. Now keep the negative criticism at bay, embrace your fears, and overcome them to march forward toward your conquest.

Awaken the giant

Know that - We are designed for success. We have enough power and energy within us to do what we want to do. We can use this power wherever we want to. Normally this energy is in the dormant stage, like a sleeping giant. But to move forward and achieve success, you need to awaken the giant to massive action. Equipped with the tools and techniques and pumped up with the energy, we can rouse this giant within us and push him to attain a phenomenal success.

At this stage, as you're geared up to start your own business, in this next chapter, I want to elaborate on the Franchise business. If you have the required funds to invest as a franchise fee to start a business, I can assure you; this is one of the surest and quickest way to establish yourself in the business world. For more details, read on.

And which you're on your way to entrepreneurship, let me tell you about some of the more common mistakes entrepreneurs make, so that you can avoid them and learn from them.

Scan this QR code to get the FREE Declarations that are a powerful self-talk. The most successful people in life have an empowering way to communicate with themselves. With these declarations you can practice positive self-talk throughout your day, and you will begin to realize more favorable rewards in life.

Or visit www.sameerindia.com/declarations

CHAPTER 5

MISTAKES THAT MOST ENTREPRENEURS DO

"I have NOT failed; I have just FOUND 10,000 ways that won't work."
– Thomas Edison

Wise words of a wise man, a scholar, and a scientist. It is this attitude that separates a successful businessman from a mediocre one. Starting and growing a business is not everyone's ballgame. It involves carefully selecting the individual components and putting them together to run a smooth machinery. But this process is easier said than done.

In my Business Startup Seminars, I meet all kinds of entrepreneurs and having interacted with many, I see their fears and mistakes. A first generation entrepreneur is bound to face failures and make mistakes in the beginning having treaded into unchartered waters. But it is important to treat these as learning lessons and grow. As we analyze this pattern from success stories and through the knowledgeable interactions at my seminar, we were able to identify the common mistakes.

List of Mistakes that most entrepreneurs do

1. Thinking that you know everything

I find this trait mostly in the second or third generation entrepreneurs. While this is not a norm, it's definitely more than average trend. The moment you feel you know it all; you're on a downward path. In order to succeed, you should first accept that you have a lot to learn. It is this attitude that can take you a long way. In today's dynamic market scenario, without continuous learning you'd be left behind in the rat race.

The moment you say, "I know everything," it closes the doors to learning. These three words are the biggest hurdle to mankind.

> "You're always a STUDENT, never a master. You have to keep moving FORWARD." – Famous cinematographer, Conrad Hall

With the ever-evolving ways of this world and with this fast paced, technology-driven environment, new strategies, new tools, and techniques keep evolving. And to be successful, you need to work with a student mindset to learn new things and grow your business. Those entrepreneurs who have put capacity building on the back foot have setup their business for suffering. Lack of time or a know-it-all attitude can only slow down your pace. Learning is the key to growth, and the moment you stop learning is when you and your business stop growing.

2. Choosing the wrong partner

Business partnerships are like marriage. And as in any marriage, compatibility is very important. A perfect match of temperament, risk taking ability, and attitude is mandatory for a partnership to be successful. There will always be testing times with differences of opinions or misunderstandings. But if handled maturely, these differences will only make the relationship stronger. Keeping an open and transparent communication channel always helps.

I have seen business partnerships fail primarily because of lack of communication or goals.

A common mistake would be to partner with someone for their personal relationships rather than business goals. A family member or best friend may not necessarily be a good business partner. A partner has equal decision making powers as you. So sharing the same passion, entrepreneurial skills, and ideologies are very important.

Also, having complimentary skills as opposed to similar skills is very important while choosing a partner. If partners come with similar skill sets, there are chances of conflict and ego clashes. Conversely, when partners come with complementary skills, they add value and give a holistic view of business.

In my sessions, I have always emphasized on the importance of partnerships. A good business partner and a right investor are the key tools that can make or break a business's growth path. So choose wisely.

3. Underestimating the importance of technology

Large business conglomerates failed as they could not onboard on the latest technology. Businesses like Uber, Airbnb, or Amazon all run on technology.

Ola doesn't own a fleet of taxis, Amazon neither manufactures products nor does Airbnb own any hotels. It is the power of technology that built these business houses to the size they are today, in a short period of time. So remember, technology is no longer a luxury but an absolute necessity. Effective use of technology can ensure process improvement and cost reduction.

The benefits of technology cannot be undermined -

- **Maintain competitive edge** – As mentioned earlier, efficient use of technology can give you an edge over competition. Sometimes, success is not just doing different things, but doing things differently, and technology comes to the rescue at such times.
- **Data security** – Tools like cloud computing etc. along with other web security tools can manage your data storage, data mining, and data warehousing successfully anytime and anywhere without high dependency on local resources.
- **Innovation** – Technology is constantly evolving. So adopting the newer technological enhancements can only improve business performance and efficiency.

4. Financial mismanagement

One of the most common errors I have seen new entrepreneurs do is to 100 percent delegate financial matters. Financial management is the key to success. As an entrepreneur, keeping a cautious eye on the finances is critical to ensure optimal utilization of available resources. Equip your business with the right team of financial advisors who know their work, but always be apprised about your finances for rationalized decision-making process. Align your decision with the business aspiration goal.

5. No proper hiring

Leadership is not about doing everything yourself, but building a team that can run as a well-oiled engine to give the desired results. The key is to hire the right talent for each job. Contrary to popular belief, multitasking results in burnout and in low productivity. So delegation is your *mantra* to success. So talent acquisition department needs to be very effective.

In the startup stage of business though, hiring decisions need special attention considering the slim margins and shoe-string budgets. Hiring decisions should be then based on the accurate forecast of incoming revenue streams to sustain the increased headcount. This is where effective financial management plays a key role.

> *"Brilliant IDEAS don't make you successful; the people you HIRE to bring those brilliant ideas to life make you successful."*

That's why talent acquisition is important and needs to be done with great care. Good talent comes with a cost, be ready to spend if really required. Our secret to hiring right is to pay right to the right competent employee who is an intrapreneur.

> *"GREAT things in business are never done by one person; they're done by a TEAM of people."*

6. Not listening to customers

Most entrepreneurs are busy in operations and they do not have time to listen to the customer who is ready to give feedback or suggestions. This creates more dissatisfied customers and this is the biggest loss to any business. At Ambica, we are able to produce right product at the right time to the right customer by mastering active listening. Understanding your customer and his needs sets the stepping stone for success. We have numerous tools like CRMs and Feedback systems that can help us gage the pulse of the customer and his perception and experience about a certain product or service. It will also help identify the weakness of your offering and offer scope for improvement. Bill Gates once said, *"Your most unhappy customers are your greatest source of learning,"* and we believe in it 100 percent.

On the hind side, the customer also feels empowered and in turn offers his loyalty to companies who empathize and value their feedback. This indirect marketing tool also promises a customer buys-in.

> *"Your most UNHAPPY customers are your greatest SOURCE of learning."*
> *– Bill Gates*

7. Keep waiting for the right time

Majority of the entrepreneurs wait for the right time to come, only then they will start business. This sometimes leaves them waiting for a lifetime. RIGHT time is not an official announcement, but an OPPORTUNITY grabbed and utilized effectively. For the launch of a product, it is always advisable to launch an MVP (Minimum Viable Product); a product with basic features, and then improvises it slowly, based on the feedback. Don't wait too long to pilot, as it may result in a loss of momentum and in this world of fierce competition, you may lose your first mover advantage, if you wait too long.

8. Not keeping up with market trends

Many entrepreneurs have a notion that my product or service is the best. They never take time to survey the customer or the competitor or the market. This leads to customers going to other businesses and is a loss to business. What separates a winner from the rest is his ability to sense the rhythm of the market and position his offering accordingly. Continuous improvement is the key. You can't be complacent if you want to be a winner. Some of the top global corporations like Kodak failed and had to file for bankruptcy as they missed the beat of the market. The R&D and Product Development divisions need to be the most active departments if you want to be the market leader. If your early validations show a different result than what you anticipated, be upbeat about accepting it and choosing the alternate route. Being adaptable to change is the first sign of an entrepreneur!

9. No focus on marketing

I find it surprising to see that many perceive Marketing to be an expense. In fact Marketing is an investment you need to make if you want to grow your business. After all, how will a customer buy your product if he does not know you exist? This simple logic is lost to so many business owners. A strategic marketing effort will help you identify your target audience and channelize a process to ensure your messaging reaches the target powerfully.

While FREE PR and referral marketing can get your business to some level, in this digital age, if you are looking for exponential growth, digital marketing needs to be an essential element of your marketing plan. A competitor analysis will also help understand how your competition is allocating their marketing spend and allow you to plan an approach, which sets you apart.

Each product or service may have its unique requirements. So choose the platform that's most engaging when launching your product or service.

10. Lacking focus and clarity in business

Many entrepreneurs start business and they get caught up in daily activities. They don't have time to focus on the main activities or the vision of the company. Focus on "finding your niche" is not always plausible for all aspiring entrepreneurs. But lack of it has plunged many in the depths of failure, harming not just the business but also the relationships with clients, partners, and associates.

Success in business does not come overnight, and those who don't have this holding capacity are bound to lose their focus. If you feel you're losing your motivation, turn your vice into an advantage. Try adopting a diversified business model.

11. No clear goal

A common albeit deadly mistake I have seen made by most young, aspiring entrepreneurs is lack of adequate emphasis on vision. They don't know what they want to achieve and they don't know what it takes to achieve it. Did you know that achieving business success has a lot to do with your personality, attitude, and vision? With an eye on a clearly defined objective, it is a lot easier to navigate your path to success.

In addition to defining your clear aim, announcing it to those who work with you will aid in your effort to expedite your journey to success.

> *"If the PLAN does not work, change the plan, not the GOAL."*

12. No business plan

> *"Failing to Plan Is PLANNING To Fail."*

A business owner without a plan is like a chef without a recipe!

Kickstart your entrepreneurial journey with a clearly defined business plan that can help make your business better through effective, disciplined, and organized approach toward work, reducing the time wasted in unproductive tasks. Never underestimate the importance of a well thought of business plan. It has been my most prized document during the course of my business. It shows me where I have to go, how soon and guides me on what I need to do to achieve my goal.

Having a business plan also helps you in defining revenue streams as well as financial planning. Another great advantage of a business plan is that it helps attract more people to your business.

13. No mentors or coach

While it might be adventurous to tread the entrepreneurial journey alone, it might be a walk in the dark at times. And at such times, you need a mentor to look up to for answers. In spite of being a guide and mentor for many business owners, I still have a mentor, who is my go-to person in my times of challenges.

From taking the critical decisions to entering into associations and partnerships, a mentor can be a beacon of hope and light. In challenging times, the right mentor can turn a difficulty into an opportunity, just like Lord Krishna was the guiding star for Arjuna in Mahabharata. As an outsider, the mentor can give an unbiased view of the situation, improving the decision-making process.

Mentors also stimulate personal and professional growth through knowledge sharing, encouragement, and support. They create benchmarks and assist in realistic goal setting while being sounding boards to bounce off ideas for an unfiltered opinion. With rich experience and networks, mentors often can save us from making irreversible mistakes. So having the right mentor is a huge asset for the business owner and his business.

But having a mentor who's a right fit is important. The mentor needs domain expertise and overall understanding of your business model to be your beacon of hope and answer to challenges.

14. Business is people oriented not system oriented

"Systems work, people don't." A system is a process, method, or course of action designed to achieve a specific result. It is repeatable to achieve the desired result without continuous intervention from top leadership. Defined systems improve efficiency and reduce overdependence on people. Systems aid strategic planning and successful execution of processes.

In a people-centric system, there is a high dependency on specific people and absence of such people can hamper efficiency. I always recommend every business owner to analyze which category his business falls under. To check, ask yourself if the functioning of the enterprise is adversely affected by absence of a person. If your answer is positive, you're building a flawed business process and in due course of time it is bound to fail.

To improve efficiency and productivity, setting up systems and processes at the onset is vital. This also improves the employee productivity, reduces costs, and boosts revenues by producing consistently high quality work. To create and setup a system, evaluating the existing mechanics of the job, time spent on each activity and the expected outcome needs to be analyzed. Potential areas for improvement can also be identified. This is a key component of the process because business systems need to be reviewed and improved with changing times.

We have seen that a system-oriented approach helps business in many ways. Some key highlights are elaborated below:

a) **Systems provide consistency**
Once a system is created and documented, it can be used by your team to produce the same products or services with the same level of consistency and minimal intervention from your side. You can monitor these processes and improvise when required. Systems can be implemented for sales, marketing, operations, employee

training, etc. Your customers are the key beneficiaries of the standardization you bring through your processes.

"CONSISTENCY is the KEY to success."

---

b) **Change is easier to undertake**
Systems make a business predictable. So in case of uncertainties and change, systems can be easily modified. Forecasting the impact of change can be more easily predicted.

c) **Training new employees is easy**
New hires can be quickly on boarded when there are standard and documented SOPs (Standard Operating Procedures) setting down expectations and processes. It also brings ease in performance assessment and appraisals.

d) **Business systems allow staff to focus on what they do best**
Identifying the right talent for the right job is made easy through implementation of appropriate systems. As the task allocation is mastered, you will find increased efficiency of your team as activities are performed on "auto-pilot" by those best equipped to handle the tasks and require minimum participation from your side. So you can focus on the high priority tasks.

e) **Business systems create value**
Implementing standardized systems add tremendous value to a firm's long-term success strategy. A system-oriented setup reduces dependency on people and function seamlessly without being significantly affected by volatility. For this purpose, documenting mundane procedures accurately proves a great starting point. Then performance of the procedure can be easily duplicated by anyone handling the task. You may choose to sell or franchise your business as you grow. Such documented and tested procedures make replicating your success much easier, giving you an edge over competition.

f) **Easy to find an investor when systems are in place**
When a business has systems in place, it attracts investors as well. This is because systems give them a guarantee of consistency in operations. Systems increase the profitability of your company as it improves business productivity, performance, and customer satisfaction. Investors get attracted to this increase in the profitability of the company.

g) **Easy to sell**
A full functional business with established business processes and systems is definitely a lucrative proposition to a buyer. I never

underestimate the importance of a great team and great people. But building strong processes that are not people-centric allows for a sustainable business.

15. Not saving for a rainy day

I find it utterly shocking to see businesses collapse due to absence of contingency planning. Having a contingency fund is of paramount importance, in your personal and professional life. Depending on financial credit would be too immature. Call it saving for a rainy day. I recommend speaking to your financial planners and plan to keep at least 3 months' worth of expenses as an emergency fund.

16. No leadership

A good leadership gives direction, vision, and confidence to the team that is striving hard to achieve a common goal. And it is not an easily acquired skill. With the right mix of attitude, perseverance, and patience a good leader evolves, who can start a business and take off on the mission to succeed. A good leader is well-read and always abreast with the latest trends and changes in the market. He is a great motivator and an inspiration for the team, encouraging them to grow along with him and the organization.

A great leader infuses energy and positivity in the team. I had the good fortune of meeting and interacting with many inspiring business leaders and each interaction has taught me at least one important message.

"Leadership is the CAPACITY to translate VISION into reality."

---

17. Why is leadership a must for a business owner?

Even a pack of wolves need an *Alpha* male and female to lead the group. Without an effective leadership, the organization is doomed for failure. A leader gives direction to the organization, defining a common goal to strive for. Most importantly, a leader has deep foresight and an ability to plan. As the trends change, it is the leader who alters plans so that the team does not wander off from their goal. A wise man once said, *"If the plan doesn't work, change the plan, not the goal."* And it is the leader who can efficiently execute this.

As the business grows, the leader needs to be closely involved in the critical aspects of business like finances, deadlines, client relations, and efficiency. He sets an example with action instead of words, for the rest to follow.

Having great communication skills is an invaluable quality in business. The ability to communicate with people from all aspect of the business world is crucial.

Leadership in business is a fine art, and if you are able to perfect it, the odds that your business will succeed increase drastically. If you don't see yourself as the ideal leader for your business, consider taking on an employee or partner who has great leadership qualities, an intrapreneur. Also, find a mentor who can hone your skills and make you feel confident to take on the lead position.

> *"There are different styles of leadership. One is leading from the FRONT; another is leading from the BACK. A good leader needs to be able to do BOTH."*

18. Mixing business with personal lives

Never mix business and personal lives, be it in financial matters or personnel matters. Numerous family-run businesses, due to the lack of efficient systems, make this mistake resulting in huge chaos and lack of accountability. Involving family in business functions without proper responsibility is also a common mistake, which not only affects business but spoils personal relationships. We may have good examples of family-run businesses who, through effective systems, are working together without any pandemonium, purely by keeping their professional relationships separate from personal. If you want to include family in business operations, see that they are properly trained and competent to do the task.

Conclusion

I know that mistakes are bound to happen, but how you deal with them and learn from them is really one of the major keys to success. Entrepreneurship, at its best, is synonymous with learning. Don't let the overnight success stories fool you. The more common story looks like this: test a product, fail, improve, and retest. Mistakes are a crucial part of this process. Of course, not all mistakes are productive. Throughout my years in the startup community, I've witnessed entrepreneurs make some of the same counterproductive mistakes again and again.

But don't let that deter you from taking up the challenge. Remember so now if you're inspired enough, let me give you a brief overview of how you can start a new business.

Scan this QR code to get the FREE Daily Planner that will help you to focus on the most important activities, keep track of them and avoid running out of time because of poor task prioritizing.

Or visit www.sameerindia.com/dailyplanner

CHAPTER 6

HOW TO START A BUSINESS

Overcoming the fears and learning from your mistakes, finally, you have made the key decision. YOU WANT TO START A BUSINESS. Applaud! Celebrate! It is definitely one of the most rewarding, life altering and important decision in your life! So take a moment and enjoy it. The ride is not going to be a smooth one. But a bumpy, rollercoaster ride is always memorable.

After the initial fiesta, now let's get a little serious and get to the basics. In this chapter, my goal is to introduce you to the business world from the absolute elementary levels and then build it up slowly.

So, let's start with WHAT is a business and HOW to get started.

The basic definition of a business can be—*an organization which understands and continuously fulfills needs and satisfies desires or solves the problems of customers by offering a right product or service and in the process makes profit*

When you're passionate about following your dreams or you've found a gap in the marketplace, which you can fill with your ideas, there's almost certainly a way to turn it into a business idea. But this is not enough to start and grow a business. Starting a business requires time, effort, and hard work. But when a business is set up with a strong foundation of high values and efficient planning process, it is sure to succeed.

Let me tell you an interesting story.

Story of Sukhiram

Once, there was a man named Sukhiram, who decided to start his own business and set up a shop. He found a nice, centralized location, invested heavily in the setup and product acquisition on credit. After a grand opening in the presence of friends and loved ones, his business started, initially with very good footfalls with exciting introductory offers. However, slowly the offers died down and the novelty wore off. The in-store traffic started declining. To counter this problem, Sukhiram further invested in expanding his product range and better marketing. He further invested in hiring additional people at the shop, who were doing roles very similar to him.

To expedite documentation and accounting, he invested in a computer, without taking the appropriate training for himself and the staff on usage of the computer. Soon, discontentment in staff further started affecting the business. Shortly, a mall opened in the vicinity, and business went down even further. Sukhiram finally had to shut down his business, and with buying so many things on credit, he went bankrupt. Sukhiram eventually turned into *Dhukhiram (Sad Person)*.

I have seen this happen to many enthusiastic, aspiring businessmen. Why do you think this happens? Where did Sukhiram go wrong?

The problem was with the basic approach of starting his business. What did he do?

1. He invested directly in infrastructure
2. Then he hired people
3. When he thought he could not handle business manually, he invested in technology (computer).

By this time, he was stuck and could not proceed, eventually resulting in failure. So what was missing? When we look at Sukhiram's story, we realize that he never reached the phase of gaining the right knowledge and did not have the right skills of running a business, which are very crucial for the success of any business. He did not have the right knowledge about the market or his customers; he neither had skills nor did he hire competent people as he was not clear of their role; he invested in technology only when he had an issue, without checking which was best suited for him. He was not prepared, when the new mall opened as he did not foresee the changes in the market. His lack of preparation and wrong start led to the shutdown of his business.

Starting and running a business requires discipline and planning, which can reduce the risk of failure. So, if you think you're ready to start your business, all you have to do is **KSTPI,** which stands for '"**Know Secrets to Profitable Investment'."**

Let me elaborate on what these five steps of starting a business are:

1. K- Knowledge

Knowledge and skills are critical to starting a new business. Having a proper knowledge base helps quick and accurate decision making. Successful entrepreneurs invest heavily in continuous improvement and learning. It makes you a better judge to situations and hones your decision making skills.

In a nutshell, knowledge building helps to:

1. Avoids failure and creates a fail proof system
2. Helps in decision making
3. Moves you from guesstimate to estimate
4. Critically evaluates situations
5. Create tools and techniques
6. Solve problems and face uncertainty
7. Builds confidence and helps in self-growth and development.

If you're thinking about starting a business, you are likely already to have an idea of what you want to sell, or at least the market you want to enter. So let us explore the knowledge a little bit in detail:

a. Knowledge about your product

I always believe that for a business to be successful, it should offer a product or service with a tangible benefit. Through research, focus groups, and even trial and error, you can gage the demand. You can use my checklist below before entering deciding your product idea:

- Is there a need for your products or services?
- Is there a problem your potential customers are facing that you can solve?
- Who needs it?
- Are there other companies offering similar products or services now?
- What is the competition like?
- How will your business fit into the market?
- What is your target market?
- Who is your target audience?
- What kind of resources will I need?
- What is your USP over your competition?

Know that satisfying an existing need or a gap is much easier than creating a need, which is very difficult and expensive. Your business must solve a problem or fulfill a need. Your product should have a ready market to ensure higher success rate.

b. Knowledge about the industry

Before entering any market segment, a thorough analysis of that domain is mandatory. The knowledge of market trends, characteristics, competition, brand leaders, etc. is an absolute MUST. Based on this, you can identify a USP that you can offer—a product or a service. If not, there is always an option of entering into a franchise business where you have a readymade business and execution plan along with complete handholding support. We have spoken about franchising as an option in our Chapter 9, wherein I have gone in depth about the smaller nuances of the business.

In today's technology-driven market, getting information about an industry that is available in public domain is not difficult. Online research, networking channels like BNI or Rotary, leading publications, and lifestyle magazines or search over any leading searching engines can open a whole breadth of information for you.

A more traditional method of professional learning involves securing the guidance of an individual more established in your industry. **Mentorship** can evolve as an extension of networking with colleagues, or it can be arranged. Mentoring can be voluntary or a paid professional service, depending on the mentor and his working methodology. But with the right mentor, the session is always rewarding.

A business cannot flourish without an efficient networking channel—online or offline. **Networking** is a way in which to relay and acquire information. Set up theme-based business lunches, attend business functions as often as your schedule will allow, and be social and mingle. Obtain memberships in as many relevant trade organizations as you can and make room in your schedule to attend some of the events they host. Attend trade shows whenever possible. Schedule conference calls with colleagues and share information.

Order subscriptions to reputable **Publications** in your field, and set aside time to read each day. Even Warren Buffet does not end his day without reading for at least an hour. So should you! A trade publication has a more narrow focus than a consumer publication, and is targeted to readers who work in a specific industry.

Go online and update yourself on current industry happenings. Set up Google alerts for your topics of interest, and bookmark a few high quality industry blogs and forums. Bookmark business reports and databases for future reference.

"Knowledge is always available to the SEEKER."

- **Knowledge about your target customer**

Identify your target customer, your prospective buyer. Unless there is a demand for your offering, all the effort is sailing toward doom. So conduct a thorough market research on your field and demographics of potential clientele and include it in your business plan. Surveys, holding focus groups and researching, SEO and public data are some of the tools you can use.

There are three different customers you'll need to think about in relation to your product, purchasers (those who make the decision or pay), influencers (who influence the purchasing decision), and the end users (who will use your product or service). You also can segregate your customers on the volumes that they buy.

c. Knowledge on the functioning of all the departments

As explained before, the seven functions are essential for running a successful business. As a business owner the main task is to build systems, teams, and strategies in every function so that it can function continuously without the intervention of the owner. As a business owner it is very important to know the working of all the departments.

d. Knowledge about raising capital

Analyzing this part is most critical. A startup needs funds either by bootstrapping or through external funding sources. Identify your sources of funds. Work with your financial consultant ahead of time to estimate your capital requirement. Your estimation sheet should include all costs covering marketing, legal, etc. (e.g., licenses and permits, equipment, legal fees, insurance, branding, market research, inventory, trade marking, grand opening, property leases, etc.), as well as other working capital needs for at least 12 months (rent, utilities, marketing and advertising, production, supplies, travel expenses, employee salaries, your own salary, etc.). This depends from business to business.

If you feel you need financial assistance, there are various ways through which you can finance your business:

- **Self-funding**

Self-funding, also known as using you own funds or savings, is an effective way of startup financing, especially when you are just starting your business. Bootstrapping your business might take longer, but the good part is that you control your own destiny.

- **Crowd funding**

It's like taking a loan, pre-order, contribution, or investments from more than one person at the same time. An entrepreneur will put up a detailed description of his business on a crowd funding platform. He will mention the goals of his business, plans for turning a profit, how much funding he needs and for what reasons, etc. and then consumers can read about the business and give money if they like the idea.

- **Join a startup incubator or accelerator**

Early stage businesses can consider Incubator and Accelerator programs as a funding option. These programs also offer access to excellent mentoring and fully equipped office spaces, which take care of your logistical needs. Found in almost every major city, these programs assist hundreds of startup businesses every year.

- **Seek loans from banks or microfinance or non-banking financial corporations**

Normally, banks are the first place that entrepreneurs go when thinking about funding. Almost every bank in India offers SME finance through various programs. Leading Indian banks have more than seven to eight different options to offer collateral free business loans.

What do you do when you can't qualify for a bank loan? Microfinance is an option. Similarly, Nonbanking Financial Corporations provide banking services without meeting legal requirement or definition of a bank.

- **Government programs that offer startup capital**

The Government of India has launched many programs to improve startup ecosystem in India. Check out the website https://www.startupindia.gov.in for more details.

- **Angel investor**

Put forth your business plan and presentation in front of angel investors and approach them to make investment in your business. If an investor finds value in your proposition, you might get your desired funds along with other angel benefits.

2. S – Skill

After knowledge the next step that an entrepreneur must focus on are skills that are required for running the business. Skill is an art of making things happen efficiently and effectively. In a constantly changing business environment, having and honing skills is an essential part of being able to meet the challenges and changes. The dramatic changes in global economies over the past 5 years have been matched with the transformation in technology in the business world. To cope with the increasing pace and change of modern times, continuously upgrading yourself has become a necessity.

Over the years, being an entrepreneur and having interacted with many of this type, I have realized that to succeed, one needs to understand and work on a set of important business skills. Without these skills, you cannot give your 100 percent.

Strategic planning skills– Strategic planning is a very important business activity. Strategic planning is where you define your company's vision for the future and list down the goals for the organization, and make decisions on allocations of resources of capital and people to achieve that goal. The key is to know how to project your company's future performance, within three to five year framework or more, supported by your well-defined business plan.

Leadership skills– Leadership is a process of getting things done through people. Leadership, a critical management skill, is the ability to inspire a group of people toward a common goal. Leadership is also the ability to take charge, assemble, mobilize, and motivate teams. You should be able to develop long-term relationships with customers, suppliers, employees, investors, and other stakeholders in business.

Analytical skills– Analytical thinking is the ability to assess the present state of your business, to determine where you want to be in the future, and what to do in order to close the gap between the present and the future stages. An entrepreneur should know how to gather, review, and evaluate data that is necessary for the business.

Delegation skills– Delegation means assigning the responsibility to accomplish a task to the right person to ensure successful completion of work. You should be able to delegate in such a manner that your staff carries out all the routine activities of your business. Effective delegation means having a proper control and people completing their job effectively.

Communication skills – Effective communication is the key to efficient business. Communication is a way to make interaction between people—vendors, clients, team members, or shareholders. This critical skill is what differentiates a good leader from a great one.

Negotiation skills – Negotiation skill can be an acquired skill with formal training and experience. This is a skill that is honed over a period of time with exposure to varied situations and dealing with different types of people. The key is to be diplomatic about what to say when and leading the communication in a direction that can eventually lead to a favorable outcome.

> *"In business, you don't get what you DESERVE, you get what you NEGOTIATE."*

Sales and Marketing skills- Creating successful sales and marketing strategies is essential in growing your business. The ability to analyze your competition, marketplace, and industry trends is critical to the development of your marketing strategy. You should be able to create and communicate a strong message to your target audience that generates business.

Management skills – Management involves directing and controlling a group of one or more people for the purpose of coordinating activities that will accomplish a goal. Management encompasses the deployment and direction of human resources, financial resources, and technological resources. The key is to know how to develop and implement a workable management system that will manage daily operations, nurture stakeholders, and support business growth.

Financial Management skills- Managing cash flow is the single most important activity in business. To manage cash flow one should have knowledge of assets and liabilities. Knowing what passive and active assets are is a must. To manage cash flow efficiently, timing is very important. This means taking decisions to cut down expenses or to increase investment at the right time. In its simplest form, cash flow is the movement of money in and out of your business. Cash flow is the life-blood of all growing businesses and is the primary indicator of business health. The effect of cash flow is real, immediate and, if mismanaged, totally unforgiving. The key is knowledge on how to monitor, protect, control, and put cash to work. The activity of finance is the application of a set of techniques that individuals and businesses use to manage their money, particularly the differences between income and expenditure and the risks of their investments. The need for timely budgeting and reporting of financial performance is of utmost importance. The key is to know how to interpret and analyze your financial statements, in such a way, as to identify the items that are adversely affecting your profitability.

Time Management skills – Time Management is a set of related common-sense skills that help you use your time in the most effective and productive way. Time Management is a very important skill to master. Learning this skill will empower you to optimize your time better.

3. T – Technology

One thing I can assure you is, in today's tech-world, Technology will help you master the other core requirements of entrepreneurship. It will help you gain knowledge, upgrade your skills, and manage your resources optimally.

Technology has important effects on business operations, no matter the size of your business. I have seen a significant improvement in efficiency and performance when a company embraces technology to accomplish its goals.

Technology is beneficial because:

1. It makes work simple, easy, and faster
2. It improves communication
3. Provides efficient and effective results
4. Result in wider global reach
5. Less people oriented
6. It's easy to control, check, audit, and review
7. Is reachable and accessible across the globe
8. Keeps record and storage of important data
9. Is upgradable and scalable.

Use technology; don't be its slave

As people rely more and more on technology to solve problems, the ability of humans to think for themselves will surely deteriorate. It's a common perception today that people rely more and more on technology rather than their own brains to solve an issue. While saying so, we tend to ignore the fact that these growing technologies are also the invention of great human brains. If they help to solve the problem more easily than humans, should not it mean the work given to the human brain decreases? Also getting addicted to technology sometimes wastes a lot of productive time. It is important to use technology only when needed.

Technology connects people across the globe and improves communication channels through transparency and speed. It can be used to secure financial and confidential data and other important business information.

4. P– People

> *"Human resources are the most VALUABLE assets the world has. They are all needed desperately." – Eleanor Roosvelt*

So unless you're planning to be your only employee, you're going to need to hire a great team to get your company off the ground. Entrepreneurs need to give the same attention to their human resources that they give their products. Defining roles and responsibility, division of labor, feedback management are some of the important areas your attention will be required. It is important to hire people and train them to mold them for your requirement.

Some of the best companies I have seen are managed by most efficient team setups. They have an excellent leadership who believes in leading by example and created leaders within the team, making the whole setup run on auto-pilot mode. Some of my learning's here include:
- State your goals clearly – absolute clarity in defining the goals and vision for the company
- State the role clarity – complete role clarity which explains their roles and responsibility without any ambiguity
- Follow hiring protocols – a clear and defined recruitment process
- Establish a strong company culture – an enhanced culture through inspiring leadership and overall work discipline.

Make sure you outline all the positions you need to fill, and the job responsibilities that are part of each position.

5. I – Infrastructure

Infrastructure represents facilities you need to build your enterprise, whether it is a home office, a rental space, or a big office. Factors like location, equipment, and logistics need to be considered while defining your infrastructure. These are critical decisions with direct impact on your bottom line. So be careful.

Make sure your location is consistent with nature of business and your ideal customers. If you need people to come into your store, make sure that store is easy to find. Research before you invest. If your business is technology driven (online business), make sure IT infrastructure availability like internet service, electricity, or backup facility is available.

If you are renting a premise, get a clear understanding about the utilities included, lease agreement terms and tenure, so you're not stuck in an unnecessary liability. If co-working is an option you can consider, think about it as it offers all the required infrastructure at affordable rates.

Don't be the Sukhiram of our story who drowned under the burden of unnecessary liabilities. Be wise before putting in your money. A venture which is debt-free has more flexibility and control over its decision making.

Equipped with the information, now be ready to spread your wings and take the dive. There might be times when you get frustrated or even face failures, but that is not a dead end. It's just a speed breaker; learn from it, as experience is the best teacher. Make as many mistakes as you can, but remember to never make the same mistake again. Positivity and perseverance coupled with tons of energy will take you to the other side. So be ready to start. Be ready for a bright, vibrant future!

Be a businessman not a busy man

Being a businessman is all about being productive, and there's a big difference between being busy and being productive. Being busy is about working harder while being productive is about working smarter. Being busy is being all over the place, while being productive is focused. Being busy is driven by perfectionism while being productive is driven by purpose. Being busy is about being good at everything while being productive is about being great at a few important things.

The most productive and efficient people are those that own their day versus letting their day own them. They work to maximize their time to be as productive as possible, not just busy. You can be busy all day and still feel like you're behind on accomplishing your goals. The busy person spends all their time doing research, trying to learn all the possibilities, creating long to-do lists, and trying to make things perfect before they start. They spend days with nothing tangible to show for their time and effort. These people tend to be over thinkers and they have an incredible ability to expand their tasks to the amount of time they have available. A productive person gets things done; they do not waste time or put things off later.

Three simple steps to be productive:
1. Take small steps by cutting major tasks into small bits
2. Focus on the most important things in a day (two or three)
3. Follow your schedule.

Being productive is the core of every high level achiever in business. They are the go-getters who make their dreams a reality.

Find a mentor

A mentor is someone who has already done or achieved what you want to achieve and is ready to help you. An entrepreneur with a great idea, you may not know exactly what you should be doing with your business at which times to develop it into a sustainable business. A mentor can help guide you through your entrepreneurial journey.

A mentor becomes very essential for the below reasons:
- Mentors give knowledge
- Mentors help in personal and professional growth
- Mentors can identify our limitations
- Mentors give unbiased opinions
- Mentors are trusted advisers as they have no stake in business
- Mentors can be influencers that can build our network.

Qualities of a great mentor

A mentor who has experienced the highs and lows of running a business is in the perfect position to give words of advice. Your chances of success in business increases by having the right mentor, the valuable connections, timely advice, and occasional checks, together with the spiritual and moral guidance will take you on a path of success.

Keep the goal in mind then start your journey

"BEGIN with the end in mind." – Stephen Covey

Imagine having to shoot an arrow without being given a target. Where would you aim? And say you did aim at some random thing, what would the purpose be? This is an example of what a business journey would be is like without a goal in mind. When we take a trip, we can map it out or we can head in a general direction toward the destination, but if we don't have a destination in mind, our journey will take us nowhere.

Goals are what take us forward; they are the first steps to every journey. You can have all the potential in the world but without focus your abilities and talent are useless; you can't achieve anything unless a goal is focusing your effort. Hence as an entrepreneur, the starting point needs to be the end goal you want to achieve, which will drive all your actions.

"Setting goals is the first victory in achieving a dream."Goal basically means go-all-out to make things happen.

Scan this QR code to get the FREE additional bonus chapter on How to Lead Silently

Or visit www.sameerindia.com/leadsilently

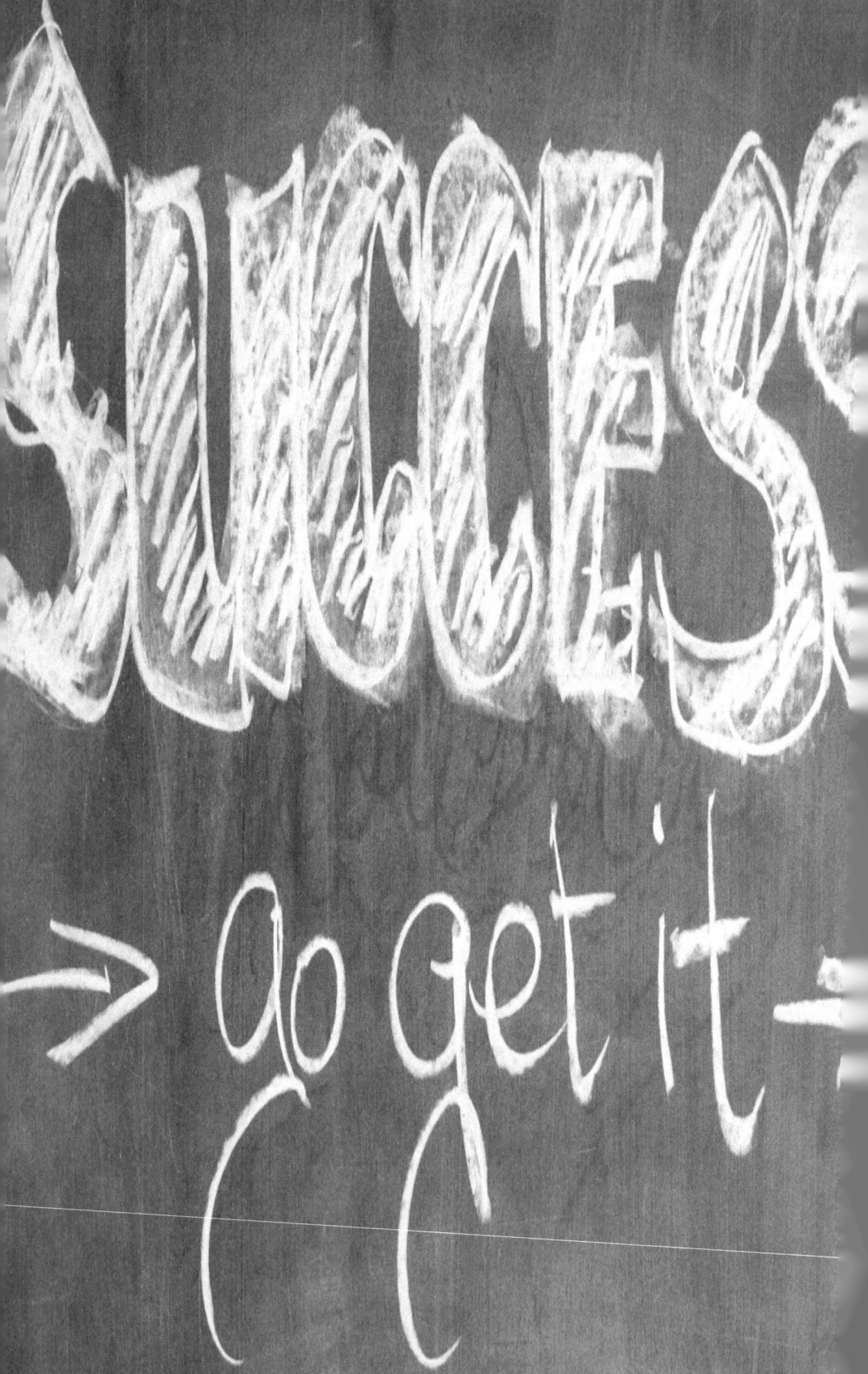

CHAPTER 7

BE FUTURE READY

1. Energy is success

*E*nergy is the soul of existence and life on this planet. It has a lasting effect on all. The energy is affected by the person's mental state—positive or negative. All great leaders exude a very powerful energy that inspires and motivates people to follow and act on the leaders' direction. So it is critical that the leaders radiate positivity to put all his followers on a progressive path. **Adolf Hitler**, one of the most powerful leaders of his time, moved the entire country on a path of destruction using negative energy he emanated. So, as I said earlier, a leader should always have a positive and encouraging spirit to the goal to add value.

I always feel that a person with positive energy is able to enjoy all aspects of his personality, personal or professional. A person with negative energy misses special moments that can be memorable. In order to achieve a goal, your power of dream should be supported by an earth-shaking passion and a drive that forces you to go beyond your ability. It is only such people who achieve the impossible with their "increased power of intention." It is a characteristic trait of successful leaders, who master positive thinking and enjoy clarity of thought that keeps them highly energized to travel great miles!

So HOW can you ensure you continue to remain energized and positive? The answer is to be proactive and take control of your physical, mental, and spiritual energy.

Did you know?

You lose energy when:
- You focus on regrets, resentment, or delve in the past
- You focus on fears, worries, or brood about the future

- Spend time with people who don't support or believe in you or worst doubt your potential
- Complain, gossip or devalue someone, be judgmental
- Poor eating habits
- Sit around, inactively, not doing anything which drives you
- When you ask over and over again, "What about me?"

You have increased energy when you do:
- Service to the society
- You focus on sharing love, knowledge, finding meaning, feeling a purpose, expressing gratitude
- Read or watch inspirational videos or books and attend seminars
- Exercise or meditate and sleep well
- Live in the moment
- Spend time with people who support you and believe in you and inspire you to believe in your ability to pursue your dreams.
- Eat healthy food
- Speak positive words, share compliments, offer help, inspire others, express gratitude out loud, make someone feel loved, encourage someone to be their most authentic self
- Do activities you're passionate about including things like working out, cooking, painting, writing, yoga, hiking, walking, swimming, being in nature, being around art, or reading inspiring books.

Now you know how you can build positive energy in yourself. So give it a try and evaluate how you feel within the first week.

"Being POSITIVE in a negative situation is not naïve, its LEADERSHIP."

Prepare for success

I have yet to find a person who wants to fail. Everyone wants to be successful. The question is whether you are ready for it? I strongly believe that everyone can achieve their dreams, accomplish their goals, and live a life that they aspire, but at the right time.

Success is a long-term goal. With the advent of technology and automation it takes people less time to produce extraordinary results and shorter time to achieve great success. We see more millionaires in their twenties today than two decades ago. I think the two main reasons instrumental for this change are:

Internet communication– Internet has transformed the way we do things. Socializing is not limited to parties and social events. People can socialize online. Mark Zuckerberg changed the way people interconnect. The effect of this technology shift is a separate discussion, but he single handedly broke the market and the way people communicate or do business. We have many such success stories, like OYO Rooms or Zomato that disrupted the market and redefined communication.

Education – The education industry has also revolutionized with the introduction of Internet technology as learning courses, videos, and live webinars are easily accessible. Expensive college degrees are not the only way to acquire high quality education anymore. Of course, degrees open the doors, but education and learning is now available to the seeker more easily than ever before.

Access to information is now much easier than it was 50 years ago. So how will you gear up to achieve your goal and be successful?

There are some tools and techniques that can help!

1. Techniques and tools for success

    a) **Thinking out loud–** As interesting as it may sound, it is also very effective. Close your eyes and visualize your dream. This technique is very powerful. Feel the experience of your success and say it out loud. Experience the happiness and increase in the energy as if it is true. Imagine your family enjoying the fruits of your success. Be very detailed in experiencing your moments. Try and do it regularly. This enhances your capacity to work toward your dream. It gives you a strong belief to take action.

b) **Raising one's level in mind** – Many of my students have expressed their concern about their ability to achieve their goal. They often doubt their capabilities and put themselves down. Here is an exercise I often do in our seminars. Close your eyes and visualize yourself as you are. From here, your dream appears high and unattainable. Now slowly imagine you're growing in size. The bigger you get, the closer your dream appears. As you keep growing, expanding beyond your physical expanse, you get bigger in size than your target and more. Soon, the dream is but a tiny dot and easily achievable. This exercise has proved to boost the confidence levels of my students, giving them the strength to dream big and achieve. it!

c) **Clarity in mind** – I have often seen my students in a confused state of mind when they come for my sessions. I often tell them the importance of the WH Questions. Knowing the How, When, What, Why, and Who of the business and goals is critical. Without this clarity, your business or life moves from place to place like a ship without a captain. But with clarity, you run your business and your life "with purpose" and focus on create amazing results both for you and for your customers.

d) **Internal dialog (the power of self-talk)** – Internal dialog is the voice inside your head that tells you what to do. It is the decision making channel in your brain that applies logic and reasoning to the course of action. A self-aware person is able to put reasoning in this thought process through self-talk. He does not allow the subconscious mind to take control. He is positive and keeps control of his mind through positive thinking. Tell yourself, "I got this," "I can handle this," "I believe in myself"… This has a powerful effect on your mind and increases your abilities through positive thinking.

But one thing I have seen is the tone of your thoughts has a deep impact on your actions. A positive mindset is emphasized through a reassuring, calm, and compassionate tone. It redefines a subtle acceptance of the person and increased confidence. So keep in mind, be gentle and calm.

2. How to be happy always

In my opinion, in order to be happy one needs to have equanimity, which is basically being in a state in which you are not affected by a situation, and you are focused on understanding that whatever ups and downs happen they are only temporary.

Some positive thoughts that have helped me always are –

Be Future Ready

- Day or Night, I am prepared to fight
- Rain or Shine, the time is mine
- Rise or fall, I am equipped for it all
- High or low, I am ready for more
- Now or never, I will not give up ever
- Win or lose, my dream I will always choose
- Ups or downs, I will not frown
- Morning or evening, I focus on winning
- Sunday or Monday, it's always my day

- SAMEER KUNCOLIEKAR

- Day or Night, I am prepared to fight
- Rain or Shine, the time is mine
- Rise or fall, I am equipped for it all
- High or low, I am ready for more
- Now or never, I will not give up ever
- Win or lose, my dream I will always choose
- Ups or downs, I will not frown
- Morning or evening, I focus on winning
- Sunday or Monday, it's always my day

"Being happy doesn't mean that everything is PERFECT. It means you've decided to look BEYOND the imperfections".

You can find umpteen ways to be happy. Like? Here you go -

1. **Enjoying the present moment is a habit that takes practice**

If you always look toward tomorrow for happiness, odds are you will do the same when you attain what you've been dreaming of. As strange it sounds, the ability to appreciate what's in front of you has nothing to do with what you actually have. It's more about how you measure the good things in your life at any given time.

2. **Finding reasons to be happy now can benefit your future**

It is said that while positive emotion tends to broaden perspective, negative emotion tends to narrow it and holds back development and progress. So be positive and good things automatically follow.

3. **Tuning into happiness can improve your health, giving many possibilities in life**

Something that most people take for granted until its compromised is health. It is observed that optimistic people have a stronger immune system than their negative counterparts. This may be due to their tendency to take better care of themselves. Exercise releases endorphins, which makes you happy. A healthy life is a happy life! Choose to be happy now and you'll have more days of good health to enjoy.

4. **Every day is a new opportunity to be better than yesterday; that pursuit can increase your self-esteem and your happiness**

It's more satisfying to set and meet an attainable goal, than it is to obsess about an imperfection. By focusing on small improvements and mini-goals, you'll naturally move yourself toward your larger dreams. Smaller achievements also increase self-esteem and confidence in self.

5. **Finding joy in the present moment, no matter how insignificant it may seem, makes a difference in other people's lives**

Living in the moment and enjoying it to the fullest has a tremendous positive impact on not only the person, but those around him. A person who's able to appreciate the small pleasures of life can spread happiness and positivity to those in his surroundings. This has a chain effect as the positivity spreads and the overall society thrives in this positive energy.

6. **Be aware, who you are and what you want to be?**

As I have mentioned earlier, the single most important goal of life is to strive for excellence and contentment. As one gets engrossed in business, you tend to forget these personal goals while running behind the professional ones. But take a step back and think. Are your activities aligned to your end goal? What is your motivation? While achieving your business goals, don't forget who you are and where you want to be.

7. **Know what is an asset and liability**

When I worked in the CA's office, I realized how people spend their money which they have earned. How you spend your money decides your future in the financial world. If you buy a car to give it on rent and earn money, it is your asset. But if you purchase it for personal consumption, it incurs expense on petrol or diesel, maintenance, etc. thus making it a liability in financial world.

Investment which generates income is called as an asset, while investments which generate loss are called as a liability. People in the smart zone appreciate their asset and reduce their liability. So they make money in any market trend. Whereas the hard zone people spend their whole life making money and buying assets, but indirectly create more liability for themselves.

A deeper understanding of finance can help you understand what is the asset and liability in your balance sheet that will help you make money. It's not how much you earn, but it is how much you keep. In my years of experience, I have seen and met a lot of small businesses that collapsed due to financial illiteracy. I think over a period of time investing in asset will make you take control of your financial destiny. Financial freedom is possible only when you learn this.

During my internship at the CA's office, there was a story he once narrated about one of his clients who won a lottery over INR 1 crore but became bankrupt within 5 years. Instead of investing the money wisely, he threw lavish celebration parties for his friends. Quit his job assuming he had enough money. Spent a fortune on a big house and fancy cars. Got expensive gifts for his family and threw an extravagant reception for his daughter's wedding.

Soon, the funds started to dry out. His son, then a medical student, had to leave his education as the fees became unaffordable. It was an unfortunate situation for the entire family.

Now, this does not mean you don't enjoy the money you earn, but spend wisely, creating an asset to support your liability. Then live life king size and enjoy a bountiful life with all luxurious pleasures.

3. The Rocket story

In my seminar, I meet many entrepreneurs and business owners. On the outside, they all look the same, but as we probe deeper; I realize they fall under different stages of business. In this section, I'll take you through the key stages of a business.

When you start a business it goes through various stages. It's like launching a rocket.

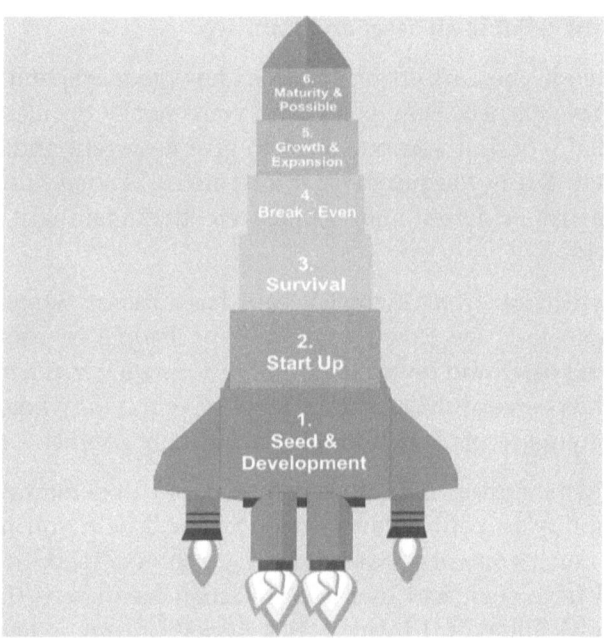

Stage 1: Seed and development

This is the start of your business lifecycle. You've got a business idea and you're eager to go ahead with it. But first you must assess just how viable your idea is.

This is where you need to work on the successful formula for starting a business **KSTPI.**

At this stage, you validate your idea with friends, family, and professional associates and do a critical evaluation. Market feasibility as well as the financial investment has to be assessed. In some ways, this is the soul-searching phase. Think once again about the idea and your commitment toward it. Setting up and growing a business is a long-term commitment analyze again if you're up for it.

Stage 2: Startup stage – Where you start building a business

Once you have validated your business idea, make it official. This is a crucial stage as more than 25 percent startups fail in the first 5 years. This stage characterizes a scenario where there is continuous improvement and edits made to your product or service based on customer and client feedback and your market assessment. There are times when you find that the revised version is a far stretch from where you started, but it is OK. Don't stop with a veil of confusion masking your judgment. This stage marks huge investments and negative cash flows. I find this stage the toughest as it is not easy looking at a negative balance sheet. But hang in there. You've just sown the seed. The roots of your plants are just starting to grow and create a solid foundation. Patience is the key.

Stage 3: Survival stage – Here you work to make cash flow correct

In this stage you are building customers and generating consistent revenue cash flow starts to improve as it helps to recover expenses. The roots of your plant are growing stronger and preparing themselves to take up the load of the growing tree.

Stage 4: Breakeven – Stage is stage where you start making profit

As the business survives and enters this new stage, you find comfort seeing a positive balance sheet. Business shows consistent revenue and a steady flow of newer customers. The working capital needs are met through the company's growing revenues. The business scenario starts to look more comfortable from this stage as a positive cash flow makes the situation look greener.

Stage 5: Growth and expansion stage – Where you are established and profit is continuous

This stage is marked by a large-scale expansion in new markets and better distribution channels. You can capitalize on your success and enter newer markets. The brand value created makes setting up in the newer markets less challenging. A pre-defined and tested sales and marketing model, operations model makes new market entry a pleasing and predictable experience.

You notice rapid growth in sales and profit. Economies of scale make production more competitive and you now have a price advantage. Companies at this stage should invest in better and improved marketing activities to maximize their return on investment. Better revenues, steady flow of customers, and positive cash flows and profits make this stage of business much more rosier than the previous stages.

This stage is marked with classic growth stage challenges like time management, managing finance and revenues, customer relationship management, while maintaining a competitive edge. Human resources management needs vital attention. If you hire experienced and smart resources with complementary skills, you can maximize on your HR investment while generating tangible value for the company. So spend more time here.

Generating a second level of command for efficient delegation is one of the most critical responsibilities you have to shoulder in this stage.

Expansion is when you are going to a different area. In this part, there is certain monotony in business as the systems are in place. The team is capable of shouldering all responsibilities and there are just a few things that require your direct attention. You experience high growth in revenue as the business sets into an auto-pilot mode. But don't let complacency set in. You'd be surprised to see your competition overtaking you. But that said don't take hasty decisions for expansion and growth. Having a mentor often helps, to validate and voice your thoughts and ideas. Use the advice of consultants to do an efficient cost-benefit analysis, before taking the plunge. Expansion should not be at the cost of current business. Value to customer should never be compromised.

Stage 6: Maturity and possible exit

This stage exemplifies steady growth and increase in profits. But it is not always a smooth sail. While growing your top line is an option, some business owners choose to exit, if an appropriate buyer expresses interest. They exit and embark on another path of entrepreneurship. Some turn into an investor, after bagging significant experience in the entrepreneurial world.

If you decide to grow the business, some critical questions need to be addressed. Some companies choose to change their leadership at the top to bring in some fresh perspective and direction for the business.

Learning

When I explain these stages at my seminar, I get astonishing replies. I came across some business owner who had pulled out in the breakeven stage and quit. Regretting his decision, he said, "If I was aware about these stages, I would have never quit." He promised to start all over again. Another person at the seminar asked me how to get out of a stage, if you're stuck? I tell them to focus on the seven functions, and check if all are working effectively.

I want to clarify here that not all businesses will experience every stage of the business lifecycle, even if they do, may not necessarily experience them in the same order. Most companies, however, experience this lifecycle in some form. So having a better understanding is always useful.

4. Market trends

Any business owner needs to be abreast with the news and trends in the market to make accurate estimates and decisions for his business. While this is a challenge in today's technology-driven world, you need to find ways to keep yourself up to speed to avoid your competition overtaking you on the road to success. Market trend analysis is simply the comparison of industry data over a set time period, designed to recognize any consistent trends or results that could be used to bap your business strategy aligning it with the general direction of your industry. Market trends tend to be heavily influenced by consumer habits and behaviors.

5. Take charge of finances

Taking charge of your finances means taking control of your future. During my seminars, I have encountered many business owners bothered with the worries of financial management—be it new entrepreneurs, family business owners, professors, and other professionals.

So a topic I discuss often is—what is the difference between money and wealth?

Money is directly related to cash you have in hand or bank, whereas wealth is related to the number of days you can maintain standards without working for it.

Access to money without a core ability to manage it is the root cause of many problems. This is where we have seen windfall gains being squandered without any value addition. A lottery is an inheritance which is wasted when financial management ability is missing. If you feel that you fall in this category I warn you to stop your spending and analyze. Now is the time to take control of your financial life. Evaluate your expenses over the past 6 months and calculate how many assets you have built to support your liabilities. How you can increase that positive value? Discuss with your mentor and realign your expenses.

I always feel that financial education should be mandated at school level. Making the youth aware of financial management and challenges since a young age will make them accountable. So they don't just learn to make money, but also to manage it effectively.

As I tell people in my seminar—"Intelligent people solve problems and produce wealth, while others just live on a month to month basis."

Scan this QR code to get the FREE Declarations that are a powerful self-talk. The most successful people in life have an empowering way to communicate with themselves. With these declarations you can practice positive self-talk throughout your day, and you will begin to realize more favorable rewards in life.

Or visit www.sameerindia.com/declarations

CHAPTER 8

FRANCHISEE – THE ULTIMATE BUSINESS MODEL

Once I had created a solution for the blood donor availability through creation of an online portal where the donor and recipient could connect, I felt the urge to do the same thing for the financial freedom of people around me. Money in today's world is a necessity and not luxury. It is one of the basic things required for people to survive and sustain. As a business owner, I wanted to help people transition from the masses to the classes. How could I help everyday normal working professional foray into the business world. Which system can I create to make this journey possible and successful? This thought kept me sleepless for many a nights.

I started analyzing various businesses and occupation to determine the best suitable path for the linkage. I wanted to find a way to transfer my experience and knowledge accumulated all these years to help people take the next big leap. I was interested in creating the business mentality in the minds of people and at the same time make a template available to them which they could easily follow. I was trying to create more job opportunities and business opportunities to contribute to my little bit toward societal development. I craved to create openings for the younger generation by expediting financial literacy and imbibing the growth mindset. It was my desire to create a massive value in the lives of multiple people all the while handholding them as they embark on the journey toward success.

An ideal scenario for societal development is the creation of a WIN-WIN situation where everyone is helping one another. This offers a twin benefit of assuring people's buy in as well as creation of a self-sustaining ecosystem. I sought to create joy and celebration in the lives of people by providing the prospects for financial independence. I didn't want to give them only a blueprint but very much wanted to be a part of their success. I kept wondering about how I could create a platform where others could sell their products and services and springboard onto the path or growth.

After meeting different people at the Business Startup Seminar, I found that there was a huge gap and a need for relevant financial education. So I took it as my mission, **'Mission Financial Education'**.

I still distinctly remember a story which my father told me, when I was small. "One day a man said to God, God I would like to know what heaven and hell are like.

God showed the man two doors. Inside the first one, was a large round table with a large pot of soup in the middle of the room. It smelled delicious and made the man's mouth water. He, however, observed that the people sitting around the table looked thin, sick, and malnourished. They appeared to be really famished. They were holding spoons in their hands with very long handles. It was possible for each one of them to reach into the pot of soup and take a spoonful, but because the handle was longer than their arms, they could not get the spoons back into their mouths. The man shuddered at the sight of misery and suffering. God said "you have seen hell."

Behind the second door, the room appeared exactly the same. There was the large round table in the middle of the room with a large pot of wonderful soup that made the man's mouth water. The people had the exact same long spoons, but they appeared to be well nourished and plump, laughing, talking, and celebrating. The man said "I don't understand." God smiled and said it is simple: love requires only one skill. These people learned early on to share, care, and feed one another. This is the reason they are happy and content. Greed makes one think only about himself, and it is the primary cause of sorrow and grief in the world.

Many a times, we are so engrossed in our personal gratification that we tend to forget our interdependence with everyone and everything around us. We stop thinking and caring about others and are only concerned with our well-being. This is what is typically observed in traditional business where everybody is obsessed about themselves and look at the market only through the prism of competition and survival. Businesses would look to demolish the competition to ensure their own existence and then eventually perish because they could not look at the bigger picture beyond themselves.

Modern day businesses have undergone a sea of change with the introduction of the franchising model of operation where interdependence and synergy are the key parameters of growth. Franchising is a beautiful concept where each person helps the other grow and creates a unique WIN-WIN situation for either parties involved. I was particularly interested in the franchisee business and decided to interact with franchisors of major brands to get a hold on what made the business model tick and flourish.

As mentioned earlier, an organized business is like a 6 wheeler truck with the management as the driver on the 7th wheel. In a same way the franchise systems works, like the train. The franchisor is the engine. It has the capacity to carry multiple numbers of coaches, which are the franchisees. The rail track is like the system. The engine carries the coaches, so the individual coaches do not require their own engine, electricity or direction.

As a franchisee you do not have to take the trouble of building an engine, you can get connected to an existing engine by signing up with the right franchisor, to establish yourself better in business. The entire franchise is like train. In franchise, the franchisors engine is already available, it has a laid track to run and you have to do is sign up as a franchisee. Screen of both depend on reference of each other. Speed of the train, depends on the speed of the engine as well as the speed of the individual coaches as well, and all have to run in proper motion to avoid derailment. Better the franchise better the train as whole. Bigger the train more people you can take and more powerful it will be. Bigger engine can be connected; bigger trains means better the network and people have already experience. A smart franchisor will always be ready to build capacity to serve more franchisee's and make the franchise stronger. Better the engine, more coaches it can pull. Apart from the engine pulling the coaches, you will observe that all the coaches are standardized; this is another characteristic of the franchise network. The operations of the coaches are limited as the engine does majority of them. In the same way, franchisee operations are limited as the franchisor has already spent time in building the right business; all the franchisee has to do is follow the same.

1. Let's look at the franchising world a little bit more in detail:

The commonly used terms in franchising:

Franchisor: the Company that lends its trade name and business system for a fee in return.

Franchisee: the Company that pays for the right to do business under the franchisors name and system.

Franchise: The contract that binds the franchisor and the franchisee. But the term franchise is also used to denote the actual business that the Franchise operates.

Franchise agreement: A written contract detailing the mutual responsibilities of franchisors and franchisees. It is typically for a several year term and requires to be renewed after the expiry of the said period. Usually a franchise agreement may not be sold, transferred, or otherwise assigned without the franchisors exclusive permission.

Franchise fee: An up-front entry, generally payable upon signing of the contract (Franchise agreement) for the right to use the franchisors name, logo, and business system. Often, the franchise fee is also the consideration paid for the initial training, site selection, operations manual, and any other support given by the franchisor before opening of the business by the franchisee. Franchise fees are amortized over the life of the franchise agreement.

Royalty: An ongoing payment that is made to the franchisor usually payable on a periodic basis, which can be weekly, biweekly or monthly, or throughout the term of the franchise agreement. Royalty payments are the compensation for the continuing services provided by the franchisor in terms of training, field services and so on. These payments can either be fixed amounts based on the percentage of gross sales, or based on a sliding scale, with graduated breakpoints.

Trademark: A distinctive name or symbol used to differentiate a particular product or service from others. A trademark has to be registered with the country's patent and trademark office. It can be used exclusively by the owner, and no one is authorized to use it without the owner's explicit permission. A portion of the franchise's value is the right to use a recognized trademark.

Definition of franchise:

The international franchise association, the chief trade association in franchising defines a franchise as a 'continuing relationship in which the franchisor provides a licensed privilege to conduct business, in addition to providing assistance in organizing, training, merchandising and management in return for a consideration from the franchise.

2. Copy first and then innovate

When we hear the word copying we find it to be synonymous with cheating. This has been largely ingrained into our mind from our early school or academic years where copying meant you did a grave crime and you would get rusticated. In the franchise world, however, copying is not frowned upon. On the contrary, the very existence of the franchising world is based on the premise that if something is successful it needs to be copied and duplicated. Be a copycat is the mantra for the franchising world.

You need to follow in the footsteps of a successful person if you want to replicate success. Never has been this saying acquired a more true meaning than in the franchising world. A franchisee is expected to follow the successful steps of the franchisor in order to achieve the same success. Similar methodology as your franchisor, same setup for outlet, same products, same service and same adaptability to change will benefit you to achieve the same growth and prosperity in a shorter span of time. In the USA, 66 percent of the products and services are sold in a similar fashion. The dictionary defines the word franchising as an authorization granted by a company to someone to sell or distribute its goods or services in a certain area.

How is buying a franchisee a shortcut to success?

As elaborated earlier, running a business involves seven primary functions. In a franchising model, these functions are performed jointly by the franchisor and the franchisee. As the business model is mutually beneficial for both parties involved, both of them have an equal concern in ensuring the success of the model. The extent of the involvement of the parties and the manner in which it is executed, however, is outlined by the mutual understanding and the agreements between the concerned parties.

Thinking outside the box of a traditional business mindset where people only sold a business, what franchise companies actually do is sell an idea. They sell the formula or recipe which can be in a variety of combinations but primarily comprises a trademark, a standard pre-defined operating system, training and consultation and marketing and promotion. The franchisee has to diligently follow the formula for success given by the franchisor to achieve its own success. In consideration for the rights and supports provided by the franchisor, the franchises have to pay as consideration an initial franchisee fee and ongoing royalty payments.

What makes the franchising model so rampant and popular is the fact that the franchisee not only gets a proven and efficient method of conducting business but also significantly benefits from the management assistance provided by the franchisor. This is in addition to the training, development, and marketing support from the franchisor. The franchisee thus inherits a total package to ensure rapid success. Franchisor routinely conducts national or regional marketing campaigns developed by professional advertising agencies and aids the franchisee run the local ad campaigns. The cumulative experience of the franchisor accumulated over the years is available to the franchisee at a nominal cost which gives the business the necessary impetus for success. It is also easier to obtain the funds from financial institutions of big brand with lot of credibility.

Types of franchising

The numerous franchising types that exist in today's market scenario can be broadly categorized into the following four major categories:

1. Product or Trade Name Franchising
2. Manufacturing Franchising
3. Business Opportunity Ventures
4. Business Format Franchising.

Models of Franchising

1. Product or trade name franchising

Product or Trade Name franchising is one of the simplest franchising methods. The manufacturer offers the franchisee the right to use his logo and his trade name to distribute his products in consideration for a fee. The manufacturer also provides some initial training and requisite assistance in operations. In this format the franchisee is merely a distributor of the products and can often sell competing or complementary products. This franchising method is mostly seen in the automobile and petroleum industries.

2. Manufacturing franchising

Manufacturing Franchising accords an organization the right to manufacture a product and sell it to the customers, using the franchisors' name and trademark. A typical example of this type of franchising can be seen in the soft drink industry. Every drink of Coca-Cola comes in easily identifiable packaging which is decided by the Coca-Cola Company. The drink tastes exactly the same all over the world. However, this does not imply that the Coca-Cola Company manufactures all the coke that is sold all over the world. It simply provides the chemical formula which contains the key ingredients. The balance work is performed by the bottlers who then add water, sugar and whatever else goes into a coke and then distributes the drink to the retailers. This method of franchising has been the preferential choice of franchising for most of the food and beverage industry.

3. Business opportunity ventures

This venture is characterized by the requirement that the business owner purchases and distributes the products of one specific company. This is also called the dealership or distributorship model. The parent company provides the customers or accounts to the business owner who either pays a fee or other consideration as compensation to the parent company. Some examples of this model include vending machine route or work from home opportunities.

4. Business format franchising

Business Format Franchising is the most popular form of franchising. Just like the product or trade name franchising business format franchising also authorizes the franchisee to use the entire business format of the franchisor. The distinct benefit of this model is that the franchisee gets a proven method for operating a business under a known trademark. He not only gets the brand from the franchisor but also a significant amount of assistance in starting and managing the franchise. An in-depth knowledge and information concerning business activities that include marketing, promotion, site selection, price suggestions, grand opening plans, management, operations, training, financing, accounting systems, and legal support or information is made available and accessible to the franchisee.

The franchisor also takes the franchisee through a fairly extensive training program. The training is not limited to the period of opening the franchise but is continuous even after the franchising unit is operational. The business owner pays a fee or royalty in return. This model also requires the franchisee to procure supplies from the franchisor. This is done to ensure complete uniformity between the way the franchisor runs and the franchisee operates.

Brands offer franchise for getting effectiveness of their services or reach of product to consumer in state-of-the-art of business concept. There are different models of franchising:

- FOFO (Franchisee Owned Franchise Operated)

In this model the franchise is completely owned by franchisee and operated by franchisee. This model is adopted by companies for faster expansion of business or brand presence and to penetrate completely new markets with the help of local businessmen. In this model the training of staffs, initial store setup is done by the franchisor and handed over to the franchisee to oversee the operations and maintain standards based on SOPs set by the franchisor. The operations are then independently managed by the franchisee. The franchisee pays a licensing fee as per the agreed terms to the franchisor. Surprise and scheduled SOP audits are done by the Company to ensure high standards are maintained. When franchisee fails repeatedly in audits, the franchisor either levies fines or pulls out from the contract eventually closing the franchisee business.

Local market knowledge if rightly coupled with the business expertise of the Company will end up fetching good profits for both the franchisor and the franchisee. A good example for this model are Fast Food Chains where in the business is owned and operated by the franchisee but regular audits are done by the Company to ensure standards are maintained as stipulated.

- FOCO (Franchisee Owned Company Operated)

This model is a win-win situation for Investor and Brands. This format relies on the fact that brands know how to represent their product or specialize in their service. This makes them confident about their ability to sell their product and services. On the opposite side the investor is looking for a business to invest in, but neither has the knowledge nor inclination about the brands product or services. FOCO model suits this scenario perfectly because both Investor and the Brand have to prosper.

This model is adopted by companies who want to reduce their capital expenditure and expand faster in an established market. The franchisee owns the business but the brand and the operations are handled by the franchisor. Business performance is reported to the franchisee on a regular basis. The franchisee can oversee the business and question the Company in case of poor performance. This model is usually signed under profit sharing basis with the franchisor getting a bigger share of the profit compared to the franchisee. Typical examples of this model are Exclusive Brand Outlets in fashion and lifestyle retail segment.

- COFO (Company Owned Franchise Operated)

In this model the Company reserves ownership of the business but shares the operation of store or branch. The brand is looking for a working partner who can invest in the business and take care of the operational cost while offering margin to cover the remaining cost and partner profit. This model is used to reduce operational expenditure for the company. The franchisor leases the operations of the business to an interested franchisee while holding trainings and conducting SOP audits to ensure standards are adhered to. The business ownership rests solely with the franchisor, who has the options of changing a franchisee, in case he finds a more profitable and efficient franchisee. This model is only in well-established markets where the company has operated and achieved high return on investment. Example: cafeterias within hospitals and corporates that are owned by the company but operated by a franchise for a lease period. Bidding happens at the end of the lease term or when the company finds out that the franchisee is not maintaining the expected standards.

- Franchise Invested Company Operated (FICO)

This model is similar to FOCO with the key difference being unlike FOCO the franchisee does not involve themselves in the business operations. Only an agreed fixed amount is paid to the franchisee by the company for the investment done by the franchisee in the business. In this model there can be multiple franchise investors for a single business unit and the Company runs the business operations with end-to-end control of the supply chain.

How did the concept of franchising emerge?

The origin of the word franchising can be traced back to the French word "'Franchise'" which means granting of powers to a peasant or self. The English verb to "enfranchise" also means to free from slavery, bondage, or legal obligation. In the middle ages, a franchise was a privilege or a right. During those times, the king would be giving permission to allow business to be conducted on his land. In essence, the king was giving someone the rights to a monopoly for a specific type of commercial activity.

With the passage of time, the franchising concept continued to evolve along with the economies of the world. In the early 1840s, a certain major ale brewery in Germany granted franchises to certain taverns for the exclusive right to sell their ale. This marked the beginning of the concept of franchising as we know it today. In 1851, the Singer Sewing Machine Company commenced granting distribution franchises for their sewing machines. Singer used written franchise contracts which are recognized as the forerunners of modern franchise agreements. In the 1880s cities began granting monopoly franchises to street car companies for utilities such as water, sewerage, gas, and electricity.

Around the turn of the century the oil refinery companies and the automobile manufacturers started to grant the right to sell their products. Over the years franchising format kept on evolving. The changes were influenced by various socio-economic conditions prevalent in different parts of the world. A major change in franchising was witnessed post World War II and during the so-called baby boom years.

The modern era of franchising began in the 1950s when Ray Kroc, a milkshake machine salesman, first discovered in San Bernardino, California a drive in restaurant operated by the McDonald brothers. Fascinated with the popularity of the restaurant as witnessed by the crowded parking lot and the tasty French fries, Kroc bought the rights to franchise the business. In doing so he laid the groundwork to build one of the most successful companies in the history of American business "McDonald's." He achieved this stupendous success through the power of franchising. The crucial reasons on why a business would go the franchising way in those days is no different than that of today. Expansion of any business is fraught with risk and requires enormous investments in terms of capital and human resources (people) to effectively run the locations. A shortage of any of these investments can adversely affect the growth as well as the brand image. This risk to growth is mitigated by the franchising way of doing business as it allows rapid expansion to occur without the business having to incur vast amounts of operating capital. The franchising model also helps creates an attractive profit picture for the franchise owner at the unit or operating level.

Single Unit and Master Franchise

The franchise model usually consists of either a unit franchise, master franchise, or a regional franchise. A single unit franchise is characterized by the fact that the franchisee is granted the right to operate a singular unit or outlet of the franchise business. This does not necessarily mean that the franchisee can operate only one unit. The franchisee also has the option of operating multiple unit franchises. This unit franchising is the simplest and most common method of franchising.

Under the master franchise concept, the franchisee is granted the rights to operate in a substantial territory which can be either a state, a country, or a region. The master franchise then can decide to setup unit franchises. The master franchise in effect operates essentially like a franchisor. The master franchise or the franchisor also has the option of dividing a territory into separate regions and creates a master franchise for each region known as regional franchise. This method is typically followed when the geographical area is large and managing it becomes a hassle for either the franchisor or the master franchisee.

Other People's Money (OPM) and Other People's Experience (OPE) - Pillars of the franchising world

- **Other People's Money (OPM)**

As the popular saying goes, it takes money to make money. This does not mean that it necessarily has to be your own money. Successful businesses are able to leverage other people's money to scale up and achieve rapid growth while realizing substantial gain for the investors and at the same time increasing their own net worth. The funding for your venture can come in a variety of forms including bank loans, investors, family and friends, venture capital and angel investors, crowd funding, and vendor financing or leasing.

There are a multitude of advantages of not using your own money which includes less personal financial risk, ability to scale up rapidly, acquire guidance from experts, and build a sustainable business. Your business size will always be limited if you financed it yourself as capital requirements for expanding may not be possible with your existing funds.

- **Other People Experience (OPE)**

We've all heard the common saying that experience is the best teacher. This might not always be the case as it is far more efficient to learn from someone else's experience. Someone who has been there and done what you want to achieve. A role model if you will. This allows you to avoid the pitfalls and mistakes that your predecessors in the same field might have made. It also provides you a running start for your business as you are already aware of what has worked and what has failed in your business area. Inventions and Innovations use existing knowledge as a stepping stone to achieve greater and better growth. We also attend school for the very same reason, to benefit from the knowledge and discoveries of those who have gone before us. There are a variety of ways to learn from someone else's experience:

- Through reading and researching
- Attending classes (online and offline)
- Mentoring with an expert in the field you are interested in
- Offering to volunteer, apprentice, or intern.
- Working with an authority in a particular field
- Following success stories and methods of your role models
- Join associations or professional groups in your area of interest to meet and connect with experienced people.

Apply what you learn. Knowledge is effective only when it's utilized.

How does OPM and OPE work for a franchisee?

The franchising business offers the benefits of both the OPM and OPE. The franchisor has already laid down the groundwork by building a successful business model. The franchisor has spent money, time, and effort on product development, technology, brand building, marketing, building a customer base, vendor development, infrastructural changes and many more. The franchisee has the advantage into tapping into this to start and expand his business. In case of an independent business you would have to spend significant money on experimentations, trials, and errors and developing the model structure for your business.

As far as experience goes, a franchisee gets the benefit of the entire experience of the franchisor as well as other franchisees in the network. The franchisor model with all its systems and SOPs mean you can enter the field without any existing knowledge on how the industry functions and still be successful. An independent business on the other hand will experience lost time and lost opportunities till the time the business owner gathers all the knowledge and experience of the business.

It is here that the franchisee needs to comprehend that the fees that they have paid to the franchisor, are for exactly these OPM and OPE that are easily accessible to them.

Myths about franchising

Franchising has provided a path breaking opportunity for multiple people who want to set their foot in the business world. This can be seen by its increasing popularity across a wide range of industries. However, the growth has also been companied by a number of misconceptions about the model resulting in a lot of potential franchisees missing the gravy train. I would like to bust some common myths about the franchising model which will allow you to take a knowledgeable and informed decision about whether you want to go the franchising route or not.

1. **Myth: Franchisors will accept anyone who shows up with a lot of money to buy a franchisee. They will gladly take your money whether you are a right fit or not.**

Truth: Franchisors are extremely conscious about their brand and will do everything in their power to ensure the continued success of their proven systems and brand value. They can only make certain this happens by on boarding the right people as franchisees.

A franchising model success is defined by the positive synergy between the franchisor and the franchisee. This makes the franchisors extremely selective on who they want to collaborate with. The franchisor also spends a lot of time and effort on ensuring the franchisees success and it is but natural that they will go through extensive checks before signing the contract with the franchisee. An evaluation process exists with a majority of them which is used to determine if there is a good fit between the two parties. Franchising involves entering into a long-term and symbiotic relationship between a franchisor and franchisee. It must be kept in mind that the evaluation is always a two-way process. It is essential that you are honest with yourself and more importantly with your franchisor as well on the goals you want to achieve with this model. You should have a clear target in mind on where you envision yourself at the end which should be shared with the franchisor. This way both of you can determine if the goal is realistic and achievable.

2. **Myth: Franchisees are essentially employees of franchisors.**

Truth: Nothing could be further from the truth than this myth about franchisees being employees of franchisors. Franchisees are necessarily business owners who are solely responsible for the daily operations, decision making, employee hiring and management, ultimately holding the key to the success of their business.

3. **Myth: The franchisor will do everything for the franchisee.**

Truth: Franchisors are true businessmen and they will provide all the necessary support to protect their brand name. However, that said franchisors will only provide training, necessary standard systems, and marketing support but the franchisee is ultimately responsible for driving revenue and profitability and running the day-to-day operations of the business.

Many first time business owners might venture into the franchising world thinking that the franchisor would run their business. They feel that there would be very minimum involvement needed from their end. Nothing could be further from the truth. A very simple thing to understand is that if the franchisor had the time to run a franchisees business, then he would not need the franchisee at all. This attitude also defeats the very purpose of franchising where both parties need to work in tandem to ensure success for the business. Failure to do so will result in business losses and rise of conflicts. It is pertinent to note that the franchise business will only get you the advantage of using the systems and processes that are tried, tested, and proven successful. The franchisee has to grab this opportunity and take care of the daily operations of the franchisee business.

4. **Myth: Investing in a franchise means buying a business.**

Truth: Most people are of the opinion that investing in a franchise means buying a business. One must keep in mind is that investing in a franchise provides you the license to operate a business under the franchisors' brand name along with the associated trademarks and operating processes, for a specified period of time. It does not mean you own the franchisor brand.

As a franchisee your strict adherence is expected to the standards, procedures, guidelines, and systems provided by the franchisor. This is also explicitly mentioned in the franchise contract agreement as well and is binding on you. As a franchisee you have the ownership to manage the day-to-day operations of the franchise and work toward driving revenue and improving profitability.

5. **Myth: It's more expensive to invest in a franchise than to start an independent business.**

Truth: Most of the time franchising is the cheaper option, but multinational brands may charge a hefty amount for owning a franchise of their brand. It is true that you might have to pay more to procure a franchise license. However, you should see a return on investment soon through brand recognition, assistance, and marketing support that a well-established franchise can offer.

It is important to note that you are not inheriting only the franchise license for your money. It is all the necessary infrastructure and support that the franchisor provides like marketing tools, standard operating procedures, training, ongoing support, guidance, etc. Remember that the very reason that the franchisor is thinking about franchising is because he has truly and effectively built systems and methods that have proven successful. You do not have to reinvent the wheel and adopt a trial and error approach for your business. The value of time that you have to spend to find all the right systems and put everything together when starting your own business is priceless. Plus, there is always a risk of not fully comprehending whether the approach you have chosen will work successfully or not. By owning a franchise, every element or tool has been given to you in order to assist in your success as a franchisee. Ultimately, franchises do not cost more than starting your own business because of time value and risk factors.

Remember, you are not just "buying" a franchise; you are essentially making an investment in yourself. Financing options are easier if the brand is established and a host of options are available including family members and small business loans.

6. **Myth: You don't have any independence in a franchise.**

Truth: it is believed that as you have signed the franchise agreement you lose all freedom of taking decisions. All the decisions are taken by the franchisor and you are merely a follower who should adhere to them. The restrictions are in place to maintain standardization across the franchise and promote brand building and long-term profit.

The franchising model lists the basic systems along with the procedures to be followed which are needed to be successful. That being said, you are accorded full flexibility within your franchise unit on who to hire and fire as well as handling the local promotions of your business. Franchisors give franchisees ample freedom to operate. One of the major perks of owning your own franchise instead of a business stems from the fact that the marketing, branding, market research and demographics, operating systems training and more are all handled by the franchisor. The franchisor has a lot of stake riding on the success of your franchise and will always have your best interest at heart. There's a relevant reason the business deploys specific tools and branding policies and expects you to adhere to them. These practices have a proven track record of success and have made the franchisor a lot of money.

Franchisors will provide only a guiding framework, but you are responsible for building and marketing the business. You have invested in the credibility of the brand, a defined marketing program, and other support systems to help you succeed. Your adherence to systems is necessary to maintain consistency in product and service quality. However, it is up to you to take independent decisions on an everyday basis as well as to come up with innovative ideas to expand the business.

Many aspiring entrepreneurs are concerned if they will get the required freedom to run the business or the franchisor would dictate all the terms. There are, however, only certain limitations which the franchisor will enforce like use of original signage, color combination, interiors of the store, etc. to maintain uniformity. Beyond these basic requirements franchisees are free to delegate as they deem fit to grow the franchise.

7. **Myth: I can't afford to buy a franchise.**

Truth: Owning a franchise is the most effective way and the easiest way to be in an organized business. If the cost benefit analysis is done it can be seen that it is always cost effective to buy a franchisee. Most people are worried that they will not have the funds to buy a franchise. A thing to remember is it is a finder's world and that there are plenty of affordable franchise businesses starting at well under INR 5,00,000/-.

It is true that there are franchise fees to be paid on a regular basis (often monthly) but these are normally defined by the nature of your business. Any additional expenses that you may incur are what you typically expect in any business, but you are getting the benefits of training and support. That said as is the case with any business, plenty of initial investments are required till the business is up and running. However, if investment is a concern you can still look at low-cost franchises which are fast becoming the rage in India.

8. **Myth: I can't be creative in a franchise business.**

Truth: Being a franchisee you are expected to follow certain protocols when it comes to pricing, branding, marketing, etc., but that is not to say there are any limits to your creativity. You will be interested in knowing that the Egg McMuffin is a creation of the McDonalds franchisee. All you need is an out of box thinking ability and the passion to grow your business and the creative ideas will automatically flow. The McDonald franchisee story is not an aberration but rather the rule. There have been multiple success stories of franchisees whose suggested menus have become best sellers for the brand. Motivational approaches for the employees deployed by the franchisees have been super successful and have been adopted by the franchisor and implemented throughout the entire franchise system.

9. **Myth: You need to have experience of running a business in order to become a franchisee.**

Truth: The reason why there are so many new entrepreneurs and professional people entering the franchisee world is because the basic concept of running a franchise is all about following proven systems and processes and acquiring the requisite training to successfully execute them.

Some of the most successful franchise owners I've known within our own franchise system and others are people who had no previous business ownership experience. Some of them came from the corporate world or the military. Many others were former teachers, car salespeople, or accountants. The common binding qualities among this diverse group of people were their ability to communicate effectively, take swift decisions, and stick to the systems that are provided to them to allow them to succeed. Therein lies the beauty of the franchising concept. It presents opportunities in every industry and comes with a plan intended for success! It provides an awesome opportunity to pursue a career in a field of your choice where you will receive training, ongoing support, marketing materials, products, and a business plan from a tried-and-tested corporate partner.

10. **Myth: Franchisors charge franchisees huge fees for their own profit.**

Truth: People worry that the franchisors are only concerned with increasing their profits and charge an enormous fee to the franchisees. This is not exactly true as the initial franchise fee accounts for the cost of training, recruiting, territory analysis, site identification, specialist equipment, stationary, franchisee launch, etc. All this is tied in with the benefit of the franchisee. Also this includes the cost of sharing a successful business model that has taken a lot of work and money from the franchisor.

Your payments to the franchisor typically consist of a one-time fee and periodic royalty payments (generally monthly) which are generally a percentage of revenue generated. There are many variables that affect royalty fees as well as payment frequency of the royalty payments. In addition some franchisees might incur what is called as a marketing fund expense which can be up to 1–2 percent of gross sales. However, the total expenses that you incur will still be far lower than if you started your own business. Additionally you have all the systems and procedures already proved successful at your beck and call to reduce your risk of failure.

There are a multitude of parameters that govern franchisee fees. Amongst them are the uniqueness and complexity of the system, the profitability and expected ROI of the business. The calculation also includes the company's costs for development, acquisition, and granting franchises. The franchise fee also widely varies among franchise companies. In order to evaluate if your franchise fee is justified you can compare it to the amount you would spend starting a similar business on your own including the necessary training and third party services cost.

Advantages of a franchisee

1. Track record of success

A successful franchise company has discovered the right technique of running a business that has been prosperous in the market with fantastic results. Another benefit of franchising is that the franchisor is required to furnish all their details in their disclosures so that you can evaluate and make an informed choice. Franchisees historically have experienced a higher rate of success than independent businesses. You can also investigate other franchisees to check if they have been successful in their business ventures before making a commitment.

2. Strong brand

The foremost advantage of franchising lies in the fact that the company has already built a brand either regionally or nationally that gives you the home field advantage because your potential customers are already aware of the brand. It makes your job of converting new customers easy because they have already developed an affinity for the brand. The need for experimentation is eliminated. You directly benefit from the brand promotion of the franchisor as your franchise also gets the spotlight. You are associated with an acknowledged brand and trade mark. People who value the brand will trust your franchise blindly.

3. Training programs

A worthy franchise company has well designed and effective training programs to help you hit the ground running by arming you with successful methods on conducting a business. Plenty of reference material is available to assist you to deal with whatever situations arise in the normal course of running a business.

4. Ongoing operational support

The franchise model is not limited to a one-time support thing but the real benefit of this model is the ongoing continuous support provided to the franchisee. A complete package inclusive of training material, help for setting up, an operations manual, and constant advice with support is provided. There is a dedicated staff to provide ongoing assistance. You are buoyed by the fact that you are not alone and help is just a call away. Experts and mentors are available when you hit rough weather or when you want to share ideas for growing the business.

Franchising companies will always want to make certain that their formula for success is duplicated by each and every franchisee. Your success story is intricately linked with the success of the franchisor. Prior expertise is not a requirement as the training received from the franchisor is sufficient to establish the skills required to operate the franchise. A franchise empowers a small business to compete with big businesses a la David versus Goliath. This is possible due to the pool of support from the franchisor as well as the franchisees network.

5. Marketing assistance

The success of any business is heavily dependent on the right kind of marketing. It can make or break a business. Here is another advantage the franchise model offers. You are given proven tools and strategies for attracting and retaining customers by the franchisor. A dedicated marketing staff will develop actual marketing plans and budgets as well as ongoing efforts to continually market your franchise. Marketing budgets average 10 percent of a company's gross profit according to industry experts. This kind of budget is unaffordable to a small startup like yours but the beauty lies in the fact that franchisor will charge you a very small percentage for managing your marketing effort. Promotional material, advertisements, hiring of professionals etc. is all managed by the franchisor.

6. Real estate assistance

Running a successful business requires the identification and location of a right site in order to maximize the footfall and revenue. Most of the franchises will have operating manuals and documentations along with the necessary support staff to help you in identifying the right site. The franchise will also help you in negotiating the best deal for the site which helps in keeping you running costs down whilst providing the best chance of speedy growth.

7. Construction assistance

Another important area where franchises support and help the franchisee is designing the layout for the franchise location along with getting you in touch with the right contractors who will complete your construction activity. Most of the projects get delayed in the eventuality of selecting a wrong contractor and this is exactly where your risk of delay gets mitigated with the franchisors' help. The franchisor also helps you select the correct mix of furniture and equipment to maximize the effectiveness of your investment.

8. Purchasing power

A good franchise can help you leverage the combined volumes during the purchasing for the entire system to negotiate lower prices. This can significantly lower your expenses and this advantage is not limited to equipment and furniture but also extends out to supplies, inventory, uniforms and any other ongoing expense. A beneficial relationship with suppliers is already established and you can tap other franchisees for sharing ideas, getting inputs, and growth strategies.

9. Risk avoidance

Perhaps the single most benefit of owning a franchise is the mitigation of risk associated with the starting of your own business. This does not mean that you don't do your homework before signing up with the franchise. You still need to choose the correct brand and location among other parameters. Being an entrepreneur is all about dealing with uncertainty. You can soar like an eagle or fall to the ground. You can make millions or lose millions as well. There is no safety net. Being a franchisee, if you start losing money you will receive unwavering support from the franchisor as well as fellow franchisees. Also if you decide to move out of the franchisee business, the chances of you finding a buyer are bright as the franchise is operating under an established business model and a reputable brand.

10. More attractive to investors

Startups are always in need of additional capital and are always on the lookout for investors to back their venture. Who do you think the investor will more readily back? Franchisee or an independent startup? The redounding answer is always a franchisee. Investors are looking for return on investment and because the franchisee belongs to a proven system of profitability and stability it becomes the obvious choice. Getting financing for a franchisee is always easier as it is backed by a reputable brand. This decisive parameter makes franchising an attractive option for many a business people.

11. Continuing innovation

The staying power of a business is directly proportional to its ability to innovate and capture the attention of its customers. If you don't have something novel then you don't really have a business. It is of course possible to perform innovation by yourself but it would involve putting in a substantial amount of time, effort, and resource. This is where the franchisee model excels. It has a dedicated department working on innovation which benefits all franchisees. Also the innovations costs get distributed over a large network resulting in lower cost per franchisee.

Disadvantages of a franchisee

Contrary to popular opinion all is not hunky dory in the franchising business. There are definitely some disadvantages associated with it, and we would be missing the complete picture if we do not take those into account.

1. Buying a franchise means entering into a formal agreement with your franchisor
2. Franchise agreements dictate how the business is run, so there will definitely be some constraints
3. There are definite boundaries on where you operate, the products you sell, and the suppliers you use
4. Bad performances by other franchisees may affect your franchise's reputation albeit no fault of yours
5. Buying a franchise means ongoing sharing of profit with the franchisor
6. Franchisors do not have any obligation to renew an agreement at the end of the franchise term.

Franchising takes a special type of person:

Owning a franchisee is not everybody's piece of cake and there are some distinct qualities that are required to become a successful franchisee:

- Willing to follow systems and procedures laid down for the business
- Flexible to adapt to merging ideas and changing situations at work
- You should have support of the family in this venture, which is fundamental to sustain and thrive
- Leadership experience for at least 5 years
- You should have the ability to take risks and be willing to invest your savings into the business
- You should have the unique combination of being entrepreneurial as well as compliant (willing to conduct business the franchisor's way)
- Be a good leader and communicator
- Be a team player
- Have basic financial knowledge
- Should have a passion and burning desire for success.

For many people, owning a franchise is an ideal way to become their own boss. This is not to say it is a risk-free option, but the presence of a tried and tested business model helps you avoid the pitfalls commonly associated with startups.

Here are some of the common mistakes prospective franchisees might make—and how to avoid them.

1. Failure to seek appropriate legal advice

It is a grave mistake to enter into any contract without a thorough understanding and implications of the terms and conditions in the contract. Most people seek legal representation during signing the contract but they don't do the required homework of the documentation or fail to appoint a representative who is well versed in the finer nuances of franchise agreements. It is important to not only select the right representative with extensive experience but also equally imperative to pick his mind on the areas which you find difficult to comprehend. Always document your concerns and get clarification from your attorney as well as the franchisor. Always make sure you have franchisor clarifications in writing. A franchisor should have no concerns clarifying your doubts or those of your legal representative.

2. Relying on instincts

You can rely on your gut feeling to make decisions, but such decisions are bound to be error prone and can lead to disastrous results. So instead of making decisions on the fly gather as much information as possible from the existing franchisees plus also conduct an additional independent probe to be doubly sure whether you want to enter an agreement into the franchisor. This will have two-fold benefits: firstly, you will make new friends who will provide you great knowledge and information. Secondly, you will also be able to learn from any of the mistake they might have made. Conduct a thorough analysis about the franchisor as well. A franchise with a long trail of lawsuits and disgruntled franchisees isn't a great fit.

3. Settling on a bad location

In the saturated and ultra-competitive market of today, modern franchises require locations that permit organic exposure and easy access. No more industrial parks or isolated locations. Today's franchisees need retail visibility, even if that is accompanied with higher rent. Be patient with picking the site. Perform as much research as possible by visiting multiple potential locations at different times and different days to get a 360 degree view. How does the traffic look? Would this spot be easily accessible? If the right location is taking more time to secure, talk to the franchise office for assistance or a time extension. The right location will make a world of difference in the franchise's success.

4. Ignoring manuals and procedures

The most awful mistake a new franchise owner can make is ignoring the proven procedures outlined by the franchise. If you don't take the manuals and processes seriously, you'll greatly limit your chances for success. The franchise has a brand and a reputation to protect. The franchisors' experience and learning has more control over your destiny than you imagine. Your success is intertwined and the more you deviate from the prescribed strategies for operations, marketing, training and service, the more likely you will encounter trouble. Have absolute clarity on what the franchise expects from you so that you can meet those expectations quickly and fully.

Don't enter the franchise business with the false impression that you'll be making the big business decisions. While you do have some autonomy as a franchisee, you have to diligently follow the operating models, guidelines, and processes set out by the franchisor. Invest your time, energy, and resources in executing the operational model with excellence. The franchisor's proven and successful ways of doing business will help you achieve a return on investment. Devote your energy on the day-to-day operation of your business.

5. Not verifying oral representations of the franchisor

Oral representations hold no value and are not legally binding as well. If your franchisor has made an oral representation of which you are uncertain, get those clarified from your fellow franchisees as well as through the franchisor. Remember it is important to have all conversations and understanding with the franchisor clearly written down and documented.

6. Not contacting enough current franchisees

Remember nobody can give you more accurate information about an organization than its own employees. Similarly the existing franchisees can provide you with a wealth of knowledge and information. If the franchisor provides you a tour of one or more existing franchises, be sure to reach out to them and seek answers on a wide spectrum of information like location, single unit or multiple unit owners, successful as well as unsuccessful franchisees, what works and what does not.

Asking questions like:

- Does the franchisor exercise excess control, or not enough?
- Is the franchisor always willing to help?
- Has the franchisor held up its end of the obligations regarding ongoing support assistance and training?

Information from franchisees from their first year in business and their experience with the franchisor can be extremely enlightening.

7. Underestimating costs

Running a business does not mean that you pay only the initial purchase and startup costs. Ongoing expenses are essential for the business to remain competitive and successful. Many startups fail to grasp this reality and land up in a situation where the requisite finances for running the business become unavailable. Careful financial planning and acumen is required to estimate the costs as well as plan for any contingencies that may arise with time.

These simple yet common mistakes must be judiciously avoided to prevent the franchise from failing. One of the biggest mistakes a franchisee can make is choose an area or an industry that he is not passionate about. It is only if you love and believe in the brand that your heart will resonate with the franchise and you will double your efforts for success. Before starting the venture take ample time to thoroughly investigate the franchise opportunity and ensure that the brand is reputable and dependable and you should be set for your journey.

Business simplified

Successful people make things simple, the unsuccessful make things complicated. The key to success is to simplify things and have the perseverance to complete what they start and that too on time. They do not make any excuses and run their business with a purpose and zeal. Let's look at a couple of examples that reinforce the point:

Example 1: Google has one of the simplest search engines. A couple of words here and there are enough to start the search. It can be used by people who are not tech savvy and creates no confusion for the user. Simplicity is like a magnet for users. The software behind the search engine solves an equation of more than 500 million variables to rank 8 billion webpages by importance and relevance.

However, the user interface which the end user encounters is something that is unbelievably simple. It merely consists of a clean white home page, featuring not more than 30 lean words, cherry six characters, and a primary colored logo and a capacious search box. Google understands that simplicity is both sacrosanct and central to its competitive advantage. The ability to give you what you want, when you want is what sets apart this search engine leader from the rest of the pack.

Example 2: Apple IPhone

While its competitors in the technology segment struggled to augment the features of digital music players, mobile and computers, Apple began their journey in the opposite direction looking for the simple solution to any design or technical challenge. The iPhones use interface that is extremely intuitive providing users with the ability to use most of the iPhone's functions without having to refer to the user manual.

The ultimate fear among the technophobic population is the inability to use a new computer, new piece of software, or a new electronic device. Confronted with this challenge, the apple iPhone flattens the learning curve considerably. Apple has always strived to create products from a user's perspective, rather than from an engineer's or a computer programmer's perspective.

If you analyze both examples closely, you will realize that both companies are successful because they have understood user or customer's needs, wants, desires, and problems. Understanding the customer pain areas, they have developed product making it an instant hit among their customers. They have taken a lot of effort in making things simple for their end users. In today's fast growing world simplicity is the answer. Just plug and play.

Many franchise brands work day and night, and invest a lot of money in R&D, hiring experts to make business simple, in turn making it simple for franchisees too. Simplicity makes it easy to copy the business model by the franchisees, thereby providing greater leverage to the brand. This makes it easy for franchises to learn, operate, and make money. It will not be wrong to say today's market is growing and getting organized due to franchise business.

A ready-made success model

"Follow the system" is a mantra in franchising and critical to franchise's success. Franchisees buy the franchisors' operating system believing that if they follow it, they will succeed and be profitable. Smart franchisors are always amenable to suggestions from their franchisees for change. Franchisors always invest money and time in building the brand, upgrading products and service, updating operation manuals and systems. Real life experiences of success and failure and the corresponding changes in the system get added in operational manual on a regular basis. This greatly benefits the franchisees.

"Challenges always bring out the best in a leader, it instigates one to have more enthusiasm, more energy and achieve more than what one can normally do."

Share your challenges –make value addition

When you buy franchisee, you may face some challenges which could be varied in nature. You can always reach out to the franchisor to get those resolved. Always remember a two-way open and honest communication is of prime importance if the franchise has to succeed. The approach to the problem should be twin fold. A temporary solution which solves the immediate need and a long-term root cause analysis approach which results in the modification of systems and procedures to prevent the problem from reoccurring.

Your inputs and suggestions are also of equal importance as a franchisee, but as the franchisor has had a better and longer experience of running the business, he may have encountered the problem earlier and could have a ready-made solution. If you are new to franchisee business, it may be a novel situation for you. It is pertinent to listen to the franchisors' suggestion and implement his suggestions and solutions. Franchisors' success lies in making you successful and he will always be fully invested in helping you find a solution to your problem.

Don't always expect everything from the franchisor

Over dependence from the franchisor can create conflicts and hamper the relationship between the franchisor and the franchisee. It is necessary to have absolute clarity about your role and you should whole heartedly participate in the training and follow the operation manual to the letter. In case you are stuck, you can always reach out for help, but it is your primary responsibility as a franchise owner to learn first.

The franchisees, who have cracked the code for success have always been the ones who have mastered the art of learning and experimenting. Follow the operation manual diligently. The franchisor is always accessible for help if you need it but it is important to be professional in your approach.

Sell more to earn more

One thing you should always master in business is selling. The better you sell the better revenue you will generate. Be proactive and teach your team the art of selling. Selling is the most critical business function. Selling is the only way of assuring rapid growth. Have proper monitoring systems to track your selling performance daily or periodically. In QSR franchises, sales are tracked thrice a day. Be creative in finding different ways to increase sale. If you have a novel idea to multiply your sale, run it by your franchisor. Tracking and analyzing, reading financial reports are main activities of your management.

Start small and finish big

As I said earlier in this book "Journey of 1000 miles begins with a single step." Take one step at a time, and learn to walk before you earn. Taking small successful steps will build your confidence and provide traction for your journey.

Most entrepreneurs go their gut feeling and invest big amounts in the business without the proper background study and end up making a loss. Acquiring the right knowledge, skill, and information is necessary before you can scale up the business. Before making a foray into the franchise world, ensure you study the market, research the franchise brand, evaluate the franchise offer, and then setup a single unit. Once you have succeeded in running the single unit, only then think of diversifying your business.

Who do you think is more important? The cell or the organ; the organ or the body? The correct answer is both carry equal weightage and both are necessary for the body to survive. Similarly in a business detailing as well as looking at the big picture both are of equal importance. You cannot ignore one or the other. Only when you have mastered the art of running a single franchise unit successfully, is it time to open multiple units. Almost all successful businesses start small before becoming big.

"A BIG business starts small."

The future of franchising in India

The concept of franchising has changed the business scenario in India at multiple levels. Franchising itself has gone through various transitional stages. From zero receptivity to gradually luring investors through minimum guarantee in the initial stage, the franchise industry is steadily inching up to a partnership model where both the franchisor and the franchisee share the pain as well as the perks equally.

Initially, the concept of franchising invited people who were looking for an investment option. They wanted to do a safe business where they do not have to build a brand. They wanted to piggy back on an established brand and run a business. Over the years companies have realized that it is not the quantity but the quality of the franchisee which is most important. Companies desire to have strong and big partners now instead of investors. Commercials have moved away from investor friendly minimum guarantee model to a retailer friendly commission-based model. Companies are increasingly looking for partners rather than pure investors.

As a model, franchising has proven itself to be highly resilient, even in times of economic downturn. Franchising can be a more attractive prospect for many people than opening their own business, as the stability of an existing model and mode of operations can mitigate a lot of the risk of opening a brand new business. Indians can rely on the fact that they are buying into an established brand with a target market that has already been identified.

Food and beverage franchises consistently dominate the franchise sector within India. One-third of new food outlets in India are established through franchise systems. QSRs and fast food outlets are the most popular, pointing to a shift in the pace of consumer lifestyles. By 2022 it is estimated that the food and beverage industry will have doubled its workforce, providing plentiful employment within India.

Retail, beauty and healthcare, and education are also attractive markets for franchising. India has become a popular tourist destination and this influx of visitor has strengthened the growth of hospitality franchises. American brands have also identified India as a market ripe for expansion. There is a strong demand for American products and service among Indian consumers in areas such as food and beverage, hospitality, retail, education, clothing, and fitness.

India's culture is richly diverse and this is reflected in the population. The needs and tastes of India's consumers are unique, and international brands who have adapted their franchise model specifically to suit the particularities of the Indian market have experienced notable success.

India was projected to regain its position as the fastest-growing economy in the world, with the country's GDP growing to 7.2 percent in the last quarter of 2017. According to estimates, this number will further rise to 7.8 percent by 2019.

This spells good news for all sectors, and in particular for the franchising industry. According to Gaurav Marya (widely known for initiating the franchise revolution in India, he is the visionary force behind the India's largest integrated franchise and retail solution company, Franchise India Brands Ltd), India has already made its place as the second-largest franchise market globally (after the United States) with around 1.5 lakh franchisees and 4,600 franchisers operating in the country. Market watchers also believe that despite the boom in franchising, India still has untapped potential within the industry. This means that the sector is set to grow even faster in the coming years.

The need of the hour is a Working Group or Regulatory Body on Franchising to frame and standardize disclosure norms and legal frameworks on the regulatory side. This will ensure that Franchisors as well as Franchisees understand and honor their commitments and responsibilities. Franchising is a stepping stone for budding entrepreneurs.

An IBM data survey suggests that 90 percent of Indian startups fail within 5 years. The prime reasons listed for this are—lack of mentorship and structure. The success rate in franchising, however, is about 85 percent. As a matter of fact, most successful startups have leveraged the franchise route for growth. Franchising is a means through which India can fight the economic disparity, and at the same time provide financial security for the business owner. It also means gainful employment for the workforce.

Economic data suggest India is ripe for a franchising boom with its burgeoning middle class helping retail sales grow 10 percent every year. This shows that there is no dearth of demand and ample opportunities are available to help cater this demand. The momentum of this sector is gathering steam with the prevalent employment condition in the country combined with the entrepreneurship zeal in the newer generation. The International Franchise Association has rated India as the 12th most valuable market for franchising.

Scan this QR code to get the FREE Daily Planner that will help you to focus on the most important activities, keep track of them and avoid running out of time because of poor task prioritizing.

Or visit www.sameerindia.com/dailyplanner

FRANCHISE
BUSINESS
CONCEPT
OPERATOR
TRADEMARK
AGREEMENT
INVESTMENT

CHAPTER 9

HOW TO CHOOSE THE RIGHT FRANCHISE

I find franchising as an incredible business opportunity. It truly can be the gateway for new entrepreneurs to learn how to start their own business and allow those who haven't felt comfortable taking that first step into entrepreneurship to take the leap. Not all franchises are the same, in fact it is the leadership at the top, like any other organization system, which proves how successful the franchise might be in its growth and scalability plans.

What I have seen in most successful franchises is that the franchisor looks to the franchisees as their partners and cares about them as much as they do their own businesses.

So when that investing opportunity comes forward, here are some tips which will help you take the plunge into the franchise business. I've personally found these tips useful to help choose the right franchise to invest in.

So when it comes to investing in a business, here is a small personal checklist which I find very beneficial in choosing the right opportunity.

Decision to own a franchise or a small business

Small business owners enjoy their flexibility and find it a challenge to abide by the rules and view the franchise system structure as an interference in their decision making process. So it is important to introspect regarding the key factors that might be most important to you while running the business. Factors like working hours, special skills, investment capacities, or exit plans are critical to evaluate as part of this decision making process.

If you feel you can abide by the structure and guidelines defined by the franchisor and be answerable to the franchisor for targets, there might not be a better business opportunity. Doing this analysis at an early stage can

Identify the total capital requirement

Generally, most franchises require a certain amount of fixed capital investment. This amount is dependent on the nature of business, but it is mandatory to make the necessary arrangement to kick start your business. Whatever is the amount, I recommend having at least twice the sum in liquid funds for working capital and other expenses. This helps achieve breakeven sooner. Estimating these numbers early on in the venture is very important for choosing a franchise that fits your budget and avoids the unnecessary heartache of falling in love with franchise systems you can't afford.

Research markets before you research franchises

Market research is crucial for the success of any business. A great product or service can fail if you don't have a consumer for that offering. I always recommend investing enough time, effort, and money in doing market research, which can be efficiently managed through various paid and free online resources. For advanced research, there are specialized agencies who specifically focus on market research using several tools and techniques. This wise investment in the nascent stage of business can eventually save a lot of money in the long run.

Interview the franchisor like you would while making the most important decision of your life

Choosing the right franchise is central to a successful business. So validate every step with great caution. Get the legal and financial documents vetted from experts like lawyers and chartered accountants. Over the years, I had the opportunity to interact with many franchises and there are some common traits among them. Their leadership swears by integrity, vision, and compassion and it augers well for their teams as well. They invest in people and give them the entire support system to ensure their success.

Once you have shortlisted a few companies, gather more information through publicly available information like website, brochures, and other marketing and financial collaterals. Based on this information, you can narrow down the company most aligned to your requirement. Communicate with the franchise team and gather more in-depth information. The responses from a healthy franchise would be more personalized and positive, in lieu of a rehearsed marketing jargon.

Franchising remains one of the safest ways to do business due to the time-tested training and support available. You pay a franchise fee and you get a format or system developed by the company (franchisor), the right to use the franchisor's name for a specific number of years and assistance. The franchisor provides a complete logistical support for setting up the franchise, including hunting for the perfect location, training and support for staff and a complete Standard Operating Procedure (SOP) for running the business, which leaves little space for ambiguity and ensures higher rate of success.

Evaluating the Franchisor

Once you have identified the line of business, the next thing is to identify among the leading franchises, which one would be a perfect match for you. For this, some of the checks are mandatory as illustrated below:

1. Check franchisor management

I strongly recommend a review of the management background and experience of key franchisor executives and support staff. It's important that they have experience in the franchise industry. The leadership team should come with cross functional skills across domains. The length of time that a franchise has been in business is not a guarantor of success, but is an indication of stability and consistency. For the newer franchise chains, review the financial projections in a bit more detail as they may have less actuals to disclose.

2. Check the various fees

There are various kinds of fees that are paid to the franchise during the tenure of business. A critical evaluation of this aspect is important to gage the investment involved and your financial capacity. The initial payment to the franchisor is the franchise fee that covers the cost of recruiting and training. The franchisor does not profit from this payment. The franchisor makes money through a regular royalty fee, which can be a percentage of the gross sales. In exchange for the right to use the franchisor's brand name and regular support, the franchisor will charge some or all of the following fees. Understand these meticulously before you take your big jump ahead.

Initial franchise fee and other expenses –Your initial franchise fee will typically range from tens of thousands of dollars to several hundred thousand dollars and may be nonrefundable. You may face significant costs to rent, build, and equip an outlet and to buy initial inventory. You also may have to pay for operating licenses and insurance and a "grand opening" fee to the franchisor to promote your new outlet.

Continuing royalty payments – You may have to pay the franchisor royalties based on a percentage of your weekly or monthly gross income. Depending on the franchisor and their franchise agreement clauses, you may pay royalties for the right to use the franchisor's brand name, even if you are losing money. You may have to also pay royalties for the duration of your franchise agreement even if the franchisor doesn't provide the services it promised and even if you decide to terminate your franchisee agreement early.

Advertising fees – You also may have to contribute to an advertising fund kitty. Some portion of the advertising fees may be allocated to national advertising or to attract new franchise owners, rather than to promote your outlet. Franchisees are often required to contribute a percentage of their sales to one or more national, regional, or local advertising funds. So always ask the franchisor about their current and future advertising plans. Ask them about the expected level of involvement from the franchisees toward the overall advertising funds.

Much of these fees are reinvested into the franchise to enable it to develop and grow, but everybody is in business to make money and the franchisor is no exception. If the franchisor can't make a satisfactory profit from the franchise, they may simply walk away from the business. So be sure that the initial franchise fee and the continuing fees are comparable to similar franchises.

3. Check the financials

A business without profit is a bad one. So it is absolutely vital to do a thorough due diligence before going forward with the investment in the franchise opportunity. The franchisor is required to share business plans, financial projections, and disclosure documents with you beforehand. Study the numbers carefully and use the services of experts like lawyers and CAs, before you arrive at a decision. Aligning your own financial projections based on the cost-benefit analysis is critical to measure your return on investment. Only if the numbers match with your financial capacity, go ahead.

In its infancy stage, you will have to bootstrap and self-fund, till the business kicks off. Evaluate this working capital requirement and add it to your investment plan to speculate a realistic financial investment. An error in this estimation can be lethal to the success of the franchise. As they say, *buying a car is an expense, but maintaining it well is another expense you need to factor before deciding the brand you'd want to own.* The franchise decision is not very different from the analogy. So take every step carefully.

4. Understand the training provided

While I know that franchises will always focus on training their franchisees in their own business through a detailed product and service training, I have seen some franchises focus on personnel and business training skills as well. This has an indirect benefit through increased efficiency and management skills. An assured continual support from the franchise over the tenure of business gives immense confidence and mental peace to the franchisee before taking this huge step.

5. Call or meet existing franchisees

The best feedback for the shortlisted franchise that you may get is from the other franchisees. So do connect with more than one franchisee, if possible, to gain a better understanding of the working and the systems. Use this opportunity to validate your cost projections and capital investment assumptions. Consider asking the franchisee's following questions:

- How long have you owned your franchise?
- What was it that attracted you to this franchise business?
- Do you own more than one unit, or do you have plans to own more?
- What was your professional background before you purchased your franchise?
- Did your prior experience help or hinder your business operations?
- What was the impact of running the franchisee upon your family and social life initially? How different is it now?
- Was the training what you expected it to be?
- Were the manuals helpful? Do you still use them?
- Did the franchisor do what they promised before you opened?
- Has the franchisor been reasonably available to help with problems?
- Are you earning the money that you expected?
- Were the franchisor's projections correct about the amount of capital and/or borrowing you would initially require?
- Were there any hidden fees or unexpected costs?
- Do you believe you can meet your financial goals in the future?
- What would you change about the business?
- What would you say are the benefits of having a franchisee, over starting your own business?
- Knowing what you know now, would you do it again?
- What advice would you give me?

6. Visit the franchisor

Plan a visit to franchisor headquarters. This is a great opportunity to get any final questions answered and to meet the people who will help you kick start your business. But also bear in mind that they will also evaluate you as a potential franchisee at the same time, so this final judgment is a two-way street.

7. Check Franchisor controls and restrictions

To ensure uniformity, franchisors usually control how franchisees conduct business. This restricts the franchisee's freedom to take decisions. A franchisor may control:

- **Site approval-** Many franchisors retain the right to approve locations for their outlets, and may not approve a site you select. Some franchisors conduct extensive site studies as part of the approval process as a site they approve may be more likely to attract customers.
- **Appearance standards-** Franchisors may impose design or appearance standards to ensure a uniform look among their outlets. Some franchisors require periodic renovations or design changes; complying with these requirements may increase your costs.
- **Restrictions on goods and services you sell-**Franchisors may put restrictions on the goods and services you sell. For example, if you own a restaurant franchise, you may not be able to make any changes to your menu. If you own an automobile transmission repair franchise, you may not be able to perform other types of automotive work, like brake or electrical system repairs.
- **Restrictions on method of operation** – Franchisors may define the working pattern for all their franchisees. Working hours, signatories, uniforms, or marketing collaterals might be required to be done in a certain way. They may also dictate the way you maintain your books of accounts or mandate certain discounts on certain products. Certain franchisors require the raw materials to be sourced from a specific supplier only.
- **Restrictions on sales area** – A franchisor may limit your business to a specific location or sales territory. If you have an "exclusive" or "protected" territory, it may prevent the franchisor and other franchisees from opening competing outlets or serving customers in your territory, but it may not protect you from all competition by the franchisor. For example, the franchisor may have the right to offer the same goods or services in your sales area through its own website, catalogs, other retailers or competing outlets of a different company-owned franchise. So having knowledge about these things ahead of time is very important. There have been cases of territorial disputes between franchisees, so being aware of the regulations and agreement clauses help.

1. The franchise agreement will include restrictions, limitations, rules, and guidelines about what you, as a franchisee, can and can't do once you've signed the contract. These may seem daunting at

first, but they're in place to protect the brand and its consistency across the franchise system. Franchises often place significant restrictions on what you can do, to enforce uniformity across the brand. Make sure you understand what these restrictions are. Consult an expert in franchising business to review the franchise agreement with you so you don't sign up to any unrealistic restrictions. Good franchisors will present fair franchise contracts, but it's worth getting a professional to confirm that you won't be hit with any surprises further down the line.

8. **Explore the exit**

I know you might find it strange to evaluate your exit strategy before you've even invested in a franchise, but I think it is important and should not be overlooked. Understanding the exit penalty or other implications due to any reason is pivotal.

Make your decision

Once you've completed the above steps, it's time to make your final decision. If you've carefully followed this process, you can be sure that you've made your choice for all of the right reasons. Does your franchise opportunity match all of the following?

- Matches your financial capability
- Provides you with the lifestyle you want
- Provides a good product or service that has demand in the market
- Has a majority of happy and successful franchisees

- Employs an experienced and enthusiastic staff of personnel who will help you achieve your dreams of business ownership success.

Know that not all franchisees openly share business details over cold calls. And that's not surprising either. I am sure you'd be wary to share sensitive information with strangers. So asking the right questions is the key. Be more generic than specific. If you're asking about finances, for example, it may be better to ask generally how much you can expect to make as a new franchisee, rather than specifically how much they've made.

Finally, buying a franchise is a major life decision. There is a significant investment in terms of time and money. This decision can make or break your life. So taking this decision with great care is important.

Once you have made this decision and chosen your franchise partner, you need to master the art of leadership to maximize returns on your investment. Being a leader is a skill you're born with, or it can be acquired with training and capacity building. World leaders, mentors, and various leading training courses can prepare you for this challenge. In the next part of this book, I am going to show you how to be a good leader. Steps you can take to make your journey as the business owner, at the helm of affairs, more pleasing and rewarding.

Scan this QR code to get the FREE additional bonus chapter on How to Lead Silently

Or visit www.sameerindia.com/leadsilently

CHAPTER 10

START SMALL, FINISH BIG

"Put your heart, mind, and soul into even your SMALLEST acts. This is the SECRET of success." – Swami Sivananda

Exclusive interviews with successful franchisor & franchisee's as never seen before

Interview with Gaurav Marya – Franchise Management Leader & Speaker

How did the concept of starting Franchise India get seeded in your mind?

I had an idea, while still in process of completing higher education to do businesses. In Chandigarh, Economic Times used be reach me a day later then when published. I was always keen in understanding business and felt to gain knowledge about the whole business scenario is very important. Nevertheless, back in 1999 the ET gave a lot of insight about large corporations or someone in Trade markets. It was quite evident that there was a bare minimum available for small businesses.

Back in those times business knowledge about small businesses were either available from friends and families, or peer businesses. This was the point where I incepted the idea of spreading knowledge to the entire ecosystem of SME's though a sustainable model in Franchising.

What were the challenges you faced initially?

I had travelled to US during the end of the 90's, and observed the fundamental of "The Great American Dream".

The story goes like this, during the in 60's America suffered a recession and the GDP fell 1.6%. During this phase, a large number of people lost their jobs and in being jobless, they found the magic wand of owning a business through franchising, which had just started in 1950's through fast food chains. Eventually 97% of the retail businesses in America run franchisee.

I had already got an incubated idea in my head that India is a "Shopkeepers Nation", as apart from the metros the economy of smaller cities and towns were driven locally than centrally.

The major challenge I faced were

1. To impart the knowledge and reach out to these people, who aspired to be established but lacked the channel knowledge we stated working on.

    Solution: Franchise India started a Magazine (The Franchising World), and started reaching out to the then scattered industry segments. To my surprise after each published issues, I had started getting 300 -400 letter enquiring about the concept.

2. The next challenge was; how do I cater all these 400 people in one go, with a sustainable and best practices avenue.

The Solution: We conducted a franchising exhibition in Delhi (2001) and were the first step in bringing Franchisor and Franchisee under one roof.

3. One of the next challenges was to bring the whole country together to understand the whole concept of Franchising and cater them with right type of business.

    Solution: Franchise India started its country wide office expansion and started its offices in Mumbai & Pune in 2002, while the next few years we focused on expanding licensing vertical. Interestingly during this time we had started "Retailer" magazine to educate and empower the small entrepreneurs (2003 – 2006). Further to this we had now evolved as a much wider bandwidth of country presence with opening of our offices in Bangalore & Chennai (2006) and Hyderabad & Kolkata (2007).

4. On our expansion we faced an obstruction, as there was no structured entity to cater between the Franchisor and Franchisee

    Solution: In 2008 we started FIBL which apparently is known as world's largest business brokering firm. Here our idea was to create a bridge between the business and entrepreneur so that they can harmonize partnership.

5. On the inception of harmony between two business, we had identified gaps between the knowledge transfer parameters

    Solution: Francorp was incorporated in the year 2009, to strategize and organize the business replication process of a Franchisor in a more standardized and professional way.

6. Until now we were focusing on going local, but the idea of going international was a big process hindrance

    Solution: To overcome and facilitate International brands go local in Indian market FranGlobal was started 2013, which as an arm solely focuses on cross border business inception, servicing and bridging.

The above are the few milestone hindrances we faced in the process of educating India about franchising and I am sure we are still in the nascent stage of enduring franchising as a business model. The next 25 – 50 odd years will show us a more powerful and beautiful picture of modernized and self-sufficient entrepreneurs in the country.

What would you say the secret of your success?
There is only one secret to success, stay focused, fearful and envisioned. I could have done things personally but the secret is 'the best of my team

share the same vision as mine' and contribute to the vision with a sense of ownership that matches mine and rejoice in the challenges met and success achieved. I would also like to mention here, there is no short cut to success; you need to have confidence, self-belief and unwavering faith.

As a child I was often told by my mother, Success comes only when you do your work wholeheartedly and honestly. I have abided to those words my whole life and this is envisioned to my team in Franchise India.

How Indian Brands are doing in comparison to foreign brands?

Franchise India has serviced more than 8000 brands since its inception and has catered around 80,000 entrepreneurs in the past decade in India. I would say that the Indian markets are doing exceptionally good in terms of franchising, but if you look into the market sentiments, we are still in the early stages of creating franchising as an industry. Foreign brands are entering India and are doing well, but I see a potential in Indian brand expansion globally.

How big is franchise industry in India today?

Franchise Industry in India is currently estimated to be at 51 billion USD. The growth projection year on year is calculated to be 30-35% and is forecasted to touch 150 billion USD in the next five years. It is the second largest franchisee market in India after the US. India currently has approximately 4700 operating franchisors and about 1.7 lakhs franchisees across all industry sectors like Retail, Food, Services, Healthcare, and Business Services etc. Since 2012 until now the industry has shown a growth of about 61% from net worth of 18.4 billion USD to 51 billion USD. It is also to be noted that though the industry is still very young, contributes around 2% of India's GDP.

Which is the fastest growing franchise industry?

About 35% of the franchisee concept in India some in the industry of food and beverage and the rest of the 65% constitute of the non-food brands. However it is forecasted that F&B (Gourmet & Specialty restaurants), Retail & Wellness and fulfillment businesses are on the incline in showcasing steady growth.

Which is the most preferred franchise format? and Why?

The most preferred franchise business model in India is Franchise owned and Franchise operated (FOFO) for unit franchising and Master Franchising is the most popular Biz model.

FOFO model is a model which gives the franchisee a complete ownership of their enterprise, thus giving more control over the operations activities. The franchisor therefore bears so cost in building the franchise unit. Therefore this particular model can be treated as a low risk model for both franchisor and franchisee.

What are benefits of being a franchisee over starting an independent business?
An independent business needs a lot of right people in its inception; one of the reason why 90% of startups fail in the first five years of their inception (IBM). Franchising on the other hand has a shared risk. That is both the franchisor and franchisee are at low risk, and to addition the franchisee has a replicated successful and time tested business model to comply their operation on.

What are the common mistakes done by franchisee, which leads to their failure? Usually categorize franchise buyer into three broad classes,

1. Enthusiast - People who do not perform a capacity analysis before partnering with the franchisor.
2. Experienced — these are class of aspiring franchisee owners who are already in some kind of business already. They are usually the low risk takers.
3. Seasoned — These are the least risk takers and usually are only interested in the ROI. They usually go for a FICO model of franchising business (Franchisee Invested and Company Operated)

Over the above categories, the first ones or the enthusiasts are the ones who do maximum mistakes. The category generally comprises of young or first time entrepreneurs. Usually these people want huge returns in a smaller span of time and that is where the problem lies. Any business model which projects or aspire to have returns within the first few months of their inception is designed to fail. I would suggest the financials need to be calculated well in advance with at least an operating capital of one year from the time of inception.

What are the ideal characteristics of a good Franchisee?
A well-researched and a knowledgeable franchisee are characterized as a good Franchisee. In India the three major elements can be identified as Culture, Cost and Consumption pattern. I always encourage entrepreneurs to start a business on a planned route. For example the franchisee needs to know the risks involved in their kind of business. It is essential to think about the synergies in the operational part first and then calculate their ROI.

What are the top trends shaping Franchisee industry today?
One can identify a numbers of trends in Franchise industry today, but the top 3 trends would be

1. Multi-Unit Owners — Once one master the tried and true formula franchisors have designed for their franchisee; it is more likely that he will open more units in other locations. This creates a

success streams in multiple locations, and they quickly grow their revenues and increase business sustainability.
2. Business within a Business — this particular trend in best seen in quick to serve restaurants and cafes, those who are opening stores within hospitals and schools. This is a win-win situation because the franchise does not have to worry about the customers walking in and therefore the cash generation starts from its very inception.
3. Food and Education — in a survey conducted by Franchise India, food and education sectors are rapidly growing because of the changing consumer trends in India. With the increase of spend ability, much more consumers than before are going to eat out than their conventional ways, and also now every parent is more conscious about giving their children a world class education with best technology.

What impact does franchising have on Indian economy?

India has started emanating confidence among franchise investors. India is projected to grow from US$ 672 billion in 2017 to 1.1 trillion in 2020. India is looking for better alternatives and franchising is one of the fastest solutions in expansion.

How is the Indian franchise scenario different from some of the mature market?

India is still in phase where we can still hear about the segregated industry, for e.g. Courier business or a food industry. It is still in a phase where we are still trying to bring in the fact that we all belong to franchise industry.

Mature markets on the other hand have a definite structure to franchising industry model. We are working towards to create that ideology in India.

What are the challenges in the Franchising Industry today?

Lack of basic knowledge is the biggest challenge, and we are working towards educating both entrepreneurs and brands. I might say that the concept is still in its infancy; however looking at the fast changing dynamics of Indian market the day is not far away where we can have an educated ecosystem.

What needs to change in the Franchise Industry?

I feel it is very important to emphasize on the building business synergies. What happens after that is the business automatically shows positive ROI. Every business needs a cooling period after its inception to benefit positive returns. I come across people who want instant profit. In franchising the breakeven might be lesser than an independent business but a cooling period should be allowed usually 6- 12 months.

What is the future of Franchising in India?
India is fast growing dynamic market, and factors driving the growth in this market are unique. such as diverse culture, availability of space, purchase power, modernization and many more. It is inevitable to say we are going to see a more explosive industry expansion in our future days.

What is your message for those who like to start a new Franchisee?
Franchisee is all about Confidence, Commitment and Consistency. You have to give your cent percent concentration in the business and build synergy. Once synergies are in place ROI automatically falls in place, may be more than you expect.

FRANCHISOR INTERVIEWS:

Shahnaz Husain
(Founder, Chairperson, and Managing Director of the Shahnaz Husain Group)

The Shahnaz Husain Group of Companies—with a successful track record of over four decades, the Shahnaz Husain Group is internationally recognized for organic beauty care, based on Ayurveda, the ancient herbal healing system of India. It has combined plant power with the latest scientific techniques, formulating over 380 products for beauty and health care. The Shahnaz Husain Franchise is at the core of the success of the Shahnaz Husain brand. It is an established business model, with phenomenal international goodwill. The company has a global network of franchise ventures, comprising franchise salons, spa, retail outlets, and beauty training institutes. The products have received several international awards for Quality Excellence in London, Paris, New York, Geneva, and Cannes. The brand has gone from strength to strength. It has been tested by the most exacting test of all...the test of Time.

Products and Services: Formulation or manufacture of herbal cosmetics, based on Ayurveda; Operating signature beauty salons or spa; Stores or Retail Outlets or Beauty Training Academy, as well as Franchise Ventures (salons and retail outlets).

No of years: 47 years
No of Employees: 1500 +
No of customers: 5 million

What inspired you to start this business?
Translating my dreams and ideas into reality inspired me to start my own enterprise. During my training in London, I came across instances of damage

caused by chemical substances. In a way this changed my life and career. It sowed the seeds of my desire to become an entrepreneur. It gave me the idea of introducing a totally new concept. I decided to evolve treatments that are safe and without risks. I was determined to find a natural alternative. The study of Ayurveda convinced me that it could provide the ideal answers to the demands of beauty care. My idea was to provide herbal beauty based on the principle of "care and cure." In a way, it was also my independence to spirit which also inspired me to start my own business.

From starting your own business to giving a part of your business to the world, how did this franchise journey begin?
Very early in my career, I started encouraging ordinary housewives to open salons in their own homes, in a small way. I trained them and gave them the Shahnaz Herbal franchise. This way they could be financially independent and yet, care for home and family. At that time, more than four decades ago, this system suited the women and the franchise became popular. I also adopted a highly successful method to promote the new franchise salons, by making it a point to attend their openings. It was again a very personal touch. I inaugurated the openings, gave free consultations and addressed press conferences, speaking on the benefits of Ayurvedic care. It was all based on a personal interaction, where I met people, listened to their problems, and provided the beauty solutions. Thus, I was answering a human need. My presence at the openings evoked much media coverage and a fantastic response. This method proved so successful that soon I was attending two openings on the same day, flying to two or three different cities in India on the same day. Within the first year, we opened 80 franchise salons in India. Later, I adopted it for the openings of our franchise salons and other ventures around the world. The pace was hectic, but it became a distinctive style and very much a part of the brand image. Unknowingly, in spreading Ayurveda across the globe, a brand was born.

What makes your product or service unique?
"Shahnaz Husain" is not a faceless brand name or corporate. I am the person behind the brand and I am, myself, trained in cosmetology, cosmetic therapy, and Ayurvedic beauty care. I am the reality behind the name. We also have a unique integrated system of Salon Chain and Product Excellence, which rely on each other. In fact, the products, based on natural ingredients, have grown out of salon or clinical treatments. Known for product innovation, we have evolved over 375 formulations for general beauty care, treatment of skin and scalp disorders, health and fitness. I have never relied on commercial advertising. Instead, I relied on "word of mouth," believing that a satisfied client is the best advertisement. During the last four decades, Shahnaz franchise salons, spa, retail outlets, and beauty academies have extended all over the world. The brand is ideally positioned in both domestic and

international market in Ayurvedic beauty care. The products have received Quality Excellence Awards in London, Paris, New York, Geneva, and Cannes. Shahnaz Herbal was the only Indian herbal cosmetic brand selling at Selfridges, the famous London store.

What type of franchise model do you operate?
Apart from strong branding, we provide the franchisee an established business system and business model, with proven success rate and efficacy. The fast-paced extension of the Shahnaz Husain Herbal clinics is due to the unique franchise system, by which the franchisee obtains the right to use the Shahnaz Husain Herbal name and treatments, as well as enjoy a margin of profit on the sale of products. The franchisee, in turn, has to acquire training in specialized treatments in Shahnaz Husain's school of beauty therapy and also satisfy the stringent requirements of a name that has become internationally known. The franchisee is expected to have a commitment to excellence, financial stability, an investment capacity of approximately INR 20 to INR 30 lakhs, premises of 1000 ft–1200 ft. Prior experience in beauty and cosmetics would be an added advantage although it is not absolutely essential. The Franchisee benefits from a comprehensive support program that begins from the moment you sign on. Our franchise support program has been designed with the success of our franchisees in mind. We have applied our experience in creating a system that is easy to understand and to implement. The franchisee gets Salon Support Assistance and Administrative Support. We also provide advice on selection of real estate selection and guidance on interior design, layout, and furniture.

The Franchisee immediately begins to enjoy the goodwill that has been carefully built up by Shahnaz Husain over the last four decades. Indeed, the association with an internationally acclaimed name is a major plus point. Franchisees also have the advantage of a highly successful business model and professional infrastructure. The Shahnaz Husain Group offers a pillar of support in terms of R&D and introduction of innovative products from time to time.

The benefits of the Shahnaz Husain franchise have made it a valued business opportunity for entrepreneurs. It also offers the opportunity to share the phenomenal success of Shahnaz Herbal. The brand equity itself speaks of our unprecedented global success. The Shahnaz Husain brand has established unquestioned loyalty and is ideally placed in the herbal care market as the leader, supported by a wide distribution network in India and direct product distributors abroad. The franchisee has the opportunity to start Shahnaz Husain franchise ventures, like Shahnaz Husain Herbal Salons, branch of Shahnaz Husain International Beauty Academy, or Just Shahnaz franchise retail outlets.

What were some of the major challenges that you faced in this franchise business? How did you manage to overcome them? Is there any example that you can highlight?

Selection of the franchisee is itself a challenge. We need to have stringent selection criteria. In order to derive the full benefit of our business format, it is essential that each franchisee follows all its systems and procedures. This will ensure the best chances of success. We have to help the franchisee follow the successful systems and procedures in the best possible way, without making any compromises. As each franchisee is individual and separate, there may be differences in the expression and execution of the common value. Narrowing down the differences and making the expression and execution uniform is a challenge.

Being part of a world-renowned chain has its advantages, but it also has some responsibilities. We ensure that the franchisee does not devalue the Shahnaz Husain name. We also make sure that all franchisees operate in accordance with our principles and standard. In fact, the franchisee's own success depends on it. Each outlet must be the epitome of the highest level of service, with properly qualified and dedicated staff. When we introduce new products, we need to educate the franchisees about them. That is why we offer franchisees the opportunity to refresh their knowledge and also acquire the knowledge and art of new techniques. Learning never stops. It is an ongoing process.

With the current success that the franchise business has seen, where does this company stand in its industry?

With the success of our franchise business and our product innovation, our organization is positioned as the leader in the premium segment in the Ayurvedic or herbal beauty industry. We have recently launched several products for the middle segment, which is also doing extremely well, on the strength of brand identity and brand loyalty. Apart from salons, we also have franchise retail outlets, which have extended to metro and Tier 2 cities.

What do you do to keep updated with developments happening in the industry?

We have two R&D units, which are absolutely necessary for product innovation. They keep abreast of developments in the industry in India and internationally. We have prominent participation in Trade Fairs, in India and at foreign locations. We encourage feedback from clients and franchisees. This is a business where trends keep changing, so we need to keep up with new trends. I travel abroad frequently and we also participate in international beauty shows and exhibitions.

What do you see as the future of the industry you are in?
The beauty and wellness industry in India is booming, with a tremendous potential for growth. In fact, it is said to be growing twice as fast as markets of the United States and Europe. India is also the second largest consumer market in the world. According to a KPMG report, the size of India's beauty and wellness market would be around INR 80, 370 crores by 2017–2018. This includes the beauty products, beauty salon, and spa businesses. The Spa Association of India estimates that the Spa Industry is around INR 11,000 crores and continues to grow. It is estimated that the salon and spa business together account for 31 percent of the total size of the beauty and wellness market. The compounded annual growth rate of the Beauty and Wellness business in India has been around 18 percent.

Indeed, the beauty business in India is not only booming, but is expected to treble in the next 5 years. The herbal beauty business will continue to drive the growth of the beauty industry in India.

Who do you consider as your role model?
I consider my father as my role model. A father's relationship with his daughter is always very special. In his eyes, the daughter is always a "princess," while the father is often a role model and gives a real sense of security to his child. My father gave me some valuable teachings through his own life. I will never forget an incident when my grandmother passed away. My father was very attached to her and he did not shed a single tear. When I asked him why he was so silent and holding back his emotions, he said "Who am I to challenge the Will of God?" This left a very powerful impression in my mind, that whatever is beyond our control, is the Will of the God and we have no right to question or challenge it. This has helped me face impossible and insurmountable tragedies with fortitude and courage. The most precious lesson I learnt from my father was about spiritual strength. He taught me that God is there within every human being and we must look for Godliness within ourselves. I remember when I returned from abroad and showed him all my certificates from London, Paris, and New York, he said, "You have made all the preparations for this world. What have you done for the next?" I laughed and said, "I have time, I will start later." He gave me an example by saying that one can have a perfect torch which gives light. But, the light can fail. The battery may run out. He told me that the only certainty in life is death! He smiled and said "Don't wait, start now." That is how I started my free beauty training courses for the speech, hearing, and visually impaired and now for acid attack survivors. This helped me to translate my spiritual values into reality.

Is there any person that you would give credit to for your success?
My father guided me and became my real inspiration to take up a career. When I started my business, he taught me to have faith in my own abilities.

It was he, who said, "There is no such thing as destiny, you can make your own destiny, you can be, what you will yourself to be." I decided to open my herbal clinic in my own home in a small way. It was my father from whom I borrowed INR 35,000 and started by first herbal clinic in the verandah of my home. Behind the success of one herbal clinic to the expansion into a worldwide chain lies, not only my relentless determination and hard work, but also my father's faith that I would succeed.

Does your franchise chain have presence internationally? If no, are you planning to take the franchise to the multinational level? If yes, how many countries and which?
Yes, our franchise chain has extended to several other countries. International branding is always on the cards, anyway. We have franchise salons in the UK, USA, Australia, New Zealand, Dubai, Kuwait, Abu Dhabi, Malaysia, Singapore, Russia, CIS countries, etc.

Can you share the success stories of your franchisees?
We had tied up with a clinic on Harley Street in London, to start Shahnaz Ayurveda. The tie-up was based on the immensely successful Shahnaz franchise system. Harley Street is synonymous with the finest medical care in the United Kingdom. Starting Shahnaz Ayurveda on Harley Street was indicative of the increasing worldwide popularity of Ayurveda as an alternative therapy. Ayurvedic esthetic treatments have become an important component of cosmeceuticals. Introducing our treatments on Harley Street is like an Ayurvedic coup. Cosmeceuticals is a fast emerging concept, serving as a bridge between esthetics and medicine, developed specially for medicinal and cosmetic benefits.

What is your success formula for marketing?
Our success mantra is our best quality of product and satisfaction of our valued customers who create more customers for our brand. The viral effect of this chain always rope in "long term and dedicated customers."

What are the marketing strategies that have worked for your brand?
Continuous research and development of our products on the basis of consumer feedback system created uniquely to get the real and unbiased picture
- New products added as per the future needs of our valued customers to keep them intact forever
- Increasing the width and depth of our distribution network
- Offering "value for money "to the customers.

How do you support your franchisees in marketing?
- We provide guidance on Advertisement Strategy, Market Research, Beauty Counseling, Sales Promotion, including brochures, and Product Launches.

- Product training to the franchisee and staff to ensure latest techniques at the parlors or spa are used to give 100 percent satisfaction to the end customers to keep coming back for more and more products and services.
- Proper merchandising of product range to attract customers to purchase new range of products.

How do you help the franchisees to get new customers?
- Provide proper assistance to the franchisee to create parlors with professional look and feel to attract new customers
- Local advertising campaign to communicate to the "catchment customers "through leaflets, adverting, banners, etc.

Since the opening or launch period is very crucial what kind of support do you give for the franchisee business?
- Product testers, samples, leaflets for the new customers to test first before purchase of any product
- Product-related queries resolved by customer care on top priority
- Proper training to all staff members to manage customers professionally
- Specially designated teams to "Handhold "new franchisee with regular visit and communication till they stand on their own.

What is the vision of this franchise business?
Our beauty academy is nurturing hundreds of new entrepreneurs (housewives, college students, etc.) to start their beauty parlors or spa by enrolling as our franchisee to earn handsome profits; the demand for becoming our franchisee is increasing with each year from all the towns of India which is motivating our company to keep adding more franchisee every year.

How much time would it take to start your franchisee from the date of signing the agreement?
The franchise salon can be started within 7-8 weeks; for Just Shahnaz retail outlets take only 3-4 weeks to get started;

Who are the people that invest in your franchisee?
- Housewives seeking financial independence
- Students who have completed our Diploma Course
- People with business acumen, who wish to start their own enterprise.

What would be the initial investment required if someone wants to invest in your franchisee?
For franchise salons—20-30 lakhs including interiors and furniture;

For franchise retail stores—5-8 lakhs to be invested in product stocks.

How do your franchisees raise capital normally?
As the investment is quite affordable, generally franchisees raise it from their own sources; some of them opt for personal loans from friends or banks.

When the franchisee is stuck in an operational problem that they are unable to solve? How do you support them?
We are with them till they stand on their own feet and start working independently; our dedicated team of customer care and franchise executives keeps track of all activities for prompt support.

Are periodic audits on quality done?
Our R&D team members visit the franchisee outlets every quarter to check the quality of services and products used by the franchisee; they also impart product usage training to keep the franchisee updated.

What is the average payback period for a person who invests in your franchisee?
Generally a franchisee starts earning within 6 months.

What is the average ROI that your franchisee can expect to receive?
The investment rotates faster than other businesses and our average franchisee earns between 10 and 15 percent per month on investment.

Does your franchise network have people who buy multiple franchisees or a Master Franchise?
There are many Franchisees who started with one outlet and then expanded their business after experiencing "faster profits." But, they take the franchise rights from us. We do not have Master Franchisees. We do not hand over control of franchising activities for a specified area to any other person.

What would you say is the success rate of your franchisees?
More than 90 percent of our franchisee are quite satisfied with the returns on their investment.

How do you help franchisees to succeed?
Our franchise support program has been designed with the success of our franchisees in mind. We have applied our experience in creating a system that is easy to understand and to implement. We provide:
- Technological Know How and Support
- Marketing Support
- Administrative Support
- Salon Set-up Assistance.

Is your franchisee model system oriented or people oriented?
It is system oriented, as this helps the franchisee's business grow faster due to tailor-made solutions and product support.

What are the characteristics or signs of a good franchisee?
The criteria for being considered a good franchisee are as follows:
- Entrepreneurial spirit
- Commitment to excellence
- Passion to succeed
- Dedication to following the systems and procedures
- Financial stability
- Prior experience in beauty is an advantage, but not compulsory.

What according to you are the most important qualities of a successful franchisee?
The franchisee should know which franchise to take up, for example, the franchisor should have an established brand, with brand identity and brand loyalty;
- The ability of sheer hard work
- People skills, in order to build up a good clientele
- Ensure that the Franchisor's brand name is not devalued, as the Franchisee's own success depends on it.

Why people should invest in a franchisee rather than investing in an own business?
The franchisee has the advantage of an established brand name, brand identity, and brand loyalty;
- In the case of the Shahnaz Husain franchise, the franchisee does not have to invest in R&D and manufacture of products
- Has the benefit of tried and tested specialized treatments
- Enjoys the benefits of product innovation and product demand
- Enjoys the advantage of the goodwill earned by the franchisor.

What care has to be taken while selecting a franchise brand to invest in?
- Find out about the company and its brand identity;
- Find out about the most suitable location for the business; ensure you have the required finances to take up the franchise, like royalty or franchise fee;
- Get an idea of the kind of investment needed for place, equipment, décor, etc.

What is the future of franchising?
The future of the franchising business is very bright. The growth rate is expecting to be much higher over the next 5 years. This is a business where a person without much experience can invest in a successful business model.

Are there any risks involved in starting a franchisee business?
The risk is very low, as the franchise industry is growing every year. The investment is less as it does not involve brand building, or building up a demand. In many cases, like the Shahnaz Husain Franchise, there are tailor-

made products for which brand loyalty is already established. Therefore, risk factor is low.

What leads to the failure of franchisee businesses?
- Lack of dedication and time given to the business
- Failure to build up enough clientele
- Not following the systems of the business model properly.

Does today's economy support the franchise business model?
Today's economy does support franchise business models because there is much greater awareness of global brands. The infrastructure and systems are already in place and are successful. It's a global market today and there are many markets around the world that are untapped and offer great opportunities to franchisors for extending their enterprise.

Why should entrepreneurs invest in a franchise?
As already mentioned, a franchise offers a successful business model, where the infrastructure is in place. The brand and demands are already established. There are several emerging markets.

Why should working professionals invest in a franchisee?
To provide an enterprise for family members; it is easier to run a franchise business because successful systems are in place. There is support from the franchisor.

What challenges lie in the franchising industry?
Taking up a franchise means following the systems implicitly. Those who have problems following systems may find it difficult to cope. Establishing a good working relationship with the Franchisor can sometimes pose a challenge. As each franchisee is individual and separate, there may be differences in the expression and execution. Narrowing down the differences and making the expression uniform is a challenge.

How important is it to follow the operations manual as a franchisee?
It is most important to follow the operations manual, as the Shahnaz Husain specialized salon treatments are exclusive and follow prescriptions for specific skin and hair problems and types. Each franchise outlet must have a standard look and feel. Apart from the Shahnaz Husain clinical treatments, which have been breakthroughs in the beauty business, there are several other aspects and symbols which help the franchisee to identify with the Shahnaz Husain brand. From clinic décor and operational standards to name boards and letter heads, the Shahnaz Husain brand must unify us and also help us to stand apart from others. Each outlet must be the epitome of the highest level of service, with properly qualified and dedicated staff. Each outlet must be the reflection of a highly successful international brand name.

What are the most common mistakes that a franchisee should avoid?
Trying to increase profits without building up a reputation and putting the systems in place; employing unskilled personnel; not using the systems faithfully; upholding the franchisor's brand name and enhancing it, by following the highest standards, will actually lead to making the franchisees own business a profitable one. That is why it is important that all franchisees operate in accordance with our principles and standard.

What challenges do people from a nonbusiness background face when starting a franchise?
The challenges are fewer because they have to follow an established business model and use a brand name for which a demand is already there. Also, the franchisor may have a training program for franchisees to help them run the business and learn how to make it profitable. For example, the Shahnaz Husain Group ensures proper hand-holding during the transition period.

What challenges do working professionals face when starting a franchisee?
To balance working hours and business hours is the biggest challenge; once they start giving sufficient time and attention, they will be in a better position to earn maximum profits from the franchisee business.

When is the right time to invest in a franchise business? Why?
One may start the business at anytime, but if one starts around August–September, it will be in time for the peak season of weddings and festivals. The chances are better to build up a clientele and to recover part of the investment.

What is the secret of managing people?
The secret of managing people lies in the ability to integrate and nurture them. For this one needs better communication and people skills. One should be able to organize and delegate. Motivating and encouraging people are important. To manage people, be tactful, co-operative, consistent, and sincere.

What message would you want to give to people who are interested in investing in a franchisee?
During the last 47 years, the Shahnaz Husain brand name has established unquestioned and unwavering brand loyalty. The Shahnaz Husain Group has always had its finger on the pulse of market demands. Its commitment to research and development, the launch of highly innovative formulations from time to time, the specialized salon treatments for specific problems are the reasons why the brand has developed so strongly. Today, the brand is ideally positioned in the market. By assuming total responsibility of research and the development of products, the Shahnaz Husain Group provides a pillar of support to the franchisee. By taking up the Franchise, the investor

will share in Shahnaz Husain's phenomenal success and derive the benefits of a world renowned brand name. Apart from strong branding, we provide the franchisee an established business system and business model, with proven success rate and efficacy. In order to derive the full benefit of our business format, it is essential that each franchisee follows all its systems and procedures. This will ensure the best chances of success.

A BUSINESSMAN BY PROFESSION, A PASSIONATE EDUCATIONIST AT HEART...

Pritam Agarwal – Owner of Hello Kids

In the world of education where everything is monotonous and essentially a business we, at Food Experts of Goa, decided to follow up on the story of Hello Kids preschool with the owner and founder of the school Pritam Agarwal. Pritam, hailing from a Marwadi background, business acumen and intelligence flows in his veins. After finishing school from Delhi, he got introduced to the concept of preschool early-on through the advertisements appearing in the newspaper. Fascinated with this colorful world of toddlers, he discovered his true calling in the world of education.

Contrary to the common conception from families of businessmen, of education being only for namesake before stepping into the family-owned business, Pritam's father truly valued education and knowledge. He motivated Pritam to not only complete his matriculation but also get into the prestigious Delhi University for completing his B.com. He then pursued Pritam to complete his MBA and sent him to the UK with an assumption that he would join the family business on his return. However, Pritam returned with a dream of starting a school with boarding facilities in Orissa, his native state. However, after a thorough market research, Pritam realized that heavy investment in business by bootstrapping felt like a risk due to lack of knowledge and expertise in the field of education.

Taking baby steps toward a larger goal, he decided to venture into the world of children education through the preschool concept which required a lower investment and would supplant him with the knowledge and experience in the education arena. The stepping stone of his success story was paved in Bangalore where he first started his preschool. Soon he felt that to grow at a rapid pace it was important to have good partners who share the same vision and passion. This led to the franchisee model with the agenda of achieving the growth advancement numbers as fast as possible.

His journey began in 2005 with his first school in Bangalore, providing valuable and cherished experience in running a school where he whole heartedly worked not only as an advertising guide but also as a driver, cleaner, and teacher. This is when he actually realized the benefits of franchising. Soon, the business model was upgraded and the franchisee model in 2007 and the business really took off when Pritam's wife joined him in handling the Bangalore centers.

Operating on a no-royalty business model, Hello Kids franchisees are purely dependent on the support provided by the parent organization. The mission behind the no-royalty model is to provide education at the most affordable rates. And it also offers a dual benefit, both to the franchisee and the franchiser.

Another key advantage for the franchisee is the access to deep knowledge of the founder of this 13+ years, resulting in very low attrition rates (5–10 percent) against market average of 60–70 percent. Unlike most franchises that charge a royalty, which becomes exorbitant to bear once the student count goes up, Pritam charges his franchisees a service fee which is not dependent on the number of children enrolled in the school. This becomes financially lucrative for the franchisee, while also enabling him to stay invested and derive growth benefits.

Service fee is collected every 2 years from the franchisees while extending regular support including updated curriculums, training, and skill enhancement at training centers, complete infrastructure support, etc. The centers are strategically located with close proximity to public transport for ease in daily commute.

Pritam faced significant struggle in the initial days while setting up the franchisee model due to high dependency on print media for marketing which is very expensive and time consuming. But the advent of internet brought major relief reducing training time from 4 days to a single day. This also made the business more efficient due to tremendous cost reduction. Internet also facilitated faster dissemination of knowledge and information.

Hello Kids today stands as the fourth biggest brand in terms of the number of centers in India. This is by itself no mean feat for the franchise business. Rural penetration and affordable fees make this franchise stand out in spite of stiff competition. It is a testament to the passion and perseverance of Pritam which is reflected in the exponential growth of the brand.

Pritam is a member of the ECA (Early Child Association) in the capacity as Vice President. The organization is a nonprofit organization, and focused on child development in the formative ages. Quality education methods from Finland and Singapore are slowly making an entrance in Indian markets.

Hello Kids brand has fully embraced the ECA organization and now represents more than 6000 preschool owners who are equally passionate and focused about their business.

Inter-state differences in Government regulations pose definite challenges in the preschool sector. First of all, while the government focuses on the primary education, preschool education has been neglected. Each state differs in its requirements for starting a pre-school. For example some states have a requirement of 9 sq. mt. space per child while some others have 20 sq. mt. per child. In some states, there is no requirement of preschool below the age of 4 years. The preschool is catered to by the HRD and Women development. Karnataka has an association called KCPS (Karnataka Association of Preschools) which enables interaction with the government in formulating the rules for preschool. Hello Kids is also a member of the organization and as preschool owners are 95 percent women, the rules and regulations were drafted accordingly, taking into account accessibility and convenience of children. ECA, in the absence of quality support from the government, has helped provide crucial material and training support in this regard to a lot of anganwadis across India.

Pritam considers Ratan Tata as a role model. And his other role model is his grandfather. Taking from his grandfather's motto, "Everyone can run a business but you should teach business to 5000 people;" he has tried implementing the thought in his current business model by constantly disseminating his knowledge and expertise to his franchisees. He credits his family—father, uncle, brother for his success. His wife has been the backbone of his success story by magnificently managing their 580 centers. This has given him freedom to pursue other avenues of interest as well. Hello Kids has a franchise presence internationally as well with two centers in Bangladesh and a few coming up in Sri Lanka and Nepal.

Hello Kids is full of success stories where women who were home makers, running small tuition centers are now successfully running large schools. For the challenging centers (the bottom 100 schools across 30 locations in India on national level), Pritam is personally involved to elevate them to the next level in business. The fire for growth and excellence still burns strong for Hello Kids in spite of having achieved so much in a short span. The no-royalty model of business still remains his critical USP since Hello Kids was established. Honesty and transparency, coupled with word of mouth and Google have contributed toward the steady growth of the brand. Other offline techniques like banners have also helped.

Hello Kids holds an annual meet, also known as **Business Meet** in 30 locations where Pritam along with team interacts with the franchise owners and conducts critical analysis of performance to identify gaps to be improved upon with training and collaterals. Marketing tools for expanding the business are discussed and all the mandatory material is procured by the head office in bulk to moderate the costs for everyone. The material and information is then circulated to the franchises thus providing them the necessary tools at affordable prices to succeed. Franchises on-board new students with a list of parents who have enquired with the head office.

Committed to the motto of affordability and cost control, the Hello Kids franchises are maintained in a budget-friendly way. Lavish openings are discouraged with an advice to the franchise owners to notify friends and people closest to them as well as from the surrounding vicinity to come and participate in the opening ceremony. This provides a dual benefit of providing visibility to the school as well as keeping the marketing costs down. Word of mouth essentially drives the success stories of the franchises rather than big marketing campaigns, with visitors getting a first-hand experience of the infrastructure provided. Pritam's goal is to currently achieve a third position ranking in the industry and then achieve first ranking in this field by 2020. Franchise growth is typically in the range of three to four centers a month with adequate support provided from the head office in capacity of a mentor rather than an owner.

Franchise opening typically required 10-20 days from signing of the agreement. An initial estimated investment of 5 lakhs for rural areas and 10 lakhs for urban areas is required, which encompasses the deposit as well as a 3-month working capital. Franchises typically raise capital through savings or bank loans with the head office providing all the necessary help in documentation. Operational support is provided to franchises 24/7 with direct accessibility to Pritam himself. The success of the franchise directly results in the growth of the parent company. So frequent feedback, guidance, and financial as well as intellectual support is amply provided on a consistent basis. Teams are setup with distinct responsibilities for each state, with regular information sharing happening with the franchise owners based on logistics, number of admissions, number of enquiries, number of teachers, marketing advancements, etc. In this technology-driven environment, Hello Kids now has a mobile application where all franchise owners are connected. The queries of any owner can thus be addressed not only by the head office but also by 500 other owners as well.

Quality is of paramount importance to Hello Kids with audits being conducted on a half yearly basis. Quality audits ensure adherence and compliance to the right way of doing things whilst also providing opportunities for improvement. The franchise model has worked wonders for investors with the average payback period for investment being 3–6 months. Break even number happens with around 13–14 students based on fees, rentals, etc. The success rate of Pritam's franchises can be gauged from the fact that

80 percent of the branches are exceeding the industry standards. With an attrition rate lower than the industry and special emphasis on retention, Hello Kids makes a classic success story.

The franchise model system for Hello Kids is a unique combination of system orientation and people orientation. With more than 60 percent branches in rural areas, a strong network of logistical support has been established. Phone support is provided on a 24/7 basis with all the necessary infrastructure provided for franchises to prosper and flourish. An inherent desire to excel in the field of education and passion about the field are all the characteristics that are needed for a good franchisee. As technology is constantly evolving, a willingness to adapt to this changing environment would be the key quality that differentiates a successful franchise. Sharing news and updates is now easily possible and happens more frequently. From weekly and monthly updates, they now maintain daily updates and it is of utmost importance that franchises acclimatize to this new change.

Pritam elaborates on the benefits of investing in a franchisee rather than investing in one's own school because investing in one's own setup is time consuming and a tedious process. In a franchisee setup, the owner has to focus on the business portion while the education and update support being provided by the brand. This systematizes the process and paves a way to a successful business. Pritam's commitment to knowledge and expertise sharing can be seen from the simple fact that he is willing to provide all possible support to not only franchisees but also to potential competitors. The franchising model thus rightly provides a good investment avenue for a rapid growth path.

The future of franchising in India is bright remarks Pritam citing examples of popular franchises like Digimart, Big Bazaar to name a few. The franchisee business is still fraught with some risks, like finding the right partnerships and creating the right synergies with your franchisees. The franchising agreement is like a marriage where the bond needs to be strong to survive. The success depends on the trust and faith that creates a mutually beneficial partnership. This trust factor guarantees success in the long run without any hiccups. Communication is the key ingredient in the success story of the franchise. Humans inherently are impatient and being responsive and transparent in communication provides a critical dimension toward the success story of the business.

Overseas, franchising gets tremendous exposure with content marketing as blogs and articles are extensively written about. The Indian scenario is a little different. Pritam believes that the exposure to franchising in India is expected to mature and spread rapidly in the near future. Franchising provides a new opportunity for fast-paced growth for entrepreneurs as well as working professionals due to time-tested infrastructure and expertise already in place.

Challenges to the franchisee industry arise at a maddening pace due to the rate at which new models keep evolving all the time. The mantra to success hinges on your ability to adapt to this highly flux scenario of change. The operational manual of a franchise provides a practical way of doing things which aids in answering any and all queries which may arise with time. It provides a timely and sequential guidance for franchisees to get ahead. The key parameter to keep in mind though is the personalization of decisions and policies according to what people of a particular place need. Uniformity of strategies and guidelines in a diverse environment that exists in India may not necessarily be the best possible approach.

Some of the more common mistakes that may occur by a franchisee include miscommunication before the execution of a planned marketing strategy. Consultation with the owner forms the key as it has been typically seen that education enthusiasts may experiment with new things which haven't been verified for their effectiveness thus creating impediments to the smooth operation. While the formula for success is always open to additions and deletions copyrights and patents need to be strictly adhered to as it might create legal scenarios which may prove harmful to the business. There have been examples of some clients teaching something outside the prescribed syllabus which may create problems for the organization in the long run even though the intent of the franchisee was positive.

Pritam denotes some of the key challenges of working with people who have no business background and attributes them the learning curve that everyone goes through when he tries his hand at something new. Some of the challenges faced by these new franchisees stem from the lack of adequate knowledge about incomes, expenses, and marketing. Some of the franchisees make impracticable assumptions under the belief that theories will pan out in the real world wherein a little more insight and experience is needed to guide oneself on the nuances of successful strategies. Being a franchisee is a full time business with time investment, dedication, and hard work needed to flourish. Working professionals who setup franchisees typically encounter these challenges of lack of sufficient time to focus on the franchisee.

Elaborating on the appropriate time to invest in a franchisee Pritam elucidates that as far as preschool is concerned it can be any time of the year. The thought to keep in mind though is it is an 18-month business in the preliminary phases and not a 12-month one. Expounding further he says the secret recipe of success for managing people is to always have an open ear. The strategy for success entails bottoms up approach of management style rather than a top down one especially in the people intensive industries. Your responsibility as a mentor should help nurturing of new ideas and open encouragement to suggestions for improvement. Open forums with casual meeting always encourage creative thinking and therein lies the success of your mentorship. This, however, does not mean you should condone indiscipline or lack of performance.

Finally on a parting note Pritam extols entrepreneurs and working people to invest in franchisees. It is a lucrative and budding business with a rapid growth potential and ample scope. It is still a relatively untapped market and has all the prospective signs of providing exponential advancement to the business and the brand.

Atul Tyagi – Owner of Wow Kids Franchise

Wow Kids founder Atul Tyagi started his career journey working in one of the upper echelon companies for around 15 years. During his career span he was looking for a national brand for his career advancement, but soon realized there are limited job opportunities available for his growth. It was then that a startling revelation hit him on exploring the arena of business. His wife initiated the venture with a preschool which was met with resounding success. Within a year the business had grown substantially and two additional branches were opened. It was then that the idea of franchising his brand dawned upon him.

The franchise journey began with a simple request when one of the parents of the ward in their school enquired if they could give them a franchise of

Wow Kids. Almost instantaneously the franchising idea originated in their mind as Atul had ample experience and expertise in the area of franchising. This is how the journey of franchising began for Wow Kids with centers starting in Ponda, Fatorda and eventually Panjim. Sensing the success of these franchises, it occurred to Atul to venture into expansion outside Goa. "Why not expand the brand domestically all over India," he thought and that is how the idea of creating a distant model duly complete with the requisite designs, SOPs, and solutions to expand into new horizons started taking shape.

Elaborating on the finer points about his preschool Wow Kids, Atul emphasizes that his USP that sets his brand apart from the rest of the pack is the innovative curriculum. Wow Kids is a member of four international associations which has a profound impact in creation of a pioneering curriculum with a unique mixture of primary and playful study. Typically in India the nursery curriculum is limited to the study of number, color, shape, etc., but Wow Kids focuses on the brain development of the child using the Montessori Method of teaching. Teachers are provided special training to enhance the thought process, hand-eye coordination, and all the other skills to provide an all-round development for the child using the Montessori equipment. "This technique first developed by Maria Montessori is patented and we have been using a customized version of this methodology for our franchise," says Atul. They have a production unit in UP where they make the Montessori equipment and distribute it to all their franchises.

The franchise model operated by Wow Kids differs from the current market models where 15–20 percent royalty per child is charged. It recognizes that the efforts and energies expended by the franchise owner is what pools in the students for the school. Hence a one-time fee or franchise fee which is renewable once in every 2–3 years is charged. The brand does not keep track of the profit of any particular franchise even if that franchise is getting larger number of children, with the franchise fee remaining the same irrespective of the number of children enrolled. The franchise fee ranges in the 2000 rupee per month on an average. The service and support offered by the head office does not differentiate between schools with large number or small number of children but is decidedly neutral.

Among the common problems faced by franchisee preschool, Atul says location tops the list. It is of utmost importance to select a proper location while starting a franchise as ancillary problems like infrastructure, hiring good teachers, etc. are almost always linked to location. Some of the other problems that arise include choosing the right channel partner who will dedicate their time and energy to the project. The franchise model of Wow Kids is not concentrated on big time businessmen but is rather looking for younger entrepreneurs like women who would like to initiate a startup at low cost. The success of any venture is defined by passion and dedication to the cause, which is what the brand looks for principally rather than focusing only on the money portion.

On-boarding at Wow Kids happens using an assortment of tools such as Google advertising, Facebook marketing, etc. to identify and shortlist potential franchise owners who are a right fit to the brand. Some 70–80 percent of the franchises are run by young couples wherein if the husband is potentially working in a job the wife runs the business. Internet tools have made it easier to ascertain the appropriate owners for running the franchise business. The success story of the franchise can be corroborated from the fact that we have opened more than 100 franchises in the past 2 years which is a record in itself. The brand is currently the fastest growing chain of preschools in India and was the only brand that was aired on national TV three times in the past 6 months. The brand's contribution toward society has been valued and recognized through the Social Impact award given to it. The Goa branches of the brand are 100 percent owned and managed by women. A total of nine branches exist in Goa with six branches owned by franchises.

The future for the brand and the business looks promising and bright as it is one of the easiest way to have an assured business. If you want to become an entrepreneur you do not have to reinvent the wheel, you just have to manage and run an existing setup. All the preliminary starting troubles and glitches associated with setting up a business are already taken care of while the success rate still remains high. Every person identifies a role model in his life who has helped him scale the heights of success while providing robust unflinching support in all his endeavors. Atul credits his wife Preeti Tyagi for being his role model and standing beside him during his entire journey.

Currently the brand is catering to the domestic market, but there are definite plans of expanding internationally. There are plenty of queries coming in from Nepal and Bangladesh, but we want to hold the international expansion for some time. In the next 5 years the plan is to expand the brand and have footprints in South East Asia, Dubai, Muscat, etc. The appropriate model for universal expansion is being developed as the whole shebang of study as well as physical material is supplied by the head office. "We have also kept abreast with the latest happenings in the industry through constant benchmarking of competition every 6 months in newer marketing strategies, usage of online tools, etc. With the world being driven by Internet and everything in cyberspace we constantly upgrade our website. Our affiliation with the international associations also helps us with feedbacks and improvements" asserts Atul.

Expanding on some of the success stories of the brand, Atul is quick to mention about the very first owner of the first franchise, a very confident lady who approached them and asked them about giving her a franchise. Her name was Darshana Naik and she is successfully operating the franchise in Porvorim. There was another lady who was working in the same franchise in Ponda who eventually opened her own franchise with her husband. She was a part of the Salgaonkar group and within a short span of 2 years their business prospered tremendously. "The husband eventually left the Salgaonkar group and is now a freelance trainer with us. I would like to credit him with the great deal of success that the brand has accomplished in the past few years" Atul says proudly.

Wow Kids has been successfully marketing their brand through various alternatives, right from the newspapers, FM stations, Car Boards to the billboards. The brand draws on the knowledge and know-how of the rich career experience that the owner brings to the table from his successful stint in Vodafone and other multi-national brands. These companies market their brand ultra-aggressively providing them superb brand visibility. It is important to keep yourself updated on the latest trends and tools in the marketing world. There might be varying levels of success that your brand will be able to achieve with the available tools but you will not know the most pertinent and effective one unless you have tried it out. Atul shares, "Our personal experience with Google and Facebook has by far been the most effectual since these are the right platforms to reach out to the younger crowd who have the potential to become young budding entrepreneurs."

"We provide ample support to your franchises during the establishment phase in order for them to successfully on-board new students. We have perfected certain strategies over the years that we have efficiently deployed in Goa with pronounced success. We give our franchises certain designs for operational execution and monitor their implementation. We provide a comprehensive solution to all our franchises where everything is provided starting from installation of the CCTVs, decoration of the interiors, etc. We are 100 percent hands-on with our clients ensuring the whole place is up and running as a well-oiled engine. We provide training to the people so that they have a holistic view on how the business should be handled. Our support association does not end with the inauguration of the school but continues during its entire tenure. All our SOPs are well clear, concise, and pre-defined."

Atul comes with a clear vision of making the brand one of the top five preschool chains of India within the next 3 years and crossing the mark of 300–400 branches. The typical lead time for starting a franchise from the date of signing the agreement is less than 30 days. The moment the agreement is inked the materials required for the franchise are dispatched within the next 5 days. This speed of execution is the reason they have been able to expand by 4–5 branches a month aggregating to 100 branches in 2 years. The startup cost of the franchise is low with a typical franchise capital requirement being 4–5 lakhs including all the material support. It is possible to keep the cost low due to the in-house manufacturing and established raw material sourcing process.

Atul further elaborates, "We have a well-founded and effectual monthly review system established with all our franchises and also an online system for the franchises to provide feedback. Mutual trust, ease of accessibility, and respect form the baseline of our relationship with our franchises. Starting from day one all franchises have direct access to the director. Once the initial starting hiccups are addressed and the franchise starts sailing smoothly, we do not interfere in the day to day operations of the franchise. We also have an app to monitor the number of children enrolled, information being shared, interactions taking place at the franchises, etc. We also monitor the Facebook page of the franchise at regular interval to ensure that adherence to protocols are being followed. We conduct quarterly quality audits to confirm compliance and also set an impetus for continuous improvement."

The business model is so accurately defined. The typical operation breakeven for franchises is 6–9 months with the payback period being less than 2 years. The ROI for a franchise is almost definitely governed by the location. Atul goes on to explain, "We don't provide the option of owning a master franchise to anyone unless they have proved their mettle and shown significant success in enhancing the value of the Wow kid's brand. The success rate of our franchises ranges in the 70–80 percent range because of the no-royalty model that we deploy. We have a time tested and tried formula to help our franchises thrive. We equip them with all the necessary tools for the success like school, infrastructure, brand name, feel, look, marketing strategies, and training. Providing the proper training is paramount in this arena and we make sure an environment is created where the child truly enjoys his time at the preschool and yearns for it. In this era where customer is King we provide the franchises with an understanding on how to handle the business, how to handle a visitor and turn that into an admission."

"Our franchises are 100 percent people oriented with special emphasis on building lasting relationships. A win-win situation environment is created and appropriate execution of strategy for growth to make the franchises prosperous is focused upon. One of the critical parameters for growth and success in a business is patience. Success can never be achieved overnight. It takes dedication, hard work, intelligent working, and passion to excel. We emphasize the importance of perseverance to all our franchise owners and explain to them that instantaneous success is not feasible. This practical approach also helps temper the unrealistic expectations of owners which can lead to disappointments in the future."

Many people advocate about starting your own business as against investing in a franchise. Atul meets so many of these types. There are multiple theories on the advantages and disadvantages of both approaches but not everybody is an inventor. The beauty of investing in a franchise arises out of the fact that someone has already tried a business model, learnt from his failures and is now offering it to you without the drawbacks and cost of the early failures. A lot of information and groundwork has already been done and you do not have to reinvent the wheel. A flurry of time-consuming activities like market research, registration of your brand, and marketing of the brand have already been arranged by the brand owner, and it will save the franchise owner valuable time and effort allowing him to focus exclusively on running the business.

Commenting on the parameters to analyze while deciding on investing in a franchise brand, Atul elaborates on dedication to the brand by the owners as the principal parameter. The owners should also be willing to provide unflinching support to their franchises. Franchising has a bright future because there are a lot of budding entrepreneurs who want to start their own business and franchising is one of the easiest ways of accomplishing that task. The risks involved include insufficient or tardy execution which will eventually lead to the failure of the franchise. Wow Kids has always managed to motivate and stimulate their franchises by addressing the problems faced by the franchise owners and resolving those problems. This has been mission critical for us from the beginning.

Ample support is available in today's economy to support the franchise business through easy availability of bank loans coupled with low cost interest rates for women. Franchise investment is enticing for entrepreneurs as well as working professionals as it provides the entire recipe of success along with the requisite tools and techniques. It is, however, a tremendously crowded marketplace and the key to success lies in the unique offerings your brand provides over the competition. Following SOPs to the hilt is critical for success and I have seen many examples of franchises failing because of poor execution. Common mistakes made by franchises comprise inadequate training, poor quality of service, and dearth of communication. One should also be willing to be patient and wait for his investment to start earning returns.

The key to management success according to Atul lies in the ability to have an open ear to people's issues and treating everyone at par without the creation of hierarchy. He advises those looking to enter the business field to be ready to put in long hours at least for the first couple of months. Be passionate about your venture and investigate and ascertain all facets of the business before entering the franchise ownership. Make certain that you aggressively and unequivocally thrust yourself into the execution of your operation to ensure rapid and sustainable growth.

A tete-a-tete with the beauty expert and super business woman – Asha Arondekar

Asha Arondekar is into the salon business for over 24 years and into the wellness arena for 11 years. She is the proud owner of Tatva Salons. On a quiet, cozy afternoon over coffee, Ash offers delightful insights into the captivating world of the franchise business and her brand. Her company employs around 70 people and boasts of a loyal customer base of around 1000 satisfied clientele.

Asha comes from a pharmaceutical background and started her career with her own company Pharma research in Pune which focused on pharmaceutical research where she spent 14 years. She relocated to Goa along with her husband, and to her surprise she discovered that there was a scarcity of good parlors which provided excellent services to the Goa customer base. Her inspiration to foray into the salon industry stemmed from this dearth of good salons in Goa. This gave her the inspiration to start a franchise of VLCC salon brand in Goa, the brand which she frequented for her parlor needs in Pune.

Within 2 years into opening of the franchises in Margoa and Panjim, she realized her true calling. This particular profession appealed to her immensely. This career allowed her to run a place where people entered in with a certain mood but always walked out happier and more confident. She ended up taking a backseat in her Pharma company and made the obvious decision to start her own brand in the salon business. She conducted a thorough background research about brand pricing, quality, and ambience by visiting parlors in different locations like Kerala, Thailand, Indonesia, Turkey, and Vietnam. The target audience for the brand was the middle class population which forms a chunk of the client base.

Though Asha began her journey into the Salon industry by launching her own brand, she forayed into the franchise business after a long time equipped with sufficient expertise and knowledge. Once she had transformed her salon from a two room place to a twelve room spa, she wanted to share the brand with the rest of the world. Realizing the immense potential of the franchise business which is one of the fastest growing industries, she chose to foray into it.

A unique combination of service, ambience, and price is what differentiates Tatva Salons from the competition. Tatva operates two distinct types of franchise models. One model is where the franchisee owns the place whilst the company manages it which is called as the FOCO model. In the second model scenario, the franchisee owns and manages the operation of the salon by themselves. But FOCO model remains by far the more popular one.

Starting a franchise business has had its fair share of challenges for Asha. The foremost being, choosing the right partner who shares your vision, passion, and goals for the brand along with the appropriate work ethics. Entering a franchise partnership is akin to entering a marriage where the success or failure is defined by the partner synergy. Secondly as with any business, profits are not immediate and breakeven periods may vary from 1 to 2 years. This requires a definite level of dedication which people entering the franchise business need to be cognizant of. Lastly government permits are sometimes a hassle as authorities don't differentiate between Ayurvedic centers and Spas. An Ayurvedic expert is needed on the premises if you want a license for a rejuvenation center. Also cross therapy where a client can choose a male or female therapist still remain off limits in the Goa market.

Tatva has enjoyed substantial success in the Goan market and is now ready to spread its wings outside Goa in places like Hyderabad, Ahmedabad, etc. Functioning in a manpower-driven sector which has a high turnover, Tatva has mitigated some of the risks through tie-ups with numerous associations like North East Association where most of the therapists are sourced from. The brand also plans on opening a technical training school where manpower can be trained and employed at various brand outlets thereby providing meaningful employment and contributing toward societal responsibility. The government provides special incentives toward such venture through schemes like National Skill Development Centers (NSDC).

Updating your knowledge about the happenings in the industry is of paramount importance if you want to stay ahead in the game. Asha does extensive research on the popular trends in the business through reading, traveling, and visiting different spas. In spite of the competition and challenges in this industry the future of wellness is upbeat as this is one of the industries which will not lose out to technology. For example it is not possible to get a head massage or your toenails done online. Technology leverage is being explored by introducing online appointments for ease of access and convenience.

Everyone has a role model who they look up to and aspire to be like. In case of Asha, it is Kiran Majumdar Shroff an Indian billionaire entrepreneur who had delivered a guest lecture when Asha was in college. She has taught me to think across global barriers due to which we have opened our international franchise in Zambia. Zambia is just the starting point and the target is to expand our brand footprint all across Africa. The key ingredient to our success has been through effective use of social media marketing, Just dial, database calling, and Business Network of India (BNI). We have efficiently used websites like Double Up, which promotes our offers making it accessible to a much wider audience.

Being from a pharmaceutical background, Asha has always specialized in launching her own products. She will be launching the brand's very first product for retail, which will be shipped directly to Zambia. The goal is to target the international market first and then progressively introduce them in the domestic market. A brand's success is intricately linked with the success of its franchises. Keeping this in mind, Tatva provides adequate support to its franchise partners through our website, ads write-ups and arduous software and technical training to ensure success. Comprehensive SOPs are provided from inauguration to registration support on portals like Just Dial including marketing. Elaborate assistance is provided in all aspects to enable the franchise to succeed.

Tatva's vision for the future involves being a distinguished Goan company which is renowned internationally. A typical timeframe for franchise business setup of the brand demands a 3–5 months' timeframe. Everything from identification of the location, outlay of the space to the interior structure and ambience is standardized to bring homogeneity across franchises. Franchise owners are characteristically established business owners looking for a second business setup or women entrepreneurs. The initial investment ranges from 25 to 30 lakhs with the breakeven period varying from 2 to 2.5 years. Funding of the franchise ownership is either through owned funds or through a bank.

Franchise operational issues tackled through explicit support from the brand with a win-win situation dictates the symbiotic relationship. Franchise royalty ranges in the 8-10 percent range. Local marketing is supported through help in generating creatives for greater visibility. Franchise monitoring is done through a multitude of initiatives like daily sales report, mystery audits, and weekly visits.ROI for the franchise is typically 40-60 percent with the agreement period being 5 years. The business model is a distinctive combination of system and people orientation. The true potential of a successful business is the employee talent pool in the organization.

Asha lists existence of SOPs and ready business plan as the benefits of the franchise business. Selecting a brand may involve some homework on the part of the franchise owner with a thorough research necessary on scrutinizing the reputation and ethics of the brand. The future of the franchise business is upbeat with more and more people entering into the business world. Working professional should avail the opportunity of franchise ownership to realize their growth dreams. They should, however, be willing to take risks, being patient and having an unwavering commitment to the business.

The secret recipe of successful people management demands placing yourself in the employees' shoes to understand their concerns and problems. Instilling professionalism in the workplace is a critical step toward a successful venture. Providing employees with a sense of ownership and a space to make mistakes and learn from them will guarantee their buy in to the business. This helps lay a firm foundation for growth. Asha's parting message to young budding entrepreneurs is if you are ready take the leap of faith and start your business. Be passionate about your venture and nurture it like your own baby. The business will always reward you with profit.

The Sun Shines on Sunshine -
A warm sharing session with Kush Khaitan

The Sunshine Worldwide School is a CBSE and IB (International Baccalaureate) school, started by Deepak Gupta and franchised by his son, Kush Khaitan. The institution is 15 years old and consists of 150 employees and 1000 students ranging from toddlers to 12th grade. The concept originated out of the idea that education can be an enjoyable experience, allowing children to create and develop their skills by thinking outside the box. Coming from the petroleum and stationary industry, Kush experienced the crucial importance education plays in skill development when he saw the proficiency limitation of his workforce. This is when Kush and his father discovered their true calling into the field of education and decided to start Sunshine Worldwide School.

Sunshine Worldwide School is a unique initiative as students are taught to compete against themselves rather than each other, as each student is unique and special in his or her own way. "Typically we have seen student labor through their education system by mugging up the syllabus. We wanted to make the process enjoyable for both the students as well as the parents. We wanted to unlock the child's true learning potential," Kush shared. In Sunshine, the focus is placed on self-evaluation and self-excellence as opposed to comparison and competition. This is applied to their sports day events, where students compete against their own personal best during races. They also take part in games like KhoKho, kabaddi, play volleyball and do marathons. Students are also taught not to get affected by other person's opinions and to not allow such opinions to motivate or demotivate them.

The franchising journey for Sunshine began 4–5 years ago with the notion of spreading the joy of education at an amplified pace. The idea initiated from the thought process of growing together to achieve exponential growth as there are always restrictions to what a single person can accomplish. A bulk of the franchise model developed for the school came from extensive online research and information gathering by Kush. This was in turn adeptly supported by the Franchise India consultancy that helped with the finishing touches for the franchise model.

Sunshine primarily operates four franchise models namely:

1. Master franchise model: Operates similar to a distributor by opening the franchise in a particular state.
2. Unit franchise model: Offered to those passionate about education, but limited to only opening preschools.
3. K12 franchise model: Education is offered up to the 12th grade; however, this model requires a lot of investment.
4. Partnership model: Offered to those who want to invest but do not have time to run the operations.

The franchising operations have not been without its set of problems. Existing brands in the business like KidZee, etc. offer stiff competition. Sunshine distinguishes itself from the existing market as it is a full day school. The existing preschools are only for 3 hours and Sunshine's unique concept of self-betterment is still difficult for people to grasp who are molded in the traditional education system. Sunshine also focuses on quality rather than quantity and the primary goal is not to create hundreds of franchises with no time to focus on running them efficiently. Rather than being part of a rat race for numbers Kush instead prefers to focus on excellence.

Sunshine has managed to overcome the initial hiccups of setting their base in the franchise industry by detailing the experience and concepts to franchisees. Although they are smaller players, they have a premium clientele and believe in sticking with their principles over numbers. Franchisees are given a tour of the school and given a firsthand experience about the kind of education that is provided. As the famous saying goes, seeing is believing. This personal interaction of the school is unique provided to the franchisees, has helped them partner with other brands by convincing them of the kind of education provided and the quality of the environment in which the students learn.

Sunshine Worldwide School is currently the top ranked franchise in Goa, with the competition being limited to only one or two other franchises who can boast about the same quality and class. Kush makes it a point to keep himself abreast on the new technologies, teaching methodologies and the progression of the education system which he believes is constantly evolving. Sunshine is also heading the Private School Organization in Goa as well as across India. Mr. Deepak Gupta is the former President of the association and is collaborating with other contemporary school owners and the government to take our teaching to the next level. The association is called NISA, National Independent School Association and the goal is to revolutionize the teaching methodology. At present, Sunshine does not have an international presence but they intend to expand in areas like Thailand, Dubai, and Doha.

Kush sees the future of the education system as an ever transforming structure where the future lies in the desire to take the learning to the next level. Newer teaching methods and technologies where knowledge is valued over marks and understanding the concepts cherished over mugging the syllabus, this sector is expected to undergo a sea of change. Kush considers BK Gupta to be his role model who is the owner of Indo Solar which is the largest manufacturer of solar cells in the world. Mr. Gupta started from a smaller setup and has risen up like a phoenix to the zenith of success. Kush credits his own success to his father Deepak Gupta who has always been a beacon of guiding light for him.

Elaborating on some of the success stories of his franchise, Kush mentions about a small school which was running with 10 students. On franchising with Sunshine the student count went up to 60 wherein the school was running at full capacity. This is the beauty of franchising he explains where exponential growth can be attained during a short duration due to the business model of development firmly established. The key to a successful franchise is the effective use of varied methods of marketing like social media, print media, electronic media, hoarding, posters, advertising in club areas, etc. The best of the lot is word of mouth as the parents of our students itself are our brand ambassadors. The marketing strategy for each area begins by doing research, making a plan, and deciding on the location of the place and budget. Marketing support is aptly provided through central marketing via newspapers which provides great publicity and visibility.

In order to sign up new students in the franchises, the brand is pitched to those who have inquiries about enrolling their children. For the inauguration and launch of the school, a 100 percent support is offered from the time the school is set up till the institution is fully functional. Weekly visits are done to ensure smooth functioning and issue resolution if any. Robust review mechanisms are in place where daily routine, lesson plans, and activities are closely monitored. Structured MIS systems are in effect with local and state audits done at regular frequencies. Standard operating procedures are clearly defined, and adherence to these is closely scrutinized. This ensures uniformity as well as implementation of tested and validated methods. Franchise schools must avoid the gaffe of doing things individually without consultancy. The appropriate time to invest in a preschool franchise is in the month of August.

The vision for Sunshine brand is to expand to 50 franchises by 2022. A typical time frame for the franchise business to be operational is around 2–3 months from the day of signing the agreement. Investors to the franchise business predominantly consist of teachers and business owners. Investment figures range in the 20 lakhs to 6 crore range contingent upon whether a preschool or a K-12 model is being launched. In the case of the former, it is from the franchise owners savings whereas in the case of the latter it is usually a bank loan. The typical pay back rate for investors in preschool is 2.5 years and for K-12 model, it is 5 years. The average ROI for the franchise business ranges from 1 lakh per month for preschools while 1–2 crore for K-12 school.

For the growth of the franchises, Kush feels it is imperative to train them, set goals, and have effective communication with the parents. The vital qualities that a franchise should have in order to be successful are passion, business ethics, operational sense, and effectual money management. The franchise model is system oriented but is run well by the employees who are vital cogs for the system to run effortlessly. Kush believes that the success of his franchises is 100 percent and the groundwork for success is laid down by the passion of the owner for the education sector. The ideological synching of the owner with the brand is of paramount importance in order to function competently and accomplish growth.

Start Small, Finish Big 221

The future of franchising is good, with 75 percent of the market still being untapped. Franchise ownership also comes with the benefit of vast expertise which the brand brings along with tried and tested strategies. Sunshine also provides abundant support to the franchise owners to deal with any setbacks in their operations. The failure of most franchise businesses is primarily on account of bad marketing or not meeting brand expectations. The franchise business is also fraught with risks like firm's long-term commitment, growing up pains, and ensuring your passion remains consistent throughout the business tenure.

The new fad of the growing economy, startups have emerged as people are looking to invest in something novel. According to Kush, entrepreneurs should invest in franchises as knowledge and experience can be utilized without having to put effort into research, whereas working professionals should invest in franchises as effort that would have otherwise put on capital planning could be saved. For people from a nonbusiness background, challenges in starting a franchise are twofold: hiring people and money management. They may not evaluate and select the right people due to the time constraint and may also not invest the right amount of capital, leaving them prey to under investment.

Kush's parting words of wisdom to people who want to invest in a franchise is to evaluate and research the brand they want to invest in, have a desire for it, and once they are equipped they should go ahead and take the plunge into the business world. As the astute saying goes fortune favors the brave, running a successful business inherently involves taking risks.

Lina Ashar
Founder of Kangaroo Kids Preschool

What inspired you to start this school?
In 1991, I came to India on a year-long sabbatical from college, while connecting with my roots; I landed up taking a teacher's job in suburban Mumbai, an experience which changed my life. Back then, the education system in India was still grappling with a strait jacketed approach to education, leaving no scope for an overall development of the child, which was a complete contrast to milieu of what I had studied. I chose to stay back in India to change the antiquated approach to education which existed then. Kangaroo Kids was born in 1993, the first center was situated in Bandra (W).

What were some of the major challenges that you faced in this franchise business? How did you manage to overcome them? Is there any example that you can highlight?
We faced a world of resistance at the time from everyone in the field of education. We started with very few students as most parents did not understand this new style of teaching and learning; however, when parents saw the results we grew leaps and bounds.

With franchising we were the first ones to start it in the education field and it took a few downfalls to come to finally build a strong network.

One of my partners decided to part ways overnight and it turned rather bitter with all the tactics the partner used to malign our reputation. However, the good part about this difficult time was that it pushed me to start my K-12 schools and make changes in our Franchise agreements to safeguard us. My reaction to a similar situation a few years later was rather different with the experiences I had gone through.

What do you do to keep updated with developments happening in the industry?
I am continuously researching and reading about world trends including education. I also attend various international conferences on education and other interesting topics to keep myself updated on what's happening around the world.

Can you share five success stories (case studies) of the top performing Franchisees?
All our partners got involved personally in the day to day working of their schools and put in a lot of effort to follow our curriculum and introduce learner-centric education to markets that did not know of any such concepts. They made the effort of taking our vision forward and added the personal

touch. A lot of them have also moved base to be close to the school and achieve their dream. Some of them are mentioned below:

Billabong High International School – Bhopal
Billabong High International School – Saket
Billabong High International School – Kanpur
Billabong High International School – Kelambakkam
Kangaroo Kids Preschool – Banjara Hills
Kangaroo Kids Preschool – Chord Road

What is your success formula for Marketing?
An educational and medical institute work mainly on word of mouth; over the years we have built a strong advisory base for ourselves. We believe in pull marketing, we market KKEL as a brand only to keep reminding people about us and to create awareness in places we do not exist yet.

What are the marketing strategies that have worked for your brand?
Like mentioned above an educational institute works mainly on word of mouth; all we do is amplify the same on different marketing platforms; we have also introduced parent advocacy groups.

How do you support your franchisees in Marketing?
Every year we prepare a personalized marketing plan for our franchisees after studying the hits and misses of the previous year. We also follow up on a regular basis. We have now started marketing our brand extensively around India along with building a strong digital presence on all platforms.

How do you help the franchisees to get new customers?
We have personalized marketing plans for our franchisees at all stages right from prelaunch, launch to sustenance. We help franchisees do location-specific marketing thereby increasing footfalls.

As the opening or launch period is very crucial what kind of support do you give for the Franchisee business?
We support our Franchises right from the start, from advising them on which property to pick to helping them in sourcing the best products for the school. We also have pre-launch marketing plans that our franchises follow in order to increase footfalls for admissions.

How much time would it take to start your franchisee from the date of signing the agreement?
It takes about 45 days for a Kangaroo Kids preschool to start while it takes 3–6 months for a K-12 school to start operations from the time of signing the agreement.

What would be the initial investment required if someone wants to invest in your franchisee?
The initial investment for a preschool is minimum 25–30 lakhs while it is 10–12 crores for a K-12 school.

How do your franchisees raise capital normally?
Most of our franchises have the money to invest in a new business, while some also finance the venture through a loan and the current trend is where a group of investors come together to start a school.

When the franchisee is stuck in an operational problem that they are unable to solve? How do you support them?
We have a support team where each center is assigned to one person from the team. The concerned person studies the issue at hand and if the same can be sorted on the spot they help them with ideas, if not then the higher authorities at the head office get involved to sort the issue.

How do you contribute toward the growth of your franchisees?
We hand hold our franchisees at every stage and also give them support from every department (Marketing support, Franchise support, curriculum, etc.) to make sure that our franchisees are growing continuously.

What system of review have you put in place, to receive the feedback of franchisees and monitor their performance and give advice on improvements?
We have a robust review and audit system in place. Our support team is in touch with our franchisees and receive feedback at all times and we implement as much as we can within the brand guidelines.

Are periodic audits on quality done? And how?
Yes, periodic audits are conducted. We have external agencies that do these audits and internally when trainers and our local associates visit the center they are required to fill an audit form.

What is the average payback period for a person who invests in your franchisee?

The break even period varies on the investment model. For a KK preschool, the break even period is around 18–24 months while it is around 3–4 years for a BHIS or High School.

What is the average ROI that your franchisee can expect to receive?
The ROI is around 17–25 percent; it increases in accordance with the increase in scale of operations (with respect to the center).

Does your franchise network have people who buy multiple franchisees or a Master Franchise?

Many of our partners have multiple unit franchisees; we offer master franchises internationally.

What would you say is the success rate of your franchisees?
Success is a very relative term, as some franchisees measure their success with full capacity, some consider ROI, etc. However, around 80 percent of our franchisees run successfully, while the remaining 20 percent are building a hold in new markets and will get there soon.

How do you help franchisees to succeed?
When we look at prospective franchisees, we not only look for business partners but also for partners who share our passion and vision for education. It is our pursuit to deliver quality across all our educational solution systems that sets us apart. We provide an in-depth and unparalleled training to our franchisees to ensure they are effectively imbibed into the KKEL value system. To ensure superior quality standards, KKEL also has a School Improvement Team (SIT) that reviews every school's processes on a regular basis.SIT identifies initiatives to continually improve the quality of KKEL's methods, outcomes, and people.

Is your franchisee model system oriented or people oriented?
Our model uses a mix of both. A large franchisee network always needs to have systems and processes in place. However, at the end of the day we deal with people, be it our partners or parents.

What is the future of franchising?
Franchising has emerged as one of the greatest business opportunities across the world, and an increasing number of people especially the youth are embracing it with fervor over the past 5 years. Currently, with the

uncertainties in the job market due to the economic slowdown more and more youth are seen opting for franchising to set up and run their business. Why is this so? Franchising solves two key problems typically faced by the youth—inexperience and lack of financial resources. Most youth are inexperienced and lack the know-how required to set up and maintain a startup. Lack of financial resources also is a major hindrance at this stage when one is just setting up one's career.

Running a business independently indeed can be challenging and especially so for the first timers. This is where being associated with a franchisor greatly helps. A franchisor has already established a renowned brand and has developed all the tools and systems required to run the business successfully. There is transfer of knowledge and resources—the franchisor extends the solutions and garnered information to the franchisee—greatly enhancing the learning curve. The mistakes have already been made and the lessons already learnt! Franchisors already have developed their own marketing solutions, training support, and have already established a brand for the market, drastically reducing risk—perhaps this remains the biggest advantage of franchising. The potential for high returns hence increases drastically.

In India, education franchising has evolved in a big way and has come to form a major share in the sector. This is further accentuated with the number of opportunities that have opened in the sector over the past 5 years with the rise in vocational courses like hospitality, aviation, retail, etc. Education is of prime importance to the people in the country and the sector is relatively unaffected by recession. According to a sector report by a leading financial institution, even the poorer sections of the society spend about 20 percent of their disposable incomes of education of their wards in private institutes. There is a lot of potential due to the large population of youth in the country (the largest in the world) and yet a significant number of them are yet to receive quality education. Also, the education sector in India is largely unorganized and as education franchising has already been accepted well in the country there's never been a better time to invest in education.

Irrespective of the industry chosen, the key factors that every entrepreneur should aim for are the commitment to deliver the best and a sincerity to work out the nitty-gritty' of business. Knowledge in the industry that one opts for also makes a huge difference. The most important factor is attitude—there needs to be a passion to strive and perform to the best of one's ability—this will surely guarantee success.

Are there any risks involved in starting a franchisee business?
Starting any business involves risk. However, as a franchisor has an established brand the risks reduce considerably.

Why should entrepreneurs invest in a franchisee?
Investing in a franchisee is a lot easier as the brand already exists and has built a reputation around it and entrepreneur need not reinvent the wheel. They have a ready model to start off.

Why should working professionals invest in a franchisee?
Investing in a franchisee business is beneficial for a working professional as it saves a lot of time as ready business model is available. They need not spend time in reinventing the wheel.

What challenges lie in the franchising industry?
Like all franchisee-driven business models, there are certain challenges that can be faced in this business also. The key one is to maintain benchmark standards across the franchisee set up. There may be certain issues of scale but an identified standard set of processes and practices can be implemented across all institutes. Although the sector will never have a shelf life, thereby making it an attractive proposition to invest in, it is important to be passionate about education. Keeping in mind the mushrooming of players in the industry, it is important to choose a well-established brand to affiliate with that follows benchmark processes, will provide quality solutions and marketing assistance.

How important is it to follow the operations manual as a franchisee?
A Brand is built over time and stands for certain values. It is essential for all franchisees to maintain the same. Hence following an operational manual to the T is very important. If not followed, it will affect the brand image in the long run.

Every Brand has guidelines which need to be followed; you will never see a Mc Donald's in blue or green. The same standardization needs to be followed in schools as well, as parents come for the brand and the teaching methodologies.

What are the most common mistakes that a franchisee should avoid?
As parents have a preconceived notion about the brand franchisee needs to make sure they do not deviate from marketing guidelines making it look like a different brand; they need to follow the curriculum and teaching methodology to the T, as that is the main reason why parents come to us. Also there is a need to be sync with the brand from an operational perspective.

What challenges do people from a nonbusiness background face when starting a franchise?
People from a nonbusiness background find it difficult to understand the nuisances of the category as it is a very different business; also different companies have different business models and the day to day working of preschool or school is different from business or accounting angle.

What challenges do working professionals face when starting a franchisee?
Working professionals lack time; they find it difficult to dedicate time to the business, which is the most important in the initial period till the schools settle and start running on auto.

When is the right time to invest in a franchise business? Why?
Every business has its seasons and it is important to start in the right season.

What message would you want to give to people who are interested in investing in a franchisee?
Thoroughly research about the industry and the company you would like to invest in, also study the agreement properly to make sure you are collaborating with the right company on the right terms. In short make a SWOT analysis of the industry with respect to key brands and study USP of each of the brands. Also be clear with your own objectives why you want to open a preschool or school which will make your decision easier.

Ms. Hazel Siromoni, MD,
Maple Bear South Asia

Part of one of the fastest growing international educational brands with 350+ schools in 15 countries, Maple Bear South Asia brings the very best of globally reckoned Canadian early childhood and elementary school practices to India, Bangladesh and Sri Lanka. We offer Pre-school, Elementary and Day Care Programs, delivered in a safe, secure and stimulating environment that instills in students a passion for lifelong learning.

Today, more than 6,500 students in 100+ Maple Bear schools in South Asia are benefitting from the Canadian methodology and curriculum developed by our own team of experts, and this number is steadily growing.

Maple Bear South Asia is a joint venture between Maple Bear Global Schools Ltd, Canada and ModiEdutech (Modi Group).

Products and Services:

No of years: 13
No of employees: 19
No of customers: 100+ schools in India, Bangladesh and Sri Lanka

Are periodic audits on quality done?
Maple Bear schools benefit from our distinguished academic faculty of Canadian trainers, curriculum writers, and quality assurance personnel.

The Maple Bear program is a living, breathing curriculum that is constantly being updated. We have a large faculty of experienced teachers and education administrators that we draw upon to develop new curriculum, new training materials and methodologies and school policies. We undertake periodic student assessment at schools to benchmark student performance.

Maple Bear provides continual professional training and support for our teachers. Trainers from the Maple Bear Faculty mentor teachers and introduce them to the latest pedagogies and instructional strategies.

Every Maple Bear school undergoes inspection that covers everything from safety equipment to classroom performance. On a regular basis and drawing on the experience of training staff in schools, we review and update our curriculum to reflect the latest developments in the field of education and changes in local regulations and requirements. All Maple Bear schools have clean, secure facilities and low student-to-teacher ratios.

What type of franchise model do you operate?

Maple Bear South Asia offers a Franchisee Owned Franchisee Operated (FOFO) model that offers the best of both worlds. It allows our school franchisees to be independently owned and at the same time operate under a well-recognized brand name with globally reckoned Canadian methodology and best practices in early childhood education. They benefit from a global brand image and an outstanding support system that covers academics and curriculum, teacher training, marketing, operations, and business planning

What were some of the major challenges that you faced in this franchise business?

Challenges are a part of any business. Some of the challenges that we faced and still continue to face at Maple Bear South Asia are:

1. Gap in the requirement and availability of teachers willing to put in the hard work required to effectively implement the our progressive program and methodology
2. Lack of a clearly defined Govt. policies w.r.t. fees and enrollment age for preschools and elementary
3. Initial reluctance of parents to adopt the progressive learning methodology which goes beyond conventional worksheets and homework
4. Training the staff and teachers to consistently meet the high standards defined by the Maple Bear Canadian methodology.

With the current success that the franchise business has seen, where does this company stand in its industry?

From just three preschools when we started with in 2005, we have grown to 100+ schools in India, Bangladesh, and Sri Lanka in just over a decade. We're in 41 Indian cities and still growing. Our numbers speak for themselves.

Needless to say, we have carved a great position for ourselves in the early education sector. Maple Bear India is now in the top five brands of preschool in India with over 100 schools across the country.

What is the future of franchising?
It is very bright as far as preschool franchising is concerned. Today's young parents are more aware and concerned than ever about their kids' future. They are seeking to give their children the best possible education right from the preschool level. Therefore, opting for a preschool franchise like Maple Bear Canadian Preschools will undoubtedly prove to be a wise business decision.

Does your franchise chain have presence internationally? If no, are you planning to take the franchise to the multinational level? If yes, how many countries and which?
Yes, we are present in 15 countries—India, Sri Lanka, Bangladesh, Brazil, China, Mexico, Morocco, Singapore, South Korea, Turkey, UAE, USA, Vietnam, Kenya, and Philippines.

Can you share the success stories of your franchisees?
I can proudly say there are plenty. So many of our school owners have been so happy with the success of their first Maple Bear school that they now run as many as two to three schools. That's not all. They have also signed up to open more schools very soon. In fact, even our parents and teachers at Maple Bear have been so impressed with the system that they have gone ahead and started Maple Bear schools of their own.

What is your success formula for marketing?
Put yourself in the shoes of your target audience. If you're not convinced with your marketing idea, no one else will be.

What are the marketing strategies that have worked for your brand?
To name a few:
- a) Referral Programs – word of mouth
- b) Digital Marketing – Website, Social Media Posts, Digital Advertising
- c) Community Events.

Since the opening or launch period is very crucial what kind of support do you give for the franchisee business?
We offer all our schools with a robust marketing support that covers everything from digital to local area marketing. Right from the launch to securing and growing admissions, we support our franchise schools on everything from ATL to BTL marketing activities: Email marketing, print and digital advertising, participation in industry awards and events, social media campaigns and more.

What is the vision of this franchise business?
To bring the very best of globally reckoned Canadian early childhood and elementary school practices to India, Bangladesh, and Sri Lanka by growing our network far and wide. Our goal is to establish quality schools that will provide an excellent education experience to students for generations to come.

How much time would it take to start your franchisee from the date of signing the agreement?
2–3 months.

Who are the people that invest in your franchisee?
From retired defense personnel to lawyers to doctors to journalists to marketers to educationists and homemakers, we have people from then most versatile backgrounds and profiles who have invested in a Maple Bear Canadian Elementary and Preschools. They are all united by just one single passion and that is to make a difference in the early childhood education space and invest in a brighter future.

When the franchisee is stuck in an operational problem that they are unable to solve? How do you support them?
Our operations team is constantly there to support and troubleshoot with our franchise schools at any given point in time. Not only do we play an advisory role but also support them on ground in case such a need arises.

What is the average payback period for a person who invests in your franchisee?
3 years.

What is the average ROI that your franchisee can expect to receive?
It varies from case to case. The profit% varies from 25to 35 percent.

Does your franchise network have people who buy multiple franchisees or a Master Franchise?
Multiple franchisees.

Is your franchisee model system oriented or people oriented?
It's a combination of both.

What according to you are the most important qualities of a successful franchisee?
- a) Believing and sharing the vision of the brand
- b) Leadership skills
- c) Willingness to learn.

What care has to be taken while selecting a franchise brand to invest in?

Some of the significant factors to consider while selecting your franchise brand are:

a) The business space that brand operates in must align with your personal goals and passion
b) A proven track record of success
c) Support system for franchisees
d) Financial consideration (investment and returns).

Why should working professionals invest in a franchisee?

While starting an independent business may pose more challenges for a person from a nonbusiness background, opting to become a franchisee is better as this way they get to benefit from utilizing the knowhow and proven systems of a recognized brand name. Franchising helps reduce the risks by providing a supported environment utilizing both the resources of the franchisor, and the community of franchisees operating under the same brand.

What are the most common mistakes that a franchisee should avoid?

a) *Failure to evolve with the times*: The market space is constantly changing, and if the franchisee doesn't change with that market, they will ultimately become irrelevant. Fortunately, they are not alone on this journey of constant change, as the franchisor must also evolve to keep up with the market. However if the franchisee is too complacent with their business (or has their attention elsewhere) to adapt to change, their business will inevitably suffer.
b) *Failure to follow the system*: Despite investing in a franchise with a prescribed way of doing things, if a franchisee decides to do their thing and implement ideas that are completely at odds with the brand offer and values, it's a sure shot cause for failure.

What challenges do working professionals face when starting a franchisee?

Working professionals may find it challenging to juggle their time and focus on the business they take on as a franchisee. In such situations it is best for them to hire competent professionals who can run their business for them without compromising on the quality of service.

When is the right time to invest in a franchise business? Why?

To give yourself the best shot at starting a business, you have to be able to focus on it. Like with any other business, the best time to start is when you have the time to devote your attention to it.

What is the secret of managing people?
It's simple, do not manage people but empower them to make the best use of whatever it is they bring to the table.

What message would you want to give to people who are interested in investing in a franchisee?
Seek and talk to existing franchisees to learn about their experiences for no one can give you a better picture of the successes and challenges that lie ahead than these people who are living the life of a franchisee every day.

Interview with Karan Tanna, Founder, CEO – Yellow Tie Hospitality

Yellow Tie Hospitality is India's first organized restaurant franchise management. We grow our restaurant brand portfolio through efficient franchising management that brings sustainability to the brand. In spite of being the second largest populated country, India doesn't have a single franchise driven nationally grown restaurant brand. This is due to naïve franchise management practices in the industry; Yellow Tie has identified this gap and focused on building up back end infrastructure to support growth of brand through franchise management.

Yellow Tie sells its franchise to an aspiring franchise entrepreneur after thorough understanding of his or her background and interest. We help franchise owner to find the most appropriate site, do the complete fit outs of the site, carry recruitment and training, give them software to manage checklists and recipes, conduct audit and brush up trainings and lead all marketing and branding support so that the franchise just has to focus on delivering the last mile customer experience. We have also developed vendors and supply chain to be able to supply the required raw material to door step of franchise, which reduces dependency of franchise owner on outlet level skilled staff. We hand hold franchise with all support to increase sales and profits making them sustainable. Yellow Tie charges one-time fee and recurring royalty for supporting and sharing intellectual properties with franchises.

Yellow Tie's another vertical of business is incubation of restaurant brands that have a product differentiator and has a potential to grow through franchising. We identify brands that have a proven unit level economics and possibility of scalability due to its friendly menu and gap in market and then invest in these companies giving them growth capital and our back-end infrastructure support. These brands are still led by passionate founders and yellow tie plugs in required investments and mentoring to grow these brands.

Products and Services: Yellow Tie Hospitality has 10 brands under its portfolio. These are as under:

A. International Brands

   a) **Genuine Broaster Chicken** – This brand is the category leader in pressure fried chicken by the Broaster Company, USA
   b) Format: Casual Dining and QSR
   Cities (includes projects in fit outs): Mumbai, Patna, Kolkata, Hyderabad, Lucknow, Guwahati, Gangtok, Bangalore, Pune, Imphal, Delhi, Bhubaneshwar, and Ranchi.
   Total outlets: 20
   c) **Wrapchic** – India's first Indo-Mexican Burrito brand from the UK
   Format: QSR and Kiosk
   Cities: Chennai
   Total outlets: 1
   d) **Just Falafel** – Authentic Lebanese Food brand from Dubai
   Format: QSR and Kiosk
   Cities: Pushkar
   Total outlets: 1
   e) **Chachago** – Unique Beverages brand from Taiwan
   Format: QSR and Kiosk

B. Home-Grown Brands

   a) **Dhadoom** – The only QSR offering Global Fusion Street Food
   Format: Casual Dining, QSR, and Kiosk
   Cities: Mumbai, Pune, Kolkata, Bangalore, Ahmedabad, Surat, Vadodara, Lucknow, Jaipur, Jamshedpur, and Gurgaon
   Total outlets: 25
   b) **BB Jaan** – Hyderabadi Nizami Cuisine
   Format: Fine Dine
   Total outlets: 1
   c) **Twist of Tadka** – Modern Indian Dining
   Format: Fine Dine
   Total outlets: 1
   d) **Teddys**– Revolutionary Soft Serve Kiosk Concept
   Format: Kiosk
   Cities: Mumbai
   Total Outlets: 1

C. Incubation Center

   a) **Wok This Way** – India's first healthy, only vegetarian oriental wok brand

Format: Casual Dining and QSR
b) **Umraan Regional** – India's first QSR offering regional food from different regions of India
Format: QSR
Cities: Mumbai
Total Outlets: 2

All our formats are category leaders or unique in their own positioning, so franchise owners tend to choose us over competition. Besides, our back-end infrastructure is best in the industry with over fifty team members spread across five cities of India giving them a support during the life of their business.

No of years: Since inception (approx. 3 years)
No of Employees: The total number of employees working in YELLOW TIE Hospitality as on date (Nov 2018) is 53. These team members are spread across five locations as under:
- Mumbai : 47
- Hyderabad: 2
- Delhi: 2
- Kolkata: 2
- Bangalore: 1

What inspired you to start this business?
As I worked in Vadodara in Gujarat for General Motors, in one of my holidays when I worked for McKinsey, I visited couple of my friends in Vadodara who were my General Motors colleagues. We visited a restaurant called Goodies and it was a very nice neighborhood bistro and I packed brownies from Goodies. When I came back I shared the brownies with my family, everyone loved it and I loved it too. That triggered a thought that why not I start a restaurant and why not Goodies to Ahmedabad and that was my first venture. So actually, the product did the magic and helped me get my eureka moment.

From starting your own business to giving a part of your business to the world, how did this franchise journey begin?
As I was born and brought up in Gujarat, I always saw entrepreneurship around me. May be there were some childhood memories of my parents running a restaurant between 1990 and 1999 that always left some imprint on my mind and left a dream of one day opening my own restaurant. I worked for General Motors and McKinsey Company and there came a point when I thought if I don't take plunge into entrepreneurship today I might not be able to ever take a plunge owning to a lot of luxuries that an MNC provides. So before I could allow myself to be carried away I decided to take plunge into entrepreneurship and I believe the thought of entrepreneurship

was not forced it came very naturally to me, hence I kicked off my journey as an entrepreneur and because there were some childhood memories of my parents running a restaurant, I started my entrepreneurship in a restaurant business.

What makes your product or service unique?
Yellow Tie's business is such that the focus is on franchise management and because we offer the portfolio of brands starting from a QSR like Dhadoom (Investment: Rs. 15 lakhs) to Casual Diners like Genuine Broaster Chicken (Investment: 1 crore) to fine-dine brands like Twist of Tadka and BB Jaan (Investment: 2-3 crores) we offer the brands suiting the investments and the needs of any entrepreneur. This makes us unique and we don't have any competitors who offer the value in terms of franchise management and the portfolio of brands to choose from.

What were some of the major challenges that you faced in this franchise business? How did you manage to overcome them? Is there any example that you can highlight?
When I started the restaurant, I did not have any restaurant background and I was new to the industry so there were multiple challenges like handling the manpower at store, understanding the requirements of guests, etc. Surprisingly in this industry the guests want consistency and at the same time they also want some change, so it's very difficult to balance both. But gradually there was passion and keenness to deeply involve in the work; we encountered all these challenges. Of course, we took a while to make a good team and once you have a good team your job becomes easier. So, I would not say that there were or there are any perennial changes in this business but they are simple business problems which we need to be solved to move ahead.

What do you do to keep updated with developments happening in the industry?
The times are changing really fast. Social media has shrunk the world and now everything is accessible. Fortunately or unfortunately food industry is one which does not have any entry barriers so there are lot of new entrants and players; also the customer mindset is evolving and the customer has started to travel a lot. So there are a lot of changes that keep happening in the industry and we always have to keep pace with it. The first step is to be involved in whatever the food trends are and whatever the world is moving toward you need to adopt it and try whatever the world wants and then see whether it is applicable to the positioning of your restaurant or not. Secondly, it is important to keep reviving the brand positioning from time to time and to make it more realistic and applicable for the current scenario. We also have a lot of in-house forums where we meet and discuss the trends and we also work out the action plan on what are the changes brand-wise

that we should bring in to keep pace with the changing times and on an individual level, I also try to keep myself hands-on with whatever is going on in the industry, visit new concepts, new restaurants, talk to the industry leaders, talk to a lot of customers which will help me evolve with time and I'm very flexible to change myself in a way that benefits the business.

What do you see as the future of the industry you are in?
We are looking at a total count of 50 stores by the end of 2018 and by the end of 2019 we are expecting to reach a total count of 100 stores by extending our portfolio to multiple brands mainly by acquiring the start-ups in food service industry. We want to extend our expertise and experience to those companies that need us the most. We want to partner with the brands that have achieved good unit level economics and potential of growth through franchise but are unable to grow due to lack of expertise knowledge in this field. Our vision is to make multiple national level brands and take Indian brands on the global map.

Who do you consider as your role model?
I look up to Steve Jobs because he was a genius who kept pushing for the perfect product. He never settled for less or accepted mediocrity. On a personal level, I admire him also because he balanced his life well with his spiritual learning.

Howard Schultz, the founder of Starbucks, is also a great source of inspiration for me. After stepping in as a chairman since 2000, he returned as CEO in 2007 to bail out Starbucks out of trouble, when for Starbucks shares were dipping for the first time in two decades. He decided to step down to take care of day-to-day operations, and very analytically and tactfully took all his partners (that's what he called his employees) into confidence, focused on the product, and delighted guests by providing great quality coffee, cup after cup. It was he who got Starbucks back on track and helped regain the shareholders confidence.

Dhirubhai Ambani, whose rags-to-riches story has encouraged many Indians with dreams, is a huge source of inspiration. He thought big and gave shareholders value for their money. He infused disruption in the DNA of Reliance so that they always came up with business ideas that disrupt the industry and help the people of the nation. He is a true poster of how a "baniya" can change the world.

I not only admire but also try to emulate these three business leaders, hoping to achieve what they achieved in their lives.

What is the vision of this franchise business?
It is our vision to be the largest restaurant franchise company by 2025. However, we plan our goals quarter by quarter. We want to take Genuine

Broaster Chicken to 50 stores by 2019, including stores in South East Asia, for which Broaster Chicken USA has just awarded us the rights (for 10 countries besides India because of its great performance in India).

We aim to set up 35+ Dhadoom stores by 2019 and 100+ stores by 2010. We will take Dhadoom to global markets and have already secured a premise in Nepal.

We'll keep growing other brands in our portfolio like Wrapchic, Just Falafel, Twist of Tadka and BB Jaan, and plan to take the total store count to 250+ by 2020.

In the coming 3 years, our main focus is going to be incubating restaurant brands to scale them and looking at investing in 10 such companies (over and above the two we have already invested in—Umraan Regional and Wok This Way) by 2020.

We plan to take four of our portfolio brands global before 2019 end. We want to continue creating value for all of our stakeholders and grow with our stakeholder. We will be the biggest restaurant franchise company in India in the next 5 years.

How much time would it take to start your franchisee from the date of signing the agreement?

We have a very strict policy in place wherein we work toward completing all the civil and operational work and get the franchise running in 45 days. However, for a larger format, the franchisee will take about 60 days to get operational from the date the civil work commences.

Who are the people that invest in your franchisee?

We don't necessarily have a particular kind of customer who invest in buying our franchise. Our franchise owners are from business as well as salaried employees, mainly those who have a passion for running a restaurant.

What would be the initial investment required if someone wants to invest in your franchisee?

We have eleven different brands for a franchisor to choose from and invest as per what suits his budget. We have investment models starting from 5 lakhs to 2 crores. We usually ask our franchise owners to have 6 months of operational expenses ready besides the investment made for franchise fees, restaurant interiors, raw material sourcing, staff salaries, and rent.

What is the average payback period for a person who invests in your franchisee?

The average payback period for each franchise will differ as we have different formats and investment for different brands. Typically for a QSR and Kiosk format of a brand like Dhadoom, the payback period is 15–18 months. For a

Casual Dining Restaurant like Genuine Broaster Chicken it is 18–24 months. Whereas for a lower investment Franchise like Teddy's, the payback period is 12–15 months.

Does your franchise network have people who buy multiple franchisees or a Master Franchise?
Yellow Tie Hospitality partners with two types of investors. One is a Franchise Operator who invests in a single unit Franchise and the other is the one who partners with us for managing and operating Franchises for a territory or a region. We have Master Franchisors for all of our brands for different regions. These Master Franchise partners also help bring in potential investors who are interested in investing in single unit franchises.

What challenges lie in the franchising industry?

1. Poor franchisee infrastructure

The lack of proper guidelines to adhere to when it comes to standard operating processes and recipe cards, made work difficult for franchisee owners.

Our Solution: We have developed a holistic mobile app to help franchisees manage their store, register a complaint, order raw materials, view recipe cards, etc.

2. Lack of good manufacturers of "scalable food"

Food needs be manufactured at a central location and made available in a ready-to-eat form everywhere. Unfortunately, there are very few efficient vendors and frozen supply chains in the country.

Our Solution: We've partnered with supply chain partners who have warehouses across India. Together, we train vendors across India to manufacture scalable food in a hygienic, standardized way.

3. Legal Framework

The efficiency of our legal system in order to take care of franchisee ambiguities is not extremely evolved. This adds to the confusion when it comes to running a seamless chain of restaurants.

Our Solution: After vetting through global franchisee contracts, we've benchmarked ideal practices and customized it to suit Indian scenarios.

4. The Franchisee Mindset

Franchisee owners don't fully understand the nuances of a franchisee-franchiser relationship and tend to deviate from the brand as per his or her convenience.

Our Solution: We have employed coaches to educate franchisees on the importance of not cutting corners in the initial days of business and adhering to the standards set by brand.

5. Unregulated Franchising Market

Companies are rapidly setting up franchisees and tend to neglect the brand's basic standardization requirements and franchising support like SOPs, projects, training programs, etc. They even undercut their franchisee's fees and royalties to win or close deals.

Our Solution: Setting expectations at the very beginning has helped us a lot. We use case studies to explain why our financial model is appropriate for long-term success.

Franchisor Interview – Dheeraj Gupta, Owner of the Jumboking Franchise

What inspired you to start this business?
The idea came because I come from a business family. For some reason I did not want to join the family business as I wanted to create a brand enterprise of my own so my father was helpful enough to let me start a separate business and he did not feel bad about it.

From starting your own business to giving a part of it to the world, how did the franchising business begin?
A lot of urgent inspiration comes from a perfect model. McDonalds—they were franchising their entire brand so a lot of influence was from there; that's why I decided that it is the right way to go. I started the first three stores by myself. Later I started Franchising and went along as I understood what the merits of Franchising were.

What makes your product or service unique?
I think that it is something which varies over time. Earlier the eating population was the whole high level society compared to the inside vendors and other operators. Now as time has developed everybody has upped the way and hygiene has become much better all across; so I think it is about positioning the brand very clearly on the whole. It's about creating a niche. If the person is on the go and is in a hurry to go somewhere or to reach the work place on time then we put our stores at the location which is right there. A lot of strategic understanding of the need makes the brand. We start the proposition, then we sustain small, and keep different credits.

What kind of Franchisee Model do you operate?
The basic purpose of Franchising is that you are getting an Entrepreneur in the business. You are replacing the Store Manager with the Entrepreneur because the Entrepreneur is the one who is going to be spending money as he will be time and again more driven and will make more money as the business owner. So in FOCO, Franchisee owned and company operated model will get the center over there. In the company operated franchising it will not succeed as that is like someone using Franchisee money to grow his business. It is an act. What we endure in business is FOFO which is what qualifies as a Franchisee. That is what we do regarding Franchisee Owned and Franchisee Operated.

What have been some of the major challenges that you have faced in Franchisee business?
The biggest challenge is that the Franchisee is a business owner and he is not an employee, so he will ask a lot of questions; if he is not making money or he is not making money as per his expectations, then he is not going to be very happy. There has to be something which needs to be as a manual destiny for work. Eventually we should keep up the conscience and keep up with what he is doing as his store will pick up. This is the most difficult part in Franchising.

How did you manage to overcome this issue?
I do not think that anybody has managed to overcome this issue as Subway has 58,000 stores worldwide and it still has its own issues. So no one can overcome these issues. What you can do is to accept the feedback, keep on improving your business model, and make positive changes which are going to ensure that Franchisee works fine. In business, high risk is involved. Earlier when we used to put up ten stores then out of it on an average five

were fine and remaining five were not. Now our ratio has gone up to be eight out of ten. All ten still do not do well so we can still figure out why they did not do well. By now we have kind of figured out how we can avoid those things which can come to a conclusion that where we have selected a bad property or we have selected a Franchisee who did not have insight of the business or services.

With the current success which Franchisee business has seen where does your company stand in the QSR industry?
Of course among the Indian players we are one of the leading brands. The International players are there who have years of experience and they have come way before the Jumboking did. We do not know enough though. In our particular Frozen QSR Burger category in comparison to International players, Jumboking is very good.

What do you do to keep yourself updated with the development happening in the industry?
We have to keep our eyes and ears open. Keep getting information from the newspaper, TV, suppliers by generally being in the market. You know what is happening to keep up with the owners; Franchisees who have considered our brand over the other players in the market have decided to take the Franchisee from us.

What do you see as the future of the Industry you are in?
In Franchising, trust is the most important factor because people are investing their money. We need to just ensure that companies which are there in Franchising are honest and sincere in their effort in order to make their Franchisee succeed. If majority of them are committed for long-term growth then they will excel. Franchisee Industry has a very bright future but it has a long way to go.

Who do you consider as your role model?
When it comes to business processes then it is McDonalds and if it is about franchising policies, the way the business expansion happens then it is Subway as they are the largest Franchisee brand in the world. McDonalds is best in terms of Operations.

Is there any person that you will give credit to for your success?
There are many people, all our suppliers, the franchisees, our well-wishers, and team members. Franchising is not a one man show but it is about a whole lot of people. In our business it is about the culture of our organization. We have to remain focused on Franchising. That has to be our number one goal.

Do you have your Franchisee chain presence internationally?
No. Our presence is until the Mumbai Airport.

What are your success formulae for Marketing?

I do not know if there are any success formulae. However, we allocated certain percentage of sales to Marketing. It is not our story but the only option that we had was to slowly wait for our Franchisees to grow. All along the best way was turning to use it to increase Franchisee sales. Franchisee success is what everything revolves around.

How do you help Franchisees directly to get new customer?
We are into retail so if we do our site selection part properly and put up in very high footfall areas the customers will come. Put up a store right in the middle of where customers are that is the best way to get them. Property and Franchisee are the most important parts. In past we had very nice properties but they were not doing well and were underperforming. We realized that the Franchisees were not motivated enough so we removed them and got another Franchisee and the store started doing extremely well; so both the things are very important.

How do you choose the right person who wants a Franchisee?
Normally we look for three things:

a) They should have the amount for investment. There should not be any loan option.
b) We try to work with only full time operators. We try to avoid working with part timers who are doing a job.
c) We try to select people with some prior business experience as they will understand the value of being a part of Jumboking. They will know that they have to work harder at the business than the job.

What Franchising does is two things:

a) System prevents – after the first year once you launch what is required then it is easier to operate.
b) You are a king at your business. You can put up a second or third store. You can double or triple your income.

What will be the Initial Investment required if someone wants to invest in Jumboking Franchisee?
Around 20 lakhs+ property deposit which will come close to about 35-40 lakhs

How does your Franchisee normally raise capital?
We do not allow them to raise capital from outside. It has to be their own money. We do not want any loans, etc.

When Franchisee is stuck in any operational problem that they are unable to solve then how do you support them?
By mentoring them with the help of the Franchisee team as they do it.

How do you contribute to the growth of your Franchisees?
There are multiple ways. The three key ways would be:
   a) We keep on working on getting new products on the menu and removing products which are not working.
   b) Keep on taking our Marketing initiatives to keep the brand alive and relevant.
   c) Consistent cooperation is provided for people who are not performing properly. They have to be trained to do things correctly because everything is linked. If any Franchisee is not giving proper product then it needs to be corrected. There is an audit mechanism which ensures that every store maintains the standard that is what every customer wants as they are getting the right product which is the same at every outlet.

What is the vision of your Franchisee business?
We look at Mumbai and Pune as a 500-store market for us and then India as a much larger market. In India we can put up as many as 5,000 stores. But we are very focused on first going to Mumbai and Pune and then we will go further.

How much time does it take to start the Franchisee from the date of signing the agreement?
It depends as there are Franchisees who had signed up with us and we had property available so we could start them off immediately. However, I am talking about two extremes. On the other hand there have been cases where Franchisees had to wait for 1 year till we could find them a property. Until we could make and give them the Franchisee they could not invest anywhere else. Normally we say within 90 days the person should have finalized his property and start working.

Who are the people who invest in your Franchisees?
I think they are definitely people in age group of about 30–35 years who want to get into business and basically feel franchising is an easier way to get into business because chances of success of going up are more. Among independent restaurants which start, only 20 percent of them last beyond the first year. However, in a good Franchisee system the chances of success are up to 80 percent in the first year.

What is the average payback period for a person investing in your Franchisee?
Between 3 and 5 years.

Does your Franchisee network have people who buy multiple Franchisees?
Yes we do. In fact that is important part of the Franchisee.

What are the characteristics signs of a good Franchisee?
Somebody who makes an effort to understand why things are happening in a certain way. We have to give them a better understanding. Share the vision with them about their growth provided so that they remain focused. It is people of the Franchisee who spend their time in building this business. He will be obviously the one who will get the success and it will become the ideal Franchisee then.

Why people should invest in Franchisee rather than starting their own business?
Because of the Franchisee fee system. We charge 10 percent royalty from our Franchisees. If someone would want to do the same business by themselves they will end up paying much more as they will have to set up their own kitchen and have extra staff and extra space. They will have to have their own separate Marketing budget so why would anyone want to do that business. They are far better off in that case being a part of Jumboking.

What care has to be taken while selecting a Franchisee brand to invest in?
People should do their homework. They should go and meet a lot of existent Franchisees and get the feedback from them because if they go to the company directly then it will talk good about their own self and will not say anything bad. People should do due diligence and understand and then take a decision on what needs to be done.

What is the future of Franchising?
As long as we ensure that Franchising is done ethically the industry will do well. If there are fly by night operators, people who think of giving Franchisee and taking money at the upfront say by giving 100 Franchisees. You need to work on ensuring that each Franchisee succeeds which is a lot of hard work. If every company works on their respective Franchisee's success then it will be very a large opportunity. The system will be way stronger as they will have the entrepreneur's energy with them as a huge value addition.

What leads to the failure of Franchisee business?
Other than wrong property or Franchisee selection the company themselves are not investing enough to create a system as they want to quickly expand and grow. When they are not working, then the company will not expand as they are not ready for it.

Does the Indian economy support the Franchisee business?
Yes, it does.

Should working professional invest in a Franchisee?
No, as per me as the person would want to work and run a Franchisee business simultaneously. I will not give him the Franchisee business as I

already know that his priority will not be the Franchisee business. The store will not get the required returns.

When is the right time to invest in Franchisee business and why?
There is no right time. Just do the homework well. Search on the company you want to invest in by the Franchisor. It is always a good time to start.

What message would you want to give to the people who are investing in a Franchisee?
Do your research well on the company that you want to invest in. Be prepared for hard work. If anyone who says that you take my Franchisee and you will have guaranteed success is the one who is lying. It is hard work. You have to put in your best as there are no short cuts.

Interview of the Founder of GoliVadaPav, Venkatesh Iyer

GoliVadaPav was founded in 2004 by Venkatesh Iyer. The chain started operations with a single "Quick service restaurant." The first outlet was set up in Kalyan, a suburban locality in Mumbai.

Today GoliVadapav operates in more than 300 stores in 20 states and 100 cities of India. The expanse is from Jalandhar in North to Calicut in South and from Porbandar in West to Kolkata in East. It's a take-away, high-street model. Store size: 150–200 sq. ft. Recognitions: Harvard, IMD Switzerland and ISB Hyderabad have done a case study on GoliVadaPav; CNBC had done a book "My Journey with Vadapav;" GoliVadaPav has bagged Golden Spoon Awards for the most preferred QSR by Coca-Cola in different segments in 2013, 2014, and 2016. Travel and Leisure has featured GoliVadaPav amongst the top 20 QSR in the world.

Products and Services: Food and Beverages—The basket of products includes varieties of Vadapavs, Vada Rolls, Curry Pavs, Beverages, Desserts, and their Combos.

No of years: 14
No of Employees: 250+
No of customers: About 1 lakh customers per day

What inspired you to start this business?
I was inspired by the vision of a wealth creation and wealth distribution for a new India.

From starting your own business to giving a part of your business to the world, how did this franchise journey begin?
After we had finalized our products we looked to expand and got opportunity to associate with Aarey Milk booths of Mumbai; the booths were branded as Goli and sold Vadapav also. We faced a major external challenge and had to withdraw from Aarey. This seemed a major blow... the story was covered by media. This helped us in getting franchisee enquiries.

What makes your product or service unique?
GoliVadaPav products – Vadapav, Vada Rolls, and Curry Pav are unique as they take the authentic Mumbai Street food flavor across the country.

What type of franchise model do you operate?
We have a transfer Price Franchise model.

What were some of the major challenges that you faced in this franchise business? How did you manage to overcome them? Is there any example that you can highlight?
Challenges in the Franchise business have been standardization of products and logistics as our 300 stores are present across 100 cities. We were able to overcome them with the help of our production and supply chain partners who helped us standardize the product by increasing the shelf life of the products and helping us reach across the country.

With the current success that the franchise business has seen, where does this company stand in its industry?
We have more than 300 stores across 100 cities which indicate that we are in the right direction and we see it growing at a faster pace.

What do you do to keep updated with developments happening in the industry?
Traveling, reading, and talking to young people about entrepreneurship...

What do you see as the future of the industry you are in?
Indian fast food industry is growing every day. A lot of players are doing a great work. The food tech revolution by the likes of Swiggy, Zomato, Food Panda, and Uber Eats has revolutionized the landscape. The eating out frequency has grown... now even larger opportunity.

Who do you consider as your role model?
I am inspired by the book *Jonathan Livingston Seagull* by Richard Bach. Paulo Cohelo's *Alchemist* lines—"You have a dream.... The dream has come in the womb of the universe... it is the responsibility of the universe to fulfill the dream.... The universe conspires to help achieve your dreams..." Mahatma Gandhi's lines of "You find the purpose.... The means will follow...."

Is there any person that you would give credit to for your success?
It could have never been if I have tried alone. I am blessed to have a great team and supporting family who stood by me...

Can you share five success stories of your franchisees?
Most of our franchisees can be a case study. There are franchisees that are in the system from past 8-10 years and are extremely happy from the contribution the business has created in their lives.

What is your success formula for marketing?
We have always done frugal marketing that has brought some creative ideas...One of them has been Barter. We barter for getting visibility. Also, Harvard, IMD Switzerland and ISB Hyderabad have done case studies on GoliVadapav. This has given us recognition. I have conducted more than 400 talks on entrepreneurship.

How do you support your franchisees in marketing?
Our Franchisees are the best persons for the local knowledge. We help them with strategies to build their sales via Local Area Marketing. It's a combination of both online and offline Marketing.

How do you help the franchisees to get new customers?
It's a continuous process—local area marketing and new product launches.

Since the opening or launch period is very crucial what kind of support do you give for the franchisee business?
We have an induction program for each franchisee where we understand the trading area of the store to be launched and according to the business generators we make a concrete plan which include both offline and online. Our team members help them to implement and measure.

What is the vision of this franchise business?
We want to grow in clusters and double the store count in the next 3 years.

How much time would it take to start your franchisee from the date of signing the agreement?
One month.

Who are the people that invest in your franchisee?
- Aspiring entrepreneurs
- People interested in running a food and beverage business.

What would be the initial investment required if someone wants to invest in your franchisee?
It's 10-12 lakhs.

How do your franchisees raise capital normally?
As this business doesn't need a very high amount to start mostly it's self-funded.

When the franchisee is stuck in an operational problem that they are unable to solve? How do you support them?
We have regional team who is always in contact with the franchisee. These team members help the franchise build sales and help resolve concern if any.

How do you contribute toward the growth of your franchisees?
Right from the time when the franchisee signs.

What system of review have you put in place to receive the feedback of franchisees, monitor their performance, and give advice on improvements?
We have a feedback system where a team works on the concerns and feedbacks of the franchisee in a time-bound manner. The franchisees can share their concerns and requirements. This team also discusses monthly performance reports for the franchisees.

Are periodic audits on quality done? And how?
Yes. We have Cluster Managers who are assigned with all the stores in a cluster. These people are from an experienced background from top QSRs. They have a roster for conducting the audits and helping the stores fix the gaps.

What is the average payback period for a person who invests in your franchisee?
The franchisees recover their invested amount in 10–12 months and then they make profits.

Does your franchise network have people who buy multiple franchisees or a Master Franchise?
Yes.

What would you say is the success rate of your franchisees?
All the involved franchisees are successful in building profits. Many a time we face challenges but our strategies and the team with rich QSR experience have solutions. We having more than 300 stores across 100 cities is the testimony.

How do you help franchisees to succeed?
Training, Audits, Incentives on Sales achievement, Marketing, Concern Resolution System.

Is your franchisee model system oriented or people oriented?
It's a mix of the both. We have an ERP as well as a team in the region that helps the franchisee to drive the business.

What are the characteristics or signs of a good franchisee?
- Intent to be trained
- Good money manager
- Team building skills.

What according to you are the most important qualities of a successful franchisee?
- Consumer centric
- Involvement in the business
- Good people manager.

Why people should invest in a franchisee rather than investing in an own business?
- They get a tested model, hence chances of failure is very less
- Have to invest only a fraction of what they need in starting a new business.

What care has to be taken while selecting a franchise brand to invest in?
- The model of the business
- Success of other franchisee
- Team of the franchisee.

Can you share with us a case study of any successful franchisee in your network?
Most of our franchisees can be a case study. There are franchisees that are in the system for the past 8–10 years and are extremely happy from the contribution the business has created in their lives.

What is the future of franchising?
The future is very bright. Franchising multiplies the business quickly. For example, in India we have a lot of diversity... be it the taste, dishes, language... A Franchisee is the best person to have the correct insights which will help the franchise.

Are there any risks involved in starting a franchisee business?
The risk is of standardization and consumer experience. Both of these need strong solutions by having a team which conducts regular audits.

What leads to the failure of franchisee businesses?
Lack of involvement of franchisee and dearth of quality manpower and system at the franchise end.

Does today's economy support the franchise business model?
Yes, it does.

Why should entrepreneurs invest in a franchisee?
They get a tested model, hence chances of failure is very less.
Have to invest only a fraction of what they need in starting a new business.

Why should working professionals invest in a franchisee?
If they intent to move from Employed professionals to Entrepreneurs and by investing in franchising they get a tested model, hence chances of failure are very less.

What challenges lie in the franchising industry?
- Competition
- Employee motivation
- Resource planning.

How important is it to follow the operations manual as a franchisee?
Operation Excellence is the heart of our business. This will ensure that the product is served right to our consumers. This ensures quality of product, quick service, and cleanliness in the stores.

What are the most common mistakes that a franchisee should avoid?
- Leaving the business entirely on the team
- Not having a monitoring mechanism
- Focusing on short term cost gain and losing sight of consumer satisfaction.

What challenges do people from a nonbusiness background face when starting a franchise?
- Employing a team
- Managing resources
- Skills needed for the business.

What challenges do working professionals face when starting a franchisee?
A working professional's biggest challenge is being risk averse. Franchising business has lesser risk element than a newly owned business.

When is the right time to invest in a franchise business? Why?
Anytime... It's always the right time to invest in a franchisee business. However, I would say in the early phase of our life when we graduate from a college and want to become an entrepreneur... investing in a franchisee helps us to learn the key insights of a business and helps one to take a big leap going ahead.

What is the secret of managing people?
Understanding their Primary Motivating Factor and supporting them to realize that. Helping them develop a skill via training and setting expectations for performance.

What message would you want to give to people who are interested in investing in a franchisee?

We as entrepreneurs are here to evolve this planet to the next level through products, services, imagination, exploration, and innovation. It's like larva becoming caterpillar and then becoming butterfly… the struggle will continue. But at the end you will have a beautiful butterfly.

I think you should go on and on by being flexible… trying new business models… new products… new markets… new technologies… the journey continues… till you succeed and after that…

FRANCHISEE INTERVIEWS

An educationist, a mom—Spotlight on Ms. Chandrika Chalasani from Kangaroo Kids Franchisee

Chandrika Chalasani, the franchisee owner of Kangaroo Kids preschool does not consider herself as a business woman, but has been running the preschool franchisee for over 15 years. She has been providing employment to over 80 people including teaching and nonteaching staff and a student strength of around 385.

When we spoke to Chandrika, she was very forthcoming in sharing her thoughts, ideas, and vision for her business. She is an educationist who believes in making education as a learning experience for the kids. We touched various topics including her business model, running a franchise and her experience in the field.

"I have been running the Kangaroo Kids franchisee for 15 years. My children inspired me to start this preschool. My son was a student there in Delhi. But when we relocated to Hyderabad, I was unable to find any school that matched the standard and education pattern of Kangaroo Kids. Finally, I approached them for a franchise. Interestingly, I never explored the option of any other franchise."

Her startup story is quite interesting. Coming from the nonbusiness background, the first few months were very challenging just because it was the first experience. But the franchisor support was tremendous. As the model was tried and tested, she had a big advantage of past statistics to showcase what can be expected. The franchisor support not only included setting up the playschool but also in running it. As the curriculum was already given, the team didn't have to sweat too much about figuring out what is required for the particular age group, what do they needed to do, what was the development, what was the kind of activities that needed to be done for the children of that age, the yearly progress, etc.

The support from Kangaroo Kids franchise made things much simpler for her. Even after years of working as a franchise, the support is still ongoing. Although with experience now, Chandrika uses her liberty to making slight edits to the program whenever a better result is possible.

As an educator, Chandrika enjoys being with kids and continuously learning new things. In fact, she's so passionate about her work that in spite of being in business for over 15 years, she's still actively involved in the day-to-day working of the school. Since the initial days, the only challenge she had was convincing the parents to go for this novel, unconventional methods of education focusing on the overall child development.

However, being a working business woman comes with a price. In spite of being a franchisee with defined systems, establishing herself in the segment took almost 4 years and required a lot of hard work. It did take a toll on family life, but as any other business, slowly as the setup grew, it got easier with time.

When we interviewed Chandrika, we had a set of rapid fire questions, just to understand her business and the franchise industry as a whole, a little better. Here is a short snippet of the rapid fire:

What care should be taken while investing in a franchisee?
The most important thing is the philosophy of the franchisee should match yours. Personally it feels like education and children shouldn't be all about business and there should be balance.

Is investing in a franchisee risky?
I think there is risk in everything right, but it is already a well-established franchisee; I think this risk factor is quite less.

So what is the ideal quality a person should possess if he is planning to run a franchisee business and run it?
Faith and passion.

What sort of support did you receive when you first opened from the franchiser? How helpful was it?
They were very accessible for any and every question I had. For the initial set up they came to help us. We were given exhaustive training. Their support is very prompt. I think that was the key. When you are choosing the franchisor that you want to work with the one also needs to check how focused are they or is it just the number game or more than that.

Is there any specialty software provided by the franchiser? Do all the franchises use the same system?
Yes, we do.

What about the territory in which your franchisee operates, does it gives you favorable returns or is it limited returns?
For me, very safe returns.

While on the subject, we probed a bit more into the training programs that Chandrika does. At the onset of a franchise, Kangaroo Kids provides on-site trainings to the management team as well as the teachers for the curriculum. The interesting part is, even after 15 years, the team comes down periodically to check on the standards and the consistency in quality. They also arrange for periodic trainings for the teachers. Besides these trainings, Chandrika is very active in doing workshops and conferences to abreast herself on the latest trends in the market. Connections with industry contacts also keep her updated with the changes and happenings of the industry.

As a franchisor, Kangaroo Kids does a lot of marketing and advertising tactics. But Chandrika has only depended on word of mouth for getting her classrooms filled. The standard of education has been so good that over the years, it is the parents who have become their indirect marketeers and the school gets wonderful referrals through them.

Chandrika finds a great competitive advantage in Kangaroo Kids when comparing the level of competition with other brands. The vision of the parent brand and the value for money are the key USPs of the brand. Their curriculum is state-of-the-art, which makes Kangaroo Kids a sought after brand in preschool space.

Rina, the founder of Kangaroo Kids has maintained a wonderful relationship with her franchises. For Chandrika, she's a mentor and a friend, a person who has built a small community of her core team members and franchises together. So they all support and mentor each other instead of viewing the other as competition. This has made the entire ecosystem more conducive for growth.

The franchise has set an effective communication channel between the franchisee and franchiser. Each franchisee has a different point of contact for support and assistance. For any complaint redressal, they have an email support to document and resolve the issue at the earliest. Chandrika attributes their transparency and support as the key reason for a successful association. There were no hidden costs or surprise elements as they progressed through the years, making the relationship stronger and deeper.

While setting up the business, the franchisor team not only provided support but also helped in financial estimations to make the journey smoother for Chandrika. But the business grew quickly and the investment increased with rapid infrastructural expansion. Chandrika started with an investment of INR 15 lakhs. But the franchisor also offers opportunities for further expansions into multiple centers.

As we move toward the end of our interview, a key question popped up—CHALLENGES. Preschool industry is very populated with multiple brands focusing on various interesting aspects of education. So the newer franchisees that open up face a lot of struggle due to steep competition. However, for Chandrika, the journey has been smoother as, over the last 15 years, her center is quite established and admissions keep flowing without much effort.

Her goal is to now do even better. Getting newer infrastructure and more trained teachers. You can see her commitment and passion when she fondly talks about her 385 children in her school.

As I ask her the last question—*Her message*—to those who get into the franchisee business, she says, "I think they should go for it, provided they believe in the concept and they have the same vision as the franchiser. You need to give it a little time to settle down and not think just because it's a franchisee; return should come from the very beginning."

We agree, Ms. Chandrika. Your journey has been aspiring and we wish you bigger and better success in the coming years. With that, we draw the curtain on our interview with a dynamic educationist from the preschool industry!

Running Business and Education Successfully—Meet Prasad from Hello Kids

Today we have a discussion with Prasad S. a proud franchise owner of Hello Kids. Prasad has been associated with the brand for 6 years now and owns two franchises. The franchises are quite popular with the children strength numbering 130 in one franchise and 110 in the other. In addition the franchises have 30 staff members (18 in the first one and 12 in the second one). Prasad takes us on the interesting journey of his foray into the franchise world.

On being probed about the products and services offered by his franchise, Prasad quips that all the necessary products required in school like toys, books, uniforms etc. are supplied by the franchisor. The manufacturing unit of the brand is located in Bangalore. Prasad's vision of the school entails a place where kids are happy and relaxed, learning in a fun environment without pressure and going home joyfully at the end of the day.

Of the two franchises owned by Prasad, one is managed by him and the other is managed by his wife. His wife had a successful stint in the teaching profession and was keen to undertake the challenge of managing the franchise. Her aim was to understand parents and their mindsets and impart the appropriate knowledge. The aim of guiding the parents in the right direction has led to workshops being conducted by the franchise. These workshops also help parents determine which standard the kids need to be enrolled in. Both Prasad and his wife want a 360 degree development of the kids and use special methods for teaching. Toys and other means are used to impart practical knowledge to the kids.

We ask him what made him choose the education field from the vast array of industries to invest in. He promptly responds it was his wife's passion for teaching that encouraged him to invest in a franchise school. After doing extensive groundwork and evaluating multiple franchises for their work culture, offerings and views, they decided to opt for Hello Kids. One of the primary reasons was the no-royalty model that Hello Kids operates on. This makes it easy for middle class people to invest in the business.

Being relatively new in the business field, they had to rely extensively on the franchisor for help in everything from setting up the infrastructure, hiring the staff, and running the operations. This is where Hello Kids stepped in and provided phenomenal support in providing the materials like toys, books etc, as well as training on how to handle parent's queries and managing the operations. Hello Kids provided a rock-like support in the initial stages till Prasad gained the requisite knowledge. Today he has the required skill set and expertise to help other people setup, answer their queries, etc. One of the other positive things about Hello Kids is the director and the owner are easily accessible and meet the franchisees whenever required to resolve any issues the franchises might be facing.

He walks us through the initial phase of his journey mentioning that Hello Kids offers different packages. A package will include a set of items like limited number of toys and training about how to market the school. He mentions that marketing is the pillar of the business and is required if the franchise is to be successful. The marketing involves a variety of methods to increase visibility. The next step is the infrastructure setup which needs to be comfortable and spacious. Parent and kids should get a feeling for warmth and coziness when they come to enroll in the school. All these activities were ably supported by the Hello Kids management.

When queried about the challenges faced by him and his preparation to meet them, he promptly responds that the main challenges came from the parents and teachers. The problems with the teachers were they were bogged down by personal problems or were looking for a higher salary etc.

I am very systematic by nature and believe that for playschools everything needs to be on time and in place. The children are small and need to be taken proper care of. There will be occasional glitches of staff unhappiness but he has managed to find ways to resolve the problems and get the work done. He strongly believes that as the child has enrolled in the school and become comfortable with the teacher, the teacher should not leave without completing one year. The challenges posed by the parents on the other hand are the excessive queries which are mostly answered by online data available still continue to persist. He patiently answers all the queries raised by the parents.

The best part about the business is the joy he gets being around kids. When he sees hundreds of kids running around he feels right at him. Talking to them and interacting with them makes him realize they are such wonderful beings and God's gift to us. He cites an example of a kid who joined the school but could not utter a single word. The boy talks nonstop now and it brings a sense of contentment and satisfaction to him. It gives him immense gratification to help kids and that is what drives him not the profit that he earns from the business. The improvement that he brings in children's life is what propels him on.

The business is, however, not without its share of issues says Prasad. One of the problems frequently encountered by him includes the fact that in the absence of him or his wife the people working in the franchise cannot handle things themselves. The faculty needs to be constantly motivated and egged on toward excellence. School events which are held outside like sports day or annual day are also another source of stress due to the responsibility of taking the children and safely bringing them back. The parents leave them with us with so much trust that we have to be extra careful all the time.

He mentions that in the beginning being a franchisee did put a stress on his personal life wherein he could not devote enough time for his family. With time, however, he learned the finer nuances of the business and also got a better insight into the psyche of the children. This helped him in better understanding of his own children and workplace became like a second home. It was like he had rediscovered his passion.

Prasad tells us that all the expectations that he had when he started his journey into the business world as a franchisee have been fulfilled. He, however, cautions the would-be entrepreneurs that starting a business, establishing it, and making a profit takes time and is not for the hasty. You need to make your franchise visible in the market, limited number of toys and the main thing was about marketing, how to market it setup the infrastructure, smoothening out the initial kinks, etc. which takes time. The biggest advantage for him was he did not have to spend time on marketing as he was a franchise owner of an established brand.

Probed about the secrets to his successful stint in the business, he mentions that what has worked for him is fulfilling the commitments that he has made with the parents of the kids enrolled in his school. He has made sure that a positive environment exists in the workplace and trust relationship exists with all stakeholders.

He mentions some of the challenges while investing in a franchise is identifying a proper franchise brand and location. Some brands charge royalty percentage (percentage of your profits) and you also need to evaluate your outgoing expenses like faculty salaries and utility bills like water, electricity, etc. You also need to be aware of the return on investment and your capacity to stay invested in the business. He, however, does not find the franchise business risky, as all the support systems and procedures exist which are provided by the franchisor.

People management is the key to business success is what Prasad strongly believes. It isn't easy managing relationships with teachers, parents, caretakers, and kids. You need to be patient and understanding in your approach. You should be able to deal with adverse circumstance while remaining calm and composed a quality he looks for in his teachers as well.

Hello Kids provided all the support related to infrastructure, marketing, materials, trainings, etc. when he first opened his franchise. Everything from inputs on location and guidance on running the franchise were provided by the franchisor. Prasad swears by the services provided by the brand. The training provided included handling staff, parents, and technical issues. It also included guidelines on how to ensure teachers are on time, planning the time-table, etc.

The communication with the franchisor is two ways and always open. The training model has also evolved over time and included inputs and directions from the people trained. This is the beauty of the franchise says Prasad. They are always progressing and improving. The marketing strategy deployed during the initial phase includes door-to-door pamphlet distribution. Neighborhood awareness is created about the brand opening a school in the area as the first step of marketing. Marketing and promotional campaigns are done every 3 months. Marketing activities include banners, newspaper flyers, bus, and books.

Additionally the franchise also has an app for the parents and management. This app also allows parents to ask their queries and provide their inputs. WhatsApp is also efficiently used for parent communication. He has gotten favorable returns for both his franchises and firmly believes that the franchise brand has contributed greatly to his success. He shares a great relationship with his franchisor and frequently receives inputs, feedback, and improvement suggestions. All the requisite support from picking up inventory to hiring of staff is readily provided. This has been a pleasant journey for Prasad something he least expected when he started his journey 6 years ago.

The communication has always been two-way according to him and in case of disagreements the franchisor has always found a mutually acceptable solution. This has reinforced his firm belief in the brand. The franchisors representatives are in constant contact with help regarding hiring, syllabus updation, and novel ideas for Diwali, Christmas, and summer camps. They constantly provide inputs which keeps us on the path of continuous improvement.

The ride in the franchise business has not always been rosy according to Prasad and we ask him how he typically logs his complaints and how does the franchisor respond. He says he prefers a direct approach and connects with the concerned person to report the issue. The response time is generally 2–3 days after contacting the owner and discussing the issue. Alternatively in some cases he directly speaks with the director of the franchise about the problem faced by him. He has always received a solution from the franchisor he claims. He has had no unpleasant experiences with the franchisor so far.

On inquiring about the accuracy of the projections regarding the capital investment required for the business provided by the franchisor Prasad says they have mostly been right on the money. The parameter for success is not only how well the school is made but also how efficiently is it marketed. You need to ensure you are visible to the world is what he mentions. There is also an ongoing investment associated with the franchise business like infrastructure upgradation, new toys, etc. As children are our main focus we try to make the environment as colorful and enjoyable as possible. We also try to improve on the books and other materials used by the kids, due to which the pricing increases sometimes.

Prasad clearly mentions there were no hidden fees from the franchisors' end and everything was transparent. The initial investment made by him was close to 6 lakhs. The return on investment was about a year because he was successful in marketing his franchise and keeping his colleagues comfortable. The returns have been more or less in line with his expectations. The main thing in this business is to provide the right kind of infrastructure and the atmosphere which will attract the parents and the children. It also ensures greater outreach and visibility for the franchise.

He stays updated with the latest trends in the industry through fliers and posters provided by the franchisor. He also attends seminars to keep his knowledge updated. There is also tremendous scope for expansion in the franchise business he feels. When asked if he would like to do anything differently regarding his starting a franchise he answers with an emphatic NO. He mentions it was one of the best decisions he has undertaken. His next big goal is to start classes from Standard 1 and above. He knows this will require additional resources, investment, and knowledge.

For the young and budding entrepreneurs Prasad advices to take the franchising route. He, however, cautions them, regarding expectations of profit from year 1. He emphasizes patience of 2–3 years before you can start reaping benefits from your investment. You also need to invest a lot of time and effort toward making your venture successful. You have to do the hard work yourself and have a hands-on approach if you want to flourish. You need to be willing to make additional investments if needed even if they reduce your profits because they are needed to build a long-term sustainable business. You have to do everything in your power to make the parents and kids comfortable if you want to ensure your business grows exponentially.

From a working mom to a successful businesswoman, meet Shreya Karkhana and her 9-year-old baby—Hello Kids Lilly

Shreya Sheshank Karkhana is a vivacious and passionate business woman who's successfully running the Bangalore-based HelloKids Franchise for the past 9 years. With two centers running in a geographical area of 1 km in the name of Hello Kids Lilly, Shreya has covered a whole gamut of services from play group, daycare, and kindergarten. She also has activity classes like Bharatnatyam, abacus, etc. that makes the center one of the most sought-after.

Hello Kids Lilly employs around 35–36 employees, with a good mix of teachers, councilors, and care takers managing a collective strength of 460 students. They have a clear vision to bring joy to the process of learning. *Learn and Grow* is their motto for their little ones. With this mission, they have tried to bring fun in the overall learning process as they believe that once the child enjoys the subject, he or she will learn it faster.

When Shreya started scouting for a franchise in preschool segment back in October 2009, she was quite enamored with the marketing activities of Hello Kids. She was further convinced with the brand when she interacted with their management and their team and took her first step toward this business. Over a period of 9 years, she now owns two franchises for the same brand.

Shreya was always passionate about the field of education. After her son was born, she was hesitant going back to work leaving her little one with a caretaker. So after a thorough research and discussion with the team, in February 2010, they opened for admissions. Their first academic year 2010–2011 started with 60 students. Shreya and her team share a special bond with the Hello Kids franchise where the franchisor helped them immensely during the setup period. They took special interest in small decisions like interiors of the school etc. which showed their commitment to take this association for a long haul. With time and the franchisor support, their confidence grew and over a period of 9 years, the student strength has grown from 60 to 460. But this has come with immaculate planning and execution process followed. Shreya's passion about teaching and drive toward perfection has made the journey very interesting.

Shreya has managed to maintain the work life balance effectively due to the nature of pre-K business. The hours are 8.30 to 2.30, which makes the family life balancing much easier. An excellent and supportive franchisor has made it much more comfortable. Hello Kids has always maintained a transparent communication. They were always accessible and available to help in any challenges that Shreya faced, making this relationship stronger over the years. Pritam and Sunita, the main Hello Kids franchisor have an excellent family-like relationship with Shreya and her team.

For Hello Kids Lilly, advantages of being a part of franchise far outweigh the disadvantages. Ability to show over 540 branches and a brand value has helped them get more enrollments. Any circulars or notifications from the education department or government are automatically circulated by the franchisor, taking away the struggles of managing the outlet to a large extent.

Hello Kids franchise specifically has standardized their process by providing the entire marketing collaterals, school apparatus, and any other teaching aid or materials needed to all their franchisees. So this makes the franchisee's life much easier.

They also have exhaustive training programs charted out for the franchisee owners. Shreya has undergone NTT (Nursery Teachers' Training) and counseling programs. The franchisor also urges their key staff to undergo this training without charging any additional fee so that they can impart this knowledge to the other staff. The trainings included the curriculum walkthrough as well as on usage of the Montessori apparatus. The training has evolved significantly since 2009 as the number of franchisees grew, making the training more interactive and exhaustive with time.

The communication channel is much defined. Mostly the franchisees communicate through messages, calls. Most of their queries are answered over calls. Face to face meetings are reserved for urgent or important matters only. They have a good and knowledgeable customer support. Escalation process is also quite easy and not bureaucratic. An email can be sent to the concerned person copying their director. Necessary documents can be attached to support the issue. The franchiser teams, however, are not allowed to be in touch with the franchisees regularly, but only on need basis. The founders expect the franchisees to function independently after the initial hand-holding support is over.

As we move ahead with our interview to understand the care that needs to be taken when investing in a franchisee, Shreya is quick to share, *"Understanding the genuineness of the franchisor and your own market study is the key. When we initiated our discussions, our franchisor encouraged us to speak to the other franchisees in the area for us to get the first hand experience sharing. We spoke to them, the parents of the school and other teachers and councilors for their feedback. After all, it is a big investment and we wanted to validate not only the option we were considering, but also our ability to manage the business. Interestingly, when we decided to go ahead, we discovered 6 to 7 schools in our own area, making our setup process more challenging due to sheer competition that we'd face. But we were a part of a franchise, so a lot of the risk was mitigated."*

When we asked for the ideal qualities for someone looking to run a franchisee business, Shreya urged them to look beyond money. After all, it is the future of the kids that we're trying to shape. So let money not be the only motivation for anyone to take this step. If you offer quality education, the word of mouth publicity will get you the volumes you're looking for and help you meet your goals automatically, she feels.

In addition to word of mouth, she also invested in parking boards, banners, and newspapers for her advertising. Other than her efforts, the Hello Kids franchise do a PAN-India ad in Times of India along with digital marketing efforts like Facebook marketing, Google AdWords, etc., which they do every year. But the franchisee is responsible for the marketing in their own locality.

Shreya has a unique way of marketing her school. Instead of using traditional marketing techniques, she believes in bringing innovation in her school curriculum. As the school is continuously trying and executing new things, this works as an indirect marketing technique for her, bringing good enrollments for the school. In their region, now she is quite established giving favorable returns.

Hello Kids has provided standardized ERP software to all its franchisees, which takes care of the costs, fees, and other logistical support for the school administration.

We then moved a little more in detail toward the business and financial setup discussions. When asked about the financial projections and accuracy in predictions, Shreya felt that Hello Kids did a wonderful job at projecting their estimates based on their outlet size and the expenses involved. They were always available to guide and help out. Their research while setting up a new franchise was immaculate. So Shreya never had to go back with issues due to incorrect financial forecasts. In fact, the franchiser helped in reducing their marketing budgets by using their contacts and network, thereby transferring the benefits to the franchisees.

Over time, Shreya has expanded and invested more in the business to grow. While the franchiser is available to guide, they have provided Shreya and many like her, the flexibility to mold the curriculum to best suit their requirement. This helps the franchisees to flourish better. Unlike some other leading franchises that are more rigid in their curriculum definitions, Hello Kids has provided a breathing space for their franchisees to grow, giving them a feeling of ownership of their outlet and the brand. This is the main reason why the franchisees stick around for a longer period of time.

Hidden Costs? Not much, says Shreya.

Infrastructure development and maintenance cost need to be factored by the franchisees. If not, you might have some discontented franchisees as they don't consider that in the financial forecasts. Building renovation, apparatus purchase is needed over a period of time. So if a franchise considers only the initial franchise fee as the major investment, it will be up for disappointment. Shreya has invested about INR 15 lakhs toward franchisee fees, setup, and renovation of the premises. Being a bigger campus, the investment in infrastructure was more in their first year. However, she has consistently invested year on year to maintain their standards.

Her acute business sense helped the center achieve a break even in the first year itself. An educationist at heart, she refused to charge a high tuition fee to the students till she was confident on delivering value education to the students. Gradually, once they were established, the fees were increased.

Finally, we did a small rapid fire with Shreya on some general business questions:

As a franchisee what do you think is essential to make this type of a business model a success?
Adding a personal touch to every aspect of the business. Just like caring for your baby, you need to care for the school, taking care of minute aspects like marketing, training the support staff, teachers, etc.

How do you stay updated on industry trends?
The Hello Kids Facebook page has all updates for us. Additionally, I do extensive Google search to know the new trends in the pre-K segment. I follow activities of other schools to know if they're doing something differently, which we can incorporate in our system.

Are there any expansion opportunities for additional franchisee ownership in this system?
Of course. That's how we started the second branch in 2013-2014.

Knowing what you know now would you make this investment again? Would you go in for any other franchisee of Hello Kids also the third one?
I am happy with two branches. I don't think we'd go for the third branch.

What challenges do you foresee in the future for your business?
The biggest challenge we face is losing admissions to main stream school. Unlike a preschool, in a main stream school, once the child takes admissions, he will remain there for the next few years. But we lose a lot of students as parents prefer to put their children in a main stream school with the fear of not getting through in class 1. We lost 110 kids this year, which is very demotivating. In spite of proving ourselves, we lose students as we don't have a main stream school.

What is your next big goal?
I would like to start a main stream school from nursery to 10th std. in CBSE board.

It was a real pleasure listening to Shreya share her experience and business, her challenges, and victories. On a parting note, when we asked her for a message to the aspiring franchisee owners, she said "It's a READY opportunity. GO Grab IT."

Thank you Shreya, it was amazing listening to you and we wish you and Hello Kids Lilly a wonderful year. Wish you all the best for all your future endeavors.

An educationist or a business woman – Ritu Handa from Maple Bear

Today we strike a conversation with Ritu Handa, a franchise owner of Maple Bear for the past 6 years. She owns two franchises in Bangalore and employs a staff strength of 30 including teachers and other support functions. A total of 180 kids are part of the two franchise schools and Ritu has had a fantastic experience of the franchise business model. Maple bear specializes in preschool education and this is what attracted her in the first place.

Maple bear has provided a guiding hand from the start says Ritu, including school curriculum, training, marketing, and any additional tools required for the franchise to succeed. Any and all support be it whatever issue faced by the franchise is addressed by the franchisor and this is a big positive for the brand asserts Ritu. She says Maple Bear has always been there to support the franchises and mentor them in order to succeed.

When asked about her vision for the franchise, Ritu states that her primary goal has been to ensure that her franchise becomes one of the top most schools in the Bangalore area. She believes in making a commitment to the parents of the kids about providing the best education and a healthy environment to learn. She says their journey has begun in the right direction which can be attested by the fact that her franchise has been recognized as the second best franchisee school in Bangalore. She remains faithful to her passion of providing quality education for the children which was the very first reason she decided to get into the franchise business. Money is not the primary motivation for her; it is the joy on the children's face and their curiosity to learn which fuels her drive. She believes in creating children who are not only smart but happy as well.

Ritu says there were a multitude of options available to her for entering into the franchise business. What drove her toward this particular franchise was her attraction and craving to do something in the education sector. She is a big believer of hard work and commitment and firmly believes those are the essential pillars to success. Her motto has always been to follow her heart and work in the field which excites her with the firm belief that success will eventually follow. This is how she decided to foray into the world of franchising by opening up the Maple Bear franchise school in Bangalore.

It was easy for her to pick up any franchise she wanted, but she was looking for something more than money. She evaluated Maple Bear thoroughly and was impressed with their product and offerings including the curriculum. She felt it was one of the best to give a great exposure for children to ensure all around development.

Expanding on her journey during the past 6 years, Ritu mentions that one of the advantages she had was the exposure to the curriculum before embarking on the journey. This does not mean there were no hiccups of growing pains, proclaims Ritu. There is no substitute for hard work and even though the franchisor was rock steady in his support, the ground work for the franchise was still to be done by her. She had the hard task of not only convincing the parents about the curriculum but also to ensure that the teachers and other support staff received the requisite training to succeed. She was not a big advocate of marketing and has always thought that word of mouth was the best strategy. Once people see for themselves the safety of the kids, the learning environment, and hygiene, they become fans of the franchise school. She, however, concedes that the marketing support provided by Maple Bear is excellent and is one of the big reasons for the success of the brand.

Some of the challenges faced by Ritu were concerning the high density of preschools in the area creating a congested environment with the appropriate road access extremely limited. This created a huge competition because every mainstream school also has an affiliated preschool. So you are basically swimming against the current. You have to prove your worth and also convince the parents to enroll your children into your preschool. You also have to fight against rumors and wrong beliefs that say the children will not get admission in the first standard after enrolling in our preschool. As our preschool is only until KG, we have faced situations where parents wanted to take out their kids after 1-2 years as they had apprehensions about getting admission to Std 1 in other schools. We have, however, taken this as an obstacle to overcome by explaining the benefits and unique feature of your school compared to the competition. We believe in a 360 degree development of children and making them strong and confident to face and overcome any challenges they may face.

It gives Ritu immense satisfaction to be in the education sector where she has the opportunity to touch and influence the lives of children and help them develop. The joy on the faces of children propels her toward doubly hard work in order to keep continuously improving. This is not to say that the business is without its fair share of stress. As you're dealing with small children, the safety and security of the kids is of paramount importance. You need to keep a constant watch on the kids to ensure they do not get hurt either during playing or fighting with each other. You need to nurture their creative thinking and provide a positive outlet for their energy. As I am the owner of the school, the ultimate accountability and responsibility lies with me. I have to face the parents on a daily basis and this is the main source of stress for me.

Ritu says the business has affected her personal and family life as well, as running a preschool is akin to a 24/7 job which requires a huge investment of time and effort. My husband has been my rock pillar of strength and has been extremely supportive of my initiatives. My two children have been extremely positive and understanding in the initial stages where the venture took most of my time. The venture is much more stabilized now, and we have an efficient team in place which can handle the running of the operations in my absence. This gives me a little bit more time to have a social life now, but like I mentioned you have to be extremely responsible and caring in this critical sector in which we operate she says as a matter of fact.

Ritu says her experience with the franchisor commitments has been very good with the franchisor having fulfilled all his obligations and providing 100 percent support and training. The franchisor has not promised the moon and has been instrumental in setting realistic goals. They have been upfront about the curriculum and have always helped in solving whichever issues have arisen. This has helped build a trust bridge between the franchisor and the franchisee which has resulted in creating a win-win situation for both.

Ritu highlights the benefits of the franchise business over starting a brand new one on your own, by mentioning that brand visibility plays a critical role in the success. She toyed with the idea of starting her own school, as she had the requisite experience in the field having worked in different verticals. On weighing the pros and cons of this decision, she questioned herself as to what would attract potential customers to her school which would have been a relatively unknown brand. Maple Bear on the other hand is a brand that is well entrenched in the market which will make the job a whole lot easier. Creating the same brand visibility for herself would require substantial investment of capital and resources whereas the franchise option provides a readily established brand to encash upon. This combined with the other systemic advantages like systems, training, infrastructure, and support provided by the franchisor convinced her that the franchise route was the way to go.

When questioned on the secret of her success and the tips she would like to give to potential would be entrepreneurs, she promptly responds there is no shortcut to success. One needs to put in sweat, blood, and tears in the business through sheer hard work and smart work in order to scale the mountain of success. If you do not have the required passion and liking for the area, you will never make it in the business. You need to give your best and as they say fortune favors the brave; keep on treading the path of hard work and success will be at your doorstep. One of the major things to look for before investing in a franchise is to see if your vision and the franchise vision are the same, she advises. Otherwise you will end up spending time, money, and effort toward a wasted cause she cautions.

It is necessary to do your homework about the brand and its performance prior to investing in it recommends Ritu. This homework will also help you mitigate your risks as you are well versed with the product, the brand, and its performance. The inherent advantage of investing in a franchise is you have a ready proven business model which has all the systems and supports inbuilt. All you need is the vision, the passion, and the effort to become successful in the franchise business she says as a matter of fact. Dedication goes a long way toward defining your success she says. It is pertinent to not think of business as an 8 to 8 job but rather a 24/7 commitment. This cannot be a half-hearted effort where you spend your effort and time in multiple avenues. You have to have an inclination toward the field and you have a great responsibility as you are shaping the future generation. You will face a lot many hurdles but you need to persist with your efforts.

Ritu mentions she received valuable support from the franchisor, including a checklist listing down all the essential things to hit the ground running. Curriculum, marketing, training, interiors of the premises and infrastructure, everything is already in place. A team of Canadian people was deployed for training the leaders and teacher training. The attrition rate amongst teachers is high but it is part and parcel of the game. Ritu says in addition to the Maple Bear training programs she has also done a Masters in child development which better equipped her to make an entrance into this field. It was really a hands-on program where they were basically running a free school on the college premises. She also went through various training programs when she was working and tried to grasp as much knowledge as possible.

The training program has also gone through a lot of iterations mentions Ritu with feedback and research contributing toward the betterment of the training program. The trainers were always open to suggestions on improving the effectiveness of the program. Ritu also says the franchisor has a very hands-on approach as far as providing support to the franchisee. They have different teams like the marketing team, the social network team, and the curriculum team who are working tirelessly toward making the franchise more efficient and effective. All you need to do is to reach out to them and they are ever eager to help you out. She emphasizes that even though the marketing support is provided by the franchisor, it is also your responsibility as the business owner to understand the market needs and wants. You need to reach out to the community and find out of the box solutions and methodologies to differentiate your franchise from the rest.

You need to establish an excellent rapport with the parents and offer unique solutions and build a trustful relationship with your clients. The brand also provides a software, which is still undergoing evolution and modification to help run the business effectively.

The territory in which the franchisee operates is extremely profitable to Ritu. *"Sky is the limit, if you invest your time and energy,"* is what she says. Her two franchisees have been extremely successful.

When comparing to other brands in the similar industry, Ritu feels that Maple Bear has an excellent curriculum, giving importance to logical reasoning and similar skills, giving the students an edge over other students. These students also outshine students from many other schools in interviews in other bigger schools, as also identified by principals and teachers.

Ritu who regularly interacts with Hazel Siromani, the MD of Maple Bear India and the other franchisor team, shares a very healthy and positive relationship with them. While she gets a chance to interact with the other franchisees during conventions, her relationship is cordial. It was interesting to know that the franchisor does not assign a regular support team to visit them often after the initial days. But there is a defined communication channel, mainly depending on emails, which can be used for feedback as well. Urgent and pressing challenges are addressed over phone calls.

When Ritu started her first franchisee, the franchisor assisted in creation of accurate financial projections. But since the time she has started, Ritu has expanded and increased her investment for growth. Initially, she had invested around Rs. 15 lakhs for each of her franchisees. With a lot of hard work and efficient planning, Ritu attained breakeven almost by the end of the first year. Her returns were also much more than she expected.

We then did a rapid fire with Ritu with a set of general questions –

As a franchisee, what is important to make this business model a success?
One hundred percent personal involvement to bring life to your vision. Training to your team to show them your vision.

How do you keep yourself updated with industry trends?
Training from various institutions and effective use of Google and social media. We also attend workshops and conventions to network and gain more knowledge.

Are there any expansion opportunities for additional franchisees?
Yes. We are also looking into it by taking more franchisees. Also, we're planning to open main stream schools, but it is a herculean task. It might take some time.

What challenges do you foresee in the future for your business?
Competition with main stream schools and challenge for parents to get their wards in mainstream schools in first standard, due to limited seats. These are two major challenges.

What is your next big goal?
Expansion to own many more franchisees

What is your message for people who want to invest in franchisees?
You should definitely go ahead with the franchisees and I would love to promote Maple Bear to them as I am very happy with the product.

Ritu was very patient and forthcoming with her responses and it was definitely enthralling to hear about her experience and journey. We closed on this wonderful note and with the hope that we get an opportunity to interact with such a wonderful person again soon. We wish her bigger success in her aspiration to grow the Maple Bear franchisee in Bangalore.

Saying HELLO to the KIDS in Hello Kids Champs –Hari Babu

Today we initiate a discussion with Hari Babu who is the franchise owner of Hello Kids, Champs. He says the unique name of his franchise helps people differentiate between his franchise and other franchises of Hello Kids. Each franchise is given a novel name, he mentions with the first preference given to you to come up with a name yourself. In case you are not able to or don't want to do that, an innovative name is provided to you by the franchisor. It is essential to note that this helps to identify your venture in the crowded marketplace.

Hari mentions that as far as the products and services of the franchise go all the necessary support and help is provided by the franchisor's head office. All the necessary planning regarding the location, the setup, the furniture, the toys, etc. is done by the franchisor and thus sets the springboard for your journey. As you know for any business location is the key. The success depends on accessibility and the franchisor helps you to identify and pin point the necessary advantages for that particular area be it an affordable building or brand visibility. The interiors of the classroom including the theme are also designed by the franchisor. The franchisor thus hands you a ready blueprint for success.

Once the necessary infrastructure is setup, the franchisor helps setup the necessary system for smooth functioning of the operations. The requisite training for your teachers and staff as well as the training for the finer nuances of running the operation are also provided. They patiently answer all your questions and queries and diligently follow up on the functioning of the business. The training provided includes not only the methods of teaching and curriculum but also a variety of topics like how to apply for admissions, marketing, pros and cons of marketing, how to overcome competition, and recruitment strategies. The amazingly fast response time of the franchisor is mind boggling and it is one of the prime reasons why Hello Kids as a brand has flourished and so many people want to be associated with the brand. Many people I know start with one franchise business and end up setting many more primarily due to the responsiveness of the management.

Hari says he has been associated with the franchise for over 9 years now and already own two franchises of Hello Kids. He employs a staff of 34 people with over 220+ student strength in the two franchises combined. When he first decided to venture into the franchising world, one of his primary concerns was whether the school business was profitable. There were multiple competitors in the vicinity and they had the early bird advantage as they were already entrenched in the locality. But a big thanks to the marketing and support done by the Hello Kids management we were able to make a mark of our own.

In fact some parents have approached us and requested us to start a bigger franchise school and absolutely loved the services and facilities provided by our school. Hello Kids also runs a bigger international school called Riverstone. It is my goal to start a Riverstone school in another 2 years. This way the kids who join our preschool can continue till fifth grade. I was in a bit of dilemma when I first started Hello Kids but after 9 years I can confidently say I have made the right decisions. The fees charged by Hello Kids are not exorbitant and this combined with the fact that they do not charge high royalty fees makes this a great business decision hands down.

This also allows us to reduce fees for children from lower and middle class families and also fulfill our societal obligation of providing quality education for children of all level of strata without any discrimination. This gives us immense satisfaction and a sense of accomplishment. Hari says he has gained great knowledge and experience working with Hello Kids and feels empowered enough to open a brand for himself. However his relationship with the franchisor is so great that he feels it is more likely he will end up opening five more franchise branches in the coming year.

Quizzed on what made him choose the educational field out of the wide array of businesses to invest in, Hari says his reason was slightly different. He comes from an IT background and he met with an accident in Bangalore about 10 years ago. He was advised by the doctor against exerting himself and was told to work in a job where he could sit for 2-3 hours and complete the work. On full recovery he could go back to his IT profession. Hari confesses that this forced job change due to the accident made him move to the education field for which he developed a passion and decided to pursue the field.

The principal thing that attracted him to the franchisee model was the low investment model offered by the no royalty structure of Hello Kids. It is not always possible to invest 20-30 lakhs in a new business venture he opines. The business should always begin with a low investment and gradually grow in size. This is the reason for choosing the Hello Kids franchise. Reflecting back on his journey in the franchise world, Hari says it was not always a smooth ride. The first year was exceptionally tough as the arena was a new one for everybody involved. Only 70 branches of Hello Kids existed during that time.

The brand presence was not very big but the willingness and the desire to grow shone brightly. We worked very hard during that year and were ably supported by the marketing expertise of the head office. They equipped us with the tools to market ourselves and helped us solve the initial hiccups. They cautioned us that the business will take around a year to settle down before growth happens which is exactly what happened. We had 17 kids in our first year which grew to 35 kids in year 2 and 60+ kids in year 3. The growth potential was widely evident which kept on motivating me to put in more and more efforts. One of the major complaints I have heard from parents of children is that the school management is not sufficiently responsive. I took this as a challenge and assumed full responsibility being available 24/7 to answer any and all queries of parents. This has gotten my franchise a lot of goodwill and positive word of mouth marketing. If you check our franchise rating it is a 4.9 which has helped us retain the positive image in the crowded marketplace and enrolments keep on growing.

Hari says the main challenge that he faced in running the franchise was in the area of recruitment. He was firm in his belief that he had to recruit only those people who had the passion and the drive to impart knowledge and simultaneously learn. He recounts his experience of a lot of housewives coming for interviews who were really not interested in teaching but looking more for a part-time job. I am happy to say my perseverance has paid off says Hari who has a passionate and dedicated teaching staff of 14+ members. Most of them have been with the franchise for 6+ years which is a testament to the smooth and ethical operation of the franchise.

Recruitment and marketing was another area of concern in the initial stages says Hari. He says he has been fortunate to be able to develop a long-term relationship with most of the children due to the very fact that he is always approachable to the parents. This helps parents develop a sense of comfort for the school and the learning environment thereby getting the new admissions in the school is a whole lot easier. This has also helped spread the positive vibe about the school in the entire neighborhood. He proudly states that admissions are always full nowadays and the rush was so great that he contemplated opening a second batch post 2 p.m. He, however, decided against the idea as the afternoon time is resting time for the kids and he did not want to disturb that just for the sake of making a few bucks.

I believe in offering a quality product and maintaining a good relationship with my teaching and nonteaching staff. Attrition will always remain a problem for all businesses and ours is no exception. It is important to treat people right so that they also work like they have a stake in the business. It has always been my motto to not get stressed out. The beginning of the academic year is the most stressful where you are flooded with inquiries for admissions. You have to spend time talking with parents from morning to evening and always have a pleasant demeanor. Over the years I have gotten really good at this and it has been a smooth ride for me.

The thing that I enjoy most about my business is the time I get to spend with the kids. They really are a bundle of joy and once you see their happy and cheerful faces, you forget all your tensions and get engrossed in their little world. I look at the children and their parents as my extended family and they have reciprocated their love likewise. I get invited to the children's birthday parties and feel rejuvenated when I spend a couple of hours at work.

Hari says Hello Kids have a very structured and systematic training program for the franchises. It begins with sessions on Child psychology, Management, Marketing, and Counseling the parents which form the four pillars of your business. The area was new for us and the training definitely helped us prepare ourselves for running the venture. Hello Kids also emphasizes that each kid is unique and the solutions need to be catering to their different needs as well. The training program gives you an insight into how a child's mind functions and how to work with them effectively.

The second most important thing that the training program does is teach Hari and his team on how to efficiently interact with the parents of the children. Parents have a lot of common and uncommon questions and the training program told us how to handle those. Additionally in Bangalore there are a lot of education expos which the franchisor encourages us to attend in order to keep updated with the trends and methods in the education sector. The training program has continuously evolved over the years, and we also get visitors who share their expertise and help us continuously improve ourselves. Hello Kids is a member of early kids' education Association and through this membership we receive regular updates on child psychology, academics, and emerging trends.

When asked about the marketing strategies he used in the beginning and their effectiveness, Hari said he started his marketing on a very preliminary level by putting up hoardings, in apartments, buildings, etc. He also placed ads in the magazines and distributed flyers to improve visibility. Over time he has effectively used social media as a powerful tool to propagate his franchise. While the old marketing ideas still persist, the advent of technology has revolutionized the marketing methods. Every year newer techniques emerge which are adopted and used resourcefully.

Hari remarks that the franchisor is always available to support you and help you whenever needed. That said you need to show willingness and efforts on your part as well if you want the business to flourish. Every month there are sessions on marketing and newer techniques and tactics are discussed. We also have a WhatsApp group where we are linked with other franchises and discuss and resolve problems and issues. This group has been of enormous help as readymade solutions are already available for most problems and there is no need to reinvent the wheel.

Hari says some of the other promotional activities that he carries out are theme-based celebrations like Diwali, Sports day, etc. The events are then uploaded online to create a franchise presence. In addition a weekly planner is also in place. Technology has made it easier for parent to track the progress of their child and also be involved in their child's development. He also comments that they use U-phony software which is like a digital diary for the parents. You can connect with them via a single click and they can send their queries or notes in a jiffy. Fee reminders and important notifications are also sent through this app.

Hari then turns to the business side of things commenting that this business has given him very favorable returns and compared to other business this model is a really profitable one. He cautions, however, that there is no substitute to passion and hard work if you want this model to succeed. He mentions his franchise has won an award for good XXX at the national franchise meet which is held on a yearly basis. He introduced a novel concept of a talking tree which would interact with the students which is the main reason he received the award.

On a parting note, Hari mentions that the owner of Hello Kids is a good friend and getting into the franchise business was one of the best decisions of his life. His phone is always off the hook with queries from parents of the 200+ students enrolled in his school. He mentions admiringly that the franchisor has always attended his calls and sometimes when he couldn't he has always called back to resolve any problems faced by him. All in all it has been a win-win situation based on mutual synergy and harmony.

A heart-to-heart discussion with an educationist and a teacher – Meet Nagamani Rao from Maple Bear

Nagamani Rao is an owner of the Maple Bear franchise, an international brand offering world class pre-K education program. She's been running her franchise for around 7 years and aspires to start an elementary program in the next year or so.

Nagamani runs her center with 15 employees and has around 80 students. As a franchisor, Maple Bear has offered a complete package from the curriculum to location scouting as well as the setting up the place, setting up the infrastructure, helping with the admission process, calculation of the rate of return on investing in a particular location and technical support and assisting with the entire process till they're admitted in Maple Bear.

Nagamani is very passionate about her work. Even her vision statement corroborates her thoughts. With the thought that *"No child must be left behind when it comes to education,"* Nagamani's admission process does not select students based on any short listing process. She aims to understand and adhere to each child and their needs. The school aims to provide the children with basic foundation that will help them later on. Leaving aside the educational part, it's the social and emotional impacts that also affect the children. This is very critical in the cognitive space and this is where Nagamani is focused on.

It was interesting to know that Nagamani comes from an educational background and starting an elementary school was always on the cards. But education and business are two separate things and she was not very confident about her business skills. Finally, as the elementary school involved a big investment and concentration that she couldn't sustain, she decided on kick starting with a preschool. The next key decision was going ahead with a franchise model as they help with a readymade package, making the setup process much easier. She did an exhaustive analysis on various available options. Being from the educational field, it was important to choose a franchise that aligned to her way of thinking.

Maple Bear's curriculum and their focus on early age education were the key reasons for choosing this franchise. This is a rare model that focuses not only on early age education but also skill developing. For this, they keep themselves updated when it comes to the curriculum, the activities or factors that can harness a child's growth.

Nagamani walks us through her journey regarding his business venture by mentioning that Maple Bear had provided a clear business plan prior to the start of the business. They had also taken her to one of the existing franchises to get a clear idea on how the model functions. She also did her groundwork before taking the plunge. Maple Bear helped her setup the franchise including infrastructure, décor, and the furniture as well. They have a tie up with various vendors who provide these services that make the job of setting up a whole lot easier. Adequate support was also provided for the admission process, recruitment of students and teachers and also a clear cut idea about how the profits would be divided. This helped her make an instantaneous decision to sign up in February and open in March.

The travel has not been without speed bumps though says Nagamani. She, however, looks at every challenge as an opportunity to improve and traverse on the improvement path. She has faced challenges right from the admission to the location finalization. I was told the breakeven period would be about a year but that was also not easy. The main challenge in the preschool arena is the mindset of the parents says Nagamani. Regular schools have it easier as the child once enrolled will leave the school after graduation. This is typically not the case with a preschool venture and we have to convince the parents about the advantages and benefits of enrolling their wards in our school. As the children are small special efforts to ensure security and safety of children become an absolute necessity. This problem is not uncommon for established preschools as well.

Nagamani's passion is to instill knowledge in the young children's mind in order to shape their future. He believes preschool is the stepping stone toward a better tomorrow. Money for her is secondary and the happiness and joy that she sees on the children's faces exhilarates her. If money was the only criteria, she could have started any other business she says curtly. The franchise school also requires a 24/7 commitment and needs involvement in every operation of the business. Cash flow is of primary importance, and it is extremely important to keep enough cash flow for 1 year are her words of wisdom for the entrepreneurs eager to set foot in this business.

The franchise school has had an impact on her personal and family life she says as a matter of fact statement. The decision to start the school was motivated by her desire to spend more time with her son, and work for the benefit of society at large. However, during the initial stages she used to work long hours including Sundays and there really is no family time. Even though the passion was there, it was a very stressful time but she was lucky to have a largely supportive family. She is a fighter by nature and has successfully battled and won against the dreaded disease cancer. Her family now looks to her as a source of inspiration and she has won admiration from all quarters. She is almost a role model now for many and also runs a counseling center for people battling cancer as well.

She mentions that the franchisor was upfront and honest about the various franchise models, which were available and she could choose from. The franchisor was also particular about the business flow she says but will never compromise on the basic principles. They are with you every step of the way and guide you through any issues like extra training for staff, how to apply revenue, supplies, etc. This support system is one of the main reasons she recommends the franchise business rather than starting an independent one. Even though you may not be from the same background, the existing systems and procedures offer you a much better chance of success. This is especially true for women says Nagamani, and she has gained immense knowledge and expertise in the 7 years as she started her franchise. Franchising is the way to go she replies confidently.

Interpersonal relationships are the keys to success and this is especially true for the service industry. She has always believed in building relations and you need to build a bond with the parents who are leaving their most precious treasure (their little ones) in your hands. You need to assure them that you will maintain their trust and work with all the integrity toward making the school a successful one.

Investing in a franchise requires a lot of homework and background research before investing in the franchise business. You need to be aware of the brand presence and value, the fee structure, the amount of control given by the franchisor, the revenue model, the ROI tenure, etc. The franchise model still helps you mitigate the risks because you have an existing model which is well established and entrenched. In order to enter in the business world you should be willing to take risks says Nagamani and also should be invested in it full time if you want to scale the ladder of success. Once the location is finalized the franchisor provides all the support for the interiors of the place. They have a ready set of vendors and you don't have to spend time looking for them. Vendors are also present for supply of regular material.

The initial training provided is for the teachers as well as staff and includes the philosophy, values, and vision of Maple Bear. This helps us work toward the common goals. We have trainers come in from Canada on a regular basis. Constant knowledge upgradation takes place and in house training is also provided to the staff on how to create a comfortable environment for the children. There is also a marketing training program to help grow the business. The training program evolves with time and feedback which show the management's commitment toward continuous improvement.

The marketing strategies used by me include door to door marketing, newspaper ads, banners, and posters to improve visibility. We have also started using the online medium which is omnipresent now to improve franchise exposure. One of the good things about Maple Bear is they are ever ready to help but do not impose themselves on you. They give you the necessary space and freedom to operate and do not interfere in day to day operations. This gives you a certain level of autonomy which every business person is looking for. They are also always open to suggestions and take all feedback in a positive sense. One example I would like to quote is a change of curriculum which I proposed was well liked and implemented. I am also a part of the back thinking and pack committee which is tasked with upgrading the curriculum. We have also started using digital marketing in a big way.

We also try to improve our franchise visibility through networking. Word of mouth marketing has worked wonders for us in this business. We attend workshops, seminars, and meetings to improve our networking reach. The brand also has a special software which is used to share the entire process from taking admissions, sharing progress, fee structure, pay out, etc with the parents. This has made managing the process flow a whole lot easier.

Nagamani says that as far as the curriculum goes, Maple Bear is way ahead of the curve and miles ahead of the competition. She, however, feels they need to improve on enhancing the brand visibility.

Nagamani's relationship with her fellow franchisers is a little tricky as they are both colleagues and competitors. Even though they are working for the same brand, each franchise is striving toward increasing their market share. That said most of the owners are thoroughly professional but are focused on their individual growth. Nagamani says the communication with the franchisor is a two-way street. She has had great experience with the franchisor and even though they are geographically located in different regions of India (Delhi and Bangalore), the phone line communications are always on. The face-to-face meetings happen on a need basis and the franchisor is always available to answer any questions and solve any queries you might have.

She mentions that the turnaround time from the franchisor to any complaint raised by her is really small. She feels they are like an extended family and has only positive things to say about them. She also mentions that the financial projections including the capital investment were more or less accurate within a 10 percent variation. The investment required in the initial 3 years was high but started decreasing subsequently once the franchise stabilized. She, however, expected the breakeven period to be faster. She started with an initial investment of 30 lakhs and the breakeven period was around 3 years with the returns varying from 30 to 50 percent.

She mentions that it is critical as a franchisee that you do your homework before you make a decision to invest in the franchise business. You need to ask a lot of questions and gather all the relevant information before taking the plunge. You also need to keep updated with the latest information through networking. She is a part of the ICSE board and gets a lot of inputs through that association. She feels the market is overcrowded which is making the competition fierce and increasing the breakeven periods. As the investment required is not exorbitant, there are no entrance barriers.

Nagamani's next goal is to make an entrance into the elementary arena. She dreams of starting a sports school. She feels we have an overemphasis on education but not on all round development including sports. She believes the reason why we don't have a lot of people representing our country in Olympics is the fact that we always give importance to studies but rarely look at sports as a career. She wants to do her small part to change that. To the people who are thinking of entering the business world, she recommends franchising is the right way to start. Once you gain enough confidence and understand the finer nuances of the operations, you always have the option of expanding or starting your own setup.

Interview with Ahmed Adhly Rasheed – Kangaroo Kids

Ahmed Adhly Rasheed is the Executive Director of Islanders Education based in the Maldives, and is also the master franchisee of Kangaroo Kids Education Limited in India. Mr. Rasheed has been with the franchise for 10 years and began his journey in the franchise world in 2009. The trip began with the setting up of Kangaroo Kids preschool and a Billabong High International School together, with approximately about 600 kids.

This venture has now expanded into a Kangaroo Kids Preschool with strength of about 1,000 kids and a Billabong High International School with strength of about 780 kids from grades 1 to 12. Ahmed mentions that Addu, a city to the extreme south, and Fuvahmulah, also in the south, are the other two cities which also have franchises of Kangaroo Kids and Billabong High. The plan is to expand into another city Thinadhoo, which is located in the south. This will result into a total of four preschools and four Billabong Highs in Maldives.

When probed about the vision of the company, he promptly mentions that in 2009 when he began his journey, the education sector was in a unique spot. Private education was mostly a closed door affair predominantly dominated by the government which operated and owned the schools. It was difficult for private players to make a foray into the education sector because the market place was relatively small. It was very difficult to build a school infrastructure, which proved to be a barrier for private education to make an entrance into the market.

The government also mandated that schools are to provide free education to all Maldivians. This began changing during the 2010 time frame which presented us an opportunity to lease a government school building and start a private school. Islanders Education is essentially a family business. Leena who started Kangaroo Kids used to frequent us and stay at one of our resorts. We have seen the growth of Kangaroo Kids from close quarters, right from its very inception. Due to our proximity with Leena, we were familiar with her vision, her values, and passion for the education sector development. This made Kangaroo Kids a natural choice for us.

This is how we decided to sign up with Leena and looking back upon our journey, I sincerely believe we have made the right decision. We have been able to grow the franchise phenomenally, so much so that even the immigration officers you meet on your journey to Maldives are well aware of the brand. Kangaroo Kids and Billabong High are renowned all over Maldives. Our vision has always been to do something different than the competition and this is exactly what we have achieved in Maldives. We have made our mark in the education sector dominated by public schools and opened the doorway for private schools to enter and succeed. This has been Leena's vision as well.

When inquired about the history with the preschool franchise, Ahmed retorts that he has been an entrenched player with over 10 years of experience. He is thankful for being granted the opportunity through a government proposal to start the very first private school in Maldives. What has gravitated him toward this particular franchise is the owner's vision and passion. The owner and the curriculum developers meticulously write exactly what needs to happen in the classroom every day. The vision is scripted perfectly and the procedures structured in such a way that the franchisee can operate smoothly without the need of going back to the owner for everything. The systematic and simple methodology has greatly benefited him since he was new to the education field. This is also one of the reasons for the success of the franchise.

Ahmed mentions it has not been a bed of roses all the time but he has also faced some challenges along the way. The journey was relatively smoother compared to other franchises as there was a pre-existing rapport with Leena who was a friend as well. This established a level of comfort which was responsible for smooth sailing in the initial phases. The Kangaroo Kids has matured in the Indian market but the Maldives market offers unique challenges due to difference in culture, religion, and society. Also development of a global model requires you to make adjustments and modifications to suit the specific geographical requirements. This has been the main challenge so far says Ahmed.

The success in the education sector requires a combination of curriculum as well as the right team to successfully execute the franchise operations. As the private school is a relatively new occurrence in Maldives, the teachers trained in the public education sector may not possess the required skill set to work in the private education area. This entails the retraining of the teachers which needs to be managed properly if the franchise is to succeed.

When asked about what he enjoys the most in the running of a business, he promptly responds that he is involved in a lot of businesses in Maldives, with the education sector forming only one part of the business. Shaping young minds through proper education is what fascinates him and drives his passion. He has strived to provide quality education to Maldivians, and this has proved to be the biggest source of joy and happiness for him. The biggest thing that Kangaroo Kids has achieved is to make preschools an imminent part of the children's education. Prior to this, most Maldivians sent their kids aged 2-7 years to community school which in essence was a day care. The focus of the school from Grade 1 to Grade 10 was only on marks and not the overall development of children. This made people believe that if the children of the school are getting good grades, the school is very good. However, the truth was that schooling in Maldives was a monotonous thing, where you study with the only intent of passing and keep moving from one grade to another essentially as a robot who is trained to pass papers. It is entirely possible that you do not know the answers to the question which do not appear in the exam paper.

With the advent of Kangaroo Kids, the private school education world was opened to Maldivians. The emphasis was on overall development of the children with a special importance on preschool education. Special days and activities are planned to make learning a fun activity for the children. The primary school children do phenomenon-based learning like reading a book of Charlie and the Chocolate Factory before branching out to Geography, Language, and Poetry. The focus is on learning and understanding and not mugging up the syllabus. These were the unique offerings of Kangaroo Kids.

He proudly states that their school was the very first which preached that results are not everything, but it is the all around development and happiness of the children that is of prime importance. Most preschools in Maldives are now following the Kangaroo Kids footsteps, and Ahmed is proud of having revolutionized the education segment of Maldives. The journey of Kangaroo Kids was actually a test case scenario to see if the government and private education could gel and be successful. The landmark success of the franchise has opened up vast avenues for private and public partnerships thus making the franchise as one of the pioneers in the education field.

When queried about how the franchise business affected his personal and family life, Ahmed says that he has always been busy. He has thoroughly enjoyed doing things that made a difference and the franchise provided a great avenue. His family had always been in the retail and resort sector, but this opportunity presented a unique challenge. In the resort sector you interact with the customers only for a limited time. In the education field, however, you are associated with children for 15–16 years of their life and are instrumental in shaping their careers. You feel a sense of pride when you see them graduate and move through life. It brings a sense of nostalgia and gratification when the children meet you later and tell us how we touched their life.

Ahmed then recounts his experience with the franchise in the capacity of a franchisee owner. He vividly tells that while signing the franchise agreement no lofty promises were made. Everything that was in the franchise contract was provided including the support and systems. There were challenges along the way but Leena and her team were always available for guidance and help. The franchise owner didn't just sign the agreement and leave us in the lurch but was with us every step of the way. In addition a brand representative for the country was always available who we could call or get in touch with anytime. The relationship always had a personal touch which was instrumental in us hitting the ground running.

I can honestly tell you the benefits of franchising says Ahmed with a smile. You end up accumulating a wealth of knowledge and don't have to struggle even if you don't have any experience in the field. In our case we got knowledge and experience of sixty plus curriculum designers who have done thousands of hours of work and continue to do that work every year. If we were to do the same on our own I don't think we had the kind of resources or the investment to succeed he says frankly. The quality of the work is of prime importance if you want to sustain success in the long run and this is where Kangaroo Kids has excelled says Ahmed.

Elaborating on the success of his venture, Ahmed says it is the determination, vision, passion, and nurturing that he and his team put in that has worked wonders for them. This included his parents, teachers, and senior members of his team. Everybody was working in harmony and synergy toward a common goal. The passion and the dedication were way beyond the salary and we could see a personal commitment from everybody involved. He mentions it is critical to evaluate the franchise brand before venturing into the business. You need to be well versed with the product, the franchise people, the systems, and the infrastructure support provided and the franchisors dedication and passion to see the franchise succeed. There are multiple franchises out there and you need to make the right choice and find the synergetic partner to make it work. You also need to have the drive to design and develop the franchise. Lastly the franchisor support and presence is a vital cog in the franchise business and very often plays an important role in attainment of the goals.

Ahmed says he has received unflinching support for his venture from the franchisor with Leena herself engaging with the government even before he signed on the dotted line of the contract. She herself made the presentation to the government and was in constant touch throughout the growing pains of the franchise. The franchisor team was ever ready and eager to help. The Kangaroo Kids team came during the launch and help setup the infrastructure for the school. Everybody from the principal, teachers, and other admin staff were trained on all processes. The school thus began on a sound note and the training program has kept on improving over the years. The experience has been rewarding and enriching.

Expanding on the marketing strategies that were implemented for the franchise, Ahmed says as his franchise was one of the very first international school, there was a huge demand and not a whole lot of marketing was required. Over the years the brand grew from strength to strength and the seats were always full with very few vacancies available. As Maldives had a lot of public schools but very few private schools, there was always a rush for seats in his school. He counts himself among the few lucky ones who entered the market at the precise time. He also mentions that the basic branding of Kangaroo Kids is provided by the franchisor while the local marketing is handled by them.

Even though the initial sailing was smooth, Ahmed has been working untiringly to differentiate his brand from the competition. As is the need of any place the brand needs to adapt to the surrounding environment to assimilate with the local populace. Kangaroo Kids provides an enterprise resource and sends their curriculum through data right protected files he says. He also mentions that the brand is developing their own software which will be launched next year. The ROI for Ahmed has been quite favorable and allowed him to expand his turf.

Questioned on what competitive advantages his brand enjoys over the competition, he clarifies that there are no international preschools in Maldives which offers them a distinct advantage. He has also distinguished his franchise school by participating in global competitions as well as other programs which will eventually get integrated in the franchise format. He is not in touch with the owners of other Kangaroo Kids franchises but does meet them once a year in a get-together of sorts. He, however, values his friendship with the franchisor as in addition to the business relationship, it is also at a personal friendship level. A daily open communication channel portal is always open with the franchisor.

Ahmed informs us that any complaint regarding any issue is communicated to the franchisor via a coordinator who is the focal point for the franchise. For example if there is any issue with financing or accounting, the coordinator is contacted who then conveys the issue to the Kangaroo Kids Education Limited (KKEL) Finance Team. If required the concerned parties can then get together on a conference call to resolve the issue. One of the main difficulties faced by the franchise with the franchisor is the difference in the academic year of the franchisor and the franchisee. The key has always been successful resolution through mutual agreement and consultations.

Ahmed says that there were no projections made by the franchisor regarding the amount of capital requirement for starting the franchise. This was primarily on account of the market being different than the one in India. He also expounds that there are further investments required as the franchise grows but says he has not incurred any hidden fees or unexpected costs. He clarifies that the return on investment was in line with his expectations and the essential ingredients for success entailed hard work, passion, and dedication. One also had to stay tuned with the industry trends and technologies. Attending educational conferences is one way of doing that. He says given an opportunity he would invest in the franchise again in a heartbeat.

Asked about his future vision for the business, Ahmed responds promptly that remaining committed to the values of the franchise and the vision of providing quality education is essential. Competition will always be omnipresent but one needs to take it as a challenge and keep driving toward the goal. Growth is essential for survival and one needs to evolve with time. Ahmed's goal is to build more schools and by 2024 branch out to Sri Lanka and other markets.

On a parting note we ask Ahmed what is the advice he would like to give to people eager to invest in a franchise. He says it is necessary to be aware that just because you are a franchisee, everything will be handed to you on a silver plate. You still need to put our heart and efforts toward ensuring the success of the franchise. There is no substitute for hard work. Owning a franchise only provides you the platform to take your leap. It is entirely your grit and efforts that will see you cross the finish line. After all you need to remember, it's your business and ultimately you are responsible for the success and failure of the venture.

Turning her passion to her employment – Meet Ms. Jaya Prasad from Delhi, Maple Bear Franchisee

Our distinguished guest today is Jaya Prasad who has been associated with Maple Bear for 15 years now as a franchise owner. She owns two franchises of Maple Bear in Vasundra in Ghaziabad and Indrapuram in Delhi. She has a total of 31 employees and 286 students are enrolled in the two centers combined. Jaya's plan is to increase the admission count to 350 by this year end. The classes are from toddler to Grade 5. Jaya and her family hail from Patna, and education has always been a passion for her. Her desire to propel quality education for everyone was what attracted her to the franchise world. Her source of inspiration is her father-in-law who in spite of being a doctor by profession volunteers to open different schools.

Jaya recounts her journey with Maple Bear and how she got attracted to the franchise. She was always driven by quality not quantity and wanted to ensure that the credibility and integrity of the school be above reproach. She did her background research by looking at various schools in Patna and was flummoxed by the lack of kindergarten school and saw this as an area where she could contribute. One day in 2003, she saw an advertisement in the newspaper regarding a franchise for Maple Bear. She and her husband were impressed with the uniqueness in curriculum and setup offered by

Maple Bear and decided that this is the brand which they should sign up for. They also had a meeting with the Canadian team before signing which only reinforced their view that this is the right brand to begin their journey in the franchise world. She mentions there were many applicants for the franchise ownership and counts herself among the lucky ones to have finally received the nod for operating the franchise.

Walking us through the initial steps of her franchise business, Jaya recalls that she started the business with very few employees. All the work for the school including the equipment, furniture, etc. was done by the small team which included her husband, her business partner Shalini Jaiswal, and Hazel. The marketing began on a very preliminary note with word of mouth marketing where she and her team would go to every society in Noida and explain about the franchise school. Advertising those days was pretty expensive she laments. She started with three kids which increased to six by the first quarter and seventeen by the end of the term. Extensive training was carried out by the Canadian team of Maple Bear for the teachers as well as the staff on how to efficiently run the operations.

The brand awareness was low at the beginning but with persistent efforts from the team, we began to get more visibility. The school continued to see an increase in enrollment and by the fourth year they were already looking for a bigger place. A transport facility was also started in order to provide convenience to the parents and children. She and her husband were closely involved in the operations and would often tell stories, take classes, and even drive the transport van. She is a firm believer in dignity of labor and never considers any work as unworthy. Their commitment and dedication resulted in the school being recognized for curriculum, methodology, and quality. Such was her devotion to the franchise school success cause that she has herself cooked food for the day care students which she had started. She says the experience has helped her grow as a person and she is currently running both the school as well as the day care. Her business partner Shalini has eventually moved to the head office says Jaya.

Jaya says that Maple Bear provides everything from the curriculum to the training (teachers, staff, owners) as well as the stationary. Maple Bear is really particular with the training as well as adherence to the curriculum. Regular audits are conducted to detect process flaws and solution to all issues that are implemented. The head office is always available for resolution of queries. Jaya's vision for the company is to open additional centers of the Maple Bear franchise. She is insistent on maintaining a 20-2 student to teacher ratio in order to ensure that the quality of education does not suffer. She believes in personal attention for the students and wants the franchise credibility to be always at 100 percent. Her plan is to open smaller schools in different localities with the main center in Indrapuram to propagate the flame of quality education through the excellent curriculum of Maple Bear. Her emphasis has always been quality is a habit and she has strived hard to stay true to her motto.

The major challenge faced by Jaya for her franchise school was the hiring of the right teachers. Her expectations are high as she holds herself responsible for ensuring that the students get the best education possible. The second biggest hurdle was to establish a rapport and convince parents to enroll their precious little ones in our school. This has been resolved to a certain extent now as the brand is now well established and the franchise school has garnered an excellent reputation. Jaya believes the biggest asset that she possesses is the faith and trust of the parents and children. She immensely enjoys the company of children and frequently spends her morning reading stories to the children. It gives her great elation when the children, hug, and greet her. They are now an integral part of her family. Seeing them brings a sense of vigor and energy in her and makes her feel younger every day.

She is candid, however, to admit that it is not smooth sailing all the time. The competition is pretty fierce and new schools keep popping up which offer lower fees. The quality of education for these schools is also low but parents sometimes look at only the cost factor. Maple Bear does a lot of extracurricular activities to increase the confidence of the children and make them independent which the lower cost schools do not offer. She sheepishly says that she is a sweet person by nature but cannot tolerate indiscipline and lethargy when it comes to behaving with children. It takes a single moment to ruin a reputation built over years she mentions.

Education has always been in their blood says Jaya. It was always her husband's dream to take a leap into the franchise school business. Her mother was not very happy she admits bluntly. She has come from a wealthy background and moving to Delhi from Patna and staying in a rented house was quite a shock for her mother. She also had to worry about the impact the move would have on her two daughters who were studying in third grade and tenth grade at that time. She proudly comments that her in-laws were extremely supportive emotionally as well as financially. Her husband always had a positive state of mind and looked at each challenge as a learning opportunity. The cash flow, additional investment, and revenue generation were other things that weighed on the back of their mind, but they faced the challenges head on. They received ample support and motivation from the head office as well.

Jaya has only positive things to say about Maple Bear and says they have always delivered whatever they promised. There were initial hiccups as they were not originally from Delhi, but the head office and Hazel were always there for her. No relationship is without its ups and down she says frankly, but the positives were abundant while the lows were infrequent. Her husband initially wanted to start his own brand with senior classes. This was their original idea when they moved to Delhi. However, in 2010 they dropped the idea because of their daughter's wedding plan and they had grown so enamored with the Maple Bear franchise and their curriculum that she had her heart set on the franchise. She feels a sense of pride representing the brand and is always looking to take up more challenges like opening up the elementary section. She was one of the very first to do that and wants to keep on continuing the success of the franchise school. She has decided that she does not want to expand till twelfth grade but rather focus her energy and efforts on opening and running of smaller centers.

Quizzed on the secret recipe to her success, she enthusiastically responds that she attributes to her discipline and effective utilization of time. She is extremely punctual and believes in giving her 100 percent to whatever task she undertakes. She firmly believes that no work is menial and never says no to any task. She is detail oriented and knows every aspect of the operation first hand. Money is not the motivating factor for her, and she is a patient listener. She tries to understand each situation and takes an unbiased view of things. She is also available at any time for parents and their queries. Perseverance and dedication are ingrained qualities for her which has made her ascend the ladder of success.

She cautions that before investing in a franchise one needs to ascertain the location, the capital investment required, and the brand. You need to take into account additional expenses like salaries, utility bills, rent, etc. Her advice is to start small and then expand rather than investing a huge amount at the very beginning. The ROI calculations need to be prepared and cash flow needs to be monitored. She, however, is of the firm opinion that once the homework is done investing in a franchise is significantly less risky than starting your own business. The mantra for success is dedicate time and effort toward the cause. Treat your staff as your extended family and be nice and courteous to them she instructs. She recommends to be patient and identify a proper location as that goes a long way in determining visibility and ultimately success. Last but most important she notes is to be updated with the latest trends and tirelessly market your franchise.

Jaya lavishes praise on the franchisor for all the support he has provided to ensure her franchise becomes successful. The franchisor recommended a huge hoarding at the very beginning of the franchise which even though expensive has worked wonders for her school. They were very involved in all activities right from doing a day out to the grand opening for their franchise. She fondly remembers the opening of their franchise recollecting that all the education heads from Delhi, Noida, Gurugram, etc. visited the opening. Almost 50 school principals were also present along with the whole

Maple Bear Canada team. She is especially thankful to Hazel and Aparna Vedant for all their help in making the opening a grand success. It provided tremendous visibility for the school she concedes. The Maple Bear team is also closely involved in training and knowledge upgradation.

Jaya found the training provided by the franchisor extremely helpful. The training topics included not only the curriculum but also on how to conduct the business effectively. Along with guidance, the franchisor also recommended multiple books which were of tremendous value for Jaya and her husband. Additionally training was also provided on how to counsel. The trainings occur at regular frequencies and Jaya takes the time to attend most of them. Thirst for knowledge is what drives her to attend as many training programs as possible. The trainings have also undergone a change over the recent years with the trainings becoming more focused on not only the curriculum but also solving problems and issues faced by the franchise.

On inquiring what marketing strategies worked best for her, Jaya says they started with hoardings which gave them good visibility. They also held workshops to improve the franchise presence. Her biggest gainer in terms of marketing has been word of mouth, due to the quality of education and comfortable learning environment provided by her school. Franchisor supports in continual with audits, Skype calls, mails, etc. She has also taken initiative to solve some of the problems on her own. Jaya laments that social media is still not being effectively used by the brand. The promotions are still in the form of workshop, seminars, and banners. The franchisor team is available for the promotional activities whenever informed.

Jaya also attracts potential clients by giving the early bird discount. She also ensures her annual day is an open park affair so that everyone from Noida can come and see. In addition stage show has been a major crowd puller providing the franchise with a lot of positive visibility. Varied themes and winter and Diwali carnivals have ensured footfalls of 1000+ people. The school gets certainly highlighted at these events and results in increased enrollment for the school. Jaya also takes this occasion to once again emphasize the superiority of the Maple Bear curriculum compared to other schools and stressed this in all the discussions with parents. The franchise is truly utilizing technology with the admission process completely online. The franchise also uses a software MMBS which the parents can use to track and monitor the progress of their child as well as receive notifications and communication from the school. This has made the entire system highly proficient.

Jaya has a very good relationship with her franchisor but hardly meets them face to face. The discussions are centered on improvements and suggestions for better growth. She also helps guide newer entrepreneurs keen to join the Maple Bear franchise brand. Most of the communication takes place through emails. Her daughter has joined her in taking care of the business and focuses on the business part whereas Jaya focuses on the curriculum and day to day operations. She vouches for the franchisor saying their investment projections were mostly on the money. Of course there were additional incidental expenses like play areas, ACs, etc. However, there were no hidden fees and the initial investment for Jaya was between 40 and 50 lakhs including rental and salaries.

The ROI for her was 3 years and was pretty much in line with her expectations. She has an inquisitive mind and keeps herself updated on industry trends through reading and traveling. Her vision for the future entails starting multiple centers which she can run but does not want to take additional investment responsibilities. She is averse to increasing of fees and is a firm believer of affordable education for all. She is always ready to guide and counsel young entrepreneurs looking to invest in the franchise business. Her message is loud and clear: differentiate yourself from the crowded marketplace if you want to succeed.

Changing the way the world does business – Meet Mr. Rajkumar Kamat, Executive Director, BNI – Goa Region

One of the most dynamic personalities that we have ever met, the Executive Director of BNI in the Goa region, the founder of EP Kamat Group, Mr. Rajkumar Kamat comes across as a very affable and easy going personality. We thank him for agreeing to speak to us and taking time out of his busy schedule as we commence the interview.

"A lot of business people are in the BNI franchising system, how did you come across it?" BNI is a numero uno institute when it comes to business networking. It is Mr. Kamat who brought this great opportunity to Goa in 2007–2008, providing a huge platform for the Goan business fraternity to thrive and flourish. In the same year, Mr. Kamat was the Chairman of Microenterprises and was striving for their betterment.

"I needed to concentrate in two areas, the paperwork and marketing. For paperwork we filed with the government to reduce paperwork and sent them a proposal. For marketing we used something called the **Price Difference Rate Contract Scheme** *by the government of Goa where we file the requirement for JHRSSICT with the government. This was the key department for purchasing from micro-departments in Goa. So, the micro-industries were supposed to register with them. I came to the board of JHRSSICT and started strengthening it, as not a lot of departments were comfortable registering with them."*

"Since it's a government organization and a lot of decisions were supposed to be made from their side, we went through a lot of board meetings in the beginning before we could strengthen properly. In time, a lot of departments started procuring from JHRSSICT to increase the sales of the smaller departments through the government. But one of the drawbacks that I witnessed was that the effort was more and the result was less. There was constant stress going on to increase the result. It was that time that I thought of entering the private market instead of breaking my head with the government."

"When we were figuring out ways about how to go into it, I was invited into a BNI meeting in Pune. I went to the meeting and I was mesmerized by what I saw. I saw multiple professionals attending the meeting and passing business onto each other. I knew this was the platform we were looking for. After that, I met the national director of BNI India and that's how it started."

This is a true entrepreneur who not only identified an opportunity but also took the necessary steps to execute it successfully in the Goa region. In the BNI framework, Mr. Kamat owns two franchisees dividing Goa into two mail regions—North Goa and South Goa. Setting up BNI in Goa was a bit of a challenge due to the cultural gap. In the *susegad* Goan lifestyle, getting businessmen for an early morning breakfast meeting still remains one of the key challenges of BNI in Goa.

But Mr. Kamat is focused and passionate about BNI which he believes to be a social enterprise. *"When I got this business in the beginning, I didn't even know it was a franchisee. Handling two regions was becoming too much for me, that's when the franchisee concept was explained to me."* The beauty of BNI is that it gives people an opportunity to grow their business and generate employment, which is the best part. When Rajkumar started his entrepreneurial journey more than two decades ago, his mission was to generate employment for around 1000 people during the year 1993-1995. But as BNI Goa Region has started, as a team, it is inspiring to see more than 10,000 youth employed through business generated through BNI. And that is his driving force.

Rajkumar was so motivated to help people and enamored with the BNI concept, he unconditionally accepted BNI and its policies. With the excellent support from the National team, BNI Goa region was established.

"When you start something new, either you learn through trial and error or you follow a defined effective methods that have been put across. You learn through other people's experience and expertise. It helps you start immediately with readymade expertise" shares Rajkumar.

They never did any major promotional activity for BNI in Goa and relied heavily only on word of mouth publicity. "Initially it was a set of 10–12 people who I personally knew and who liked the concept, came in to check it out. The same *people recommended it to other people and so on. That is how things went and go on till now. We've crossed 500 people now."*

BNI at the national level has a well-defined, professionally managed team and process. They're very involved and helpful with whatever the region needs. No matter what the problem is, they efficiently cater to any and every challenge, concern, or requirement of every region. Their projections in terms of revenue cost and borrowing were immaculate. The amounts vary as per franchise, and they're very efficient in their estimations.

Rajkumar shares that the BNI platform can connect people across the globe via the BNI network through a software called BNI Connect. It is like a private social media platform used by the members of BNI in order to manage the whole franchisee business. The software stores analytical data to manage your business well. This way you can identify areas of focus too.

In his opinion, there is no platform in competition to BNI operating with the same professionalism or scale of operations across the globe. BNI was started in 1983 by Dr. Ivan Misner and they've improved significantly with time. With a focus on developing robust processes and culture, BNI is the global leader in business networking organizations. *"There have been instances where one of our members has tried venturing out and starting something similar, but it didn't work."* BNI believes in collaboration and growth, rather than competition.

Rajkumar's journey with BNI did not just end with bringing BNI to Goa region. In fact, in 2014 he was elected to be one of the members of the Franchisee Advisory Board. Currently, he heads the board. This escapade has given Rajkumar an insight into identifying the right people for the BNI franchise. He has been involved in interviewing franchisees for different regions in India. He has also been requested to interview franchisees beyond India also.

BNI also offers expansion opportunities by covering additional regions provided there is bandwidth to manage that. Key parameters like past performance, organizing strengths, etc. are evaluated for the same.

BNI has introduced various means of keeping their franchisees up-to-date on the changes and happenings within and around the BNI network. There is a platform called a Bulletin Board. From within India there is a platform called Success Flag and globally, another one called Elevate, which is extensively used by regions.

When we asked him if, given a chance, he would go for the same decision of investing in BNI again, Rajkumar says, *"Very much. More than money, it's the time that we invest. In that time, I'm passionate about what I do so it feels great."* But he foresees having some trouble with finding passionate people who'd take up regional projects that can minimize all the other challenges.

Rajkumar personifies "DREAM BIG." His next big goal is Vibrant Goa. Outsourcing work from Goa and bringing people together to collaborate with global networks is his passion. To spark and redefine Goan business based on trends now.

His advice to all aspiring franchisee owners is—if the franchisee has good experience in the line of business, then franchising is the best way to enter business. It helps in saving up on those initial 5 years that would otherwise be spent on collecting expertise and experience in the particular field. This saves time. So one can learn more in less time.

Talking to this passionate and positive person has filled us with a lot of optimism and hope. A go-getter attitude coupled with perseverance and hard work can take one a long way. Mr. Rajkumar Kamat truly exemplifies this. He is surely an example for people who want to dream big and have bigger goals. On that note, we take his leave and close the curtains on this interview.

Interview with Karthikeyan R. Naidu, franchisee of Jumboking

About your company: Omisha Enterprises is a franchisee of Jumboking and owns two stores at D N Nagar Metro Station (both the exits)
Products and Services: All approved products as per the menu of Jumboking
No of years: 2 years 6 months
No of employees: 8
No of customers: More than 30,000 customers per month catered
Vision of the company: To be the leading Franchisee of Jumboking delivering consistent quality products and excellent customer focused service.

How long have you been in the franchisee business?
30 months.

From all the vast industries in the economy, what made you choose this particular industry to invest in?
Food and Education were and are the two growing sectors. Hence, chose the former for an allied business line of operations.

What was it that attracted you about this franchise business?
Before zeroing upon this brand, a thorough market research was done. I have personally met the master franchisees of various brands. However, the transparency and clarity found in Jumboking was not seen elsewhere.

How many franchisees do you own?
Only one: Jumboking.

Take us through the initial steps on this journey:
After the research which went on for more than 4 months, we signed up with Jumboking. As mentioned earlier, the staple diet of millions and the transparency found during the first meet urged us to go ahead with Jumboking. We signed the LOI (Letter of Intent) the very next day. Within 10 days, the property for putting up the store was finalized and we went ahead with the civil and electrical and equipment work. The outlet was operational within 2 months from the date of signing of the LOI.

What are the challenges that you faced, and were you prepared for it?
I was prepared for the nuances of starting of the business. This was a completely new business model for me, as I come from an engineering and management background. I was associated with the petroleum industry in the project engineering, sales, and management divisions. However, the motive of diversification was thought of before entering this business. I was prepared to devote the next 6 months to understand the business in totality before multiplying.

What do you enjoy most about running this business?
The statement of purposes, audits, training, supply chain, and logistics are all managed by the company side. The only things as a franchisee I need to manage are the store operations and customer service. I enjoy interacting with the customers and continuously add value to the business I am in.

What is it, which stresses you in this business?
Having spent three seasons at the first store, I have matured as an entrepreneur. The business has its own variation due to flow of human traffic. Like the seasonal holidays, the long weekends, the public or bank holidays, etc. impact the business. But if the analysis is done on a yearly basis, the returns are stable and acceptable.

What was the impact of running the franchisee upon your family and social life initially? How different is it now?
Initially while starting the franchisee, I was devoting more than 13 hours a day at the store. This was primarily done to develop my team at the store, understand my customers, understand and implement the SOPs, audits, trainings, etc. and develop my business model. This was done in the initial 3 months and my family had a tough time seeing me less than usual. However, after the set up, the operations and systems have been in place and the quality of personal life has improved considerably.

How has your experience matched up to what the franchisor told you, when taking the franchisee?
I would say 90 percent of what was discussed during the meet has been fulfilled. The gap was primarily due to my assumption, which was in turn taken care of.

What would you say as the benefit of having a franchisee, over starting your own business?
In a franchise model pertaining to a QSR, the supply chain, logistics, training, product development, audits, etc. are all taken care of by the systems in place. The only focus is on customer service. The challenges against starting a new business vis-a-vis following a successful franchise module are far more and not recommended for a first time business person.

What is the secret of your success?
Persistent efforts at the store level, managing staff, and improving customer service on a daily basis are the mantras for success. There is this continuous learning and progress at the store level, which leads to success.

What care should be taken when investing a franchisee?
Identify the options, make a detailed study, understand the pros and cons, understand the roles and responsibilities of a franchisee, do not assume anything, and get all the first hand data from the franchisor. Take legal or professional help while finalizing the franchisee document and once fully comfortable, invest in that brand.

Is investing in a franchisee risky?
Of course all business comes with the risk factor. The projection if the business is based upon estimation and analysis. There are reasons for failures beyond one›s control. One should be mature enough to understand the nuances of business and only then invest.

What are the ideal qualities of someone looking to run a franchisee business?
The ideal franchisee is the one who can sincerely devote his/her 8-10 hours a day for the first 5-6 months in the business. The franchisee has to understand each and every detail of his business and then multiply the count every 6-9 months. Build a system to take care of business and grow together.

What sort of support did you receive when you first opened? How helpful was it?
The franchisor had extended support with property finalization, civil and electrical and interior works at the outlet, training, audit, SOPs, and staff management and other related activities to run the store. The basic understanding at the store level was imparted to me which helped me scale up asap.

How the initial training provided by the franchisor help you run the business?
As discussed, the initial training helped me to understand the basics. Within a fortnight the operations were well under control and the focus shifted to customer service and store success.

What training program have you gone through?
Some 2 days theoretical and 6 days practical at an audited company approved store. This was followed by test where I had to score minimum 80 percent to proceed.

Has the training program changed since the beginning?
If yes, has it improved? Yes, it has changed and improved for good. It is more comprehensive now with emphasis on documentation and video coverage of SOP.

What successful marketing strategies were implemented at the beginning of the franchisee business, and how effective were they?
We run JK of the Day promotion as BTL at the store level. Rest is local marketing through pamphlets and branding.

How involved is the franchisor in terms of support on an ongoing basis?
One hundred percent involment on a day to day basis.

How often and what marketing and promotional campaigns are provided?
Our business model is more through word of mouth. However, the newspaper and print media advertisements are in full swing.

What additional activities do you have to carry out yourself to promote your business?
None.

Was there any specialist software provided? Do all franchisees use the same system?
Yes. We have a licensed POS (Point of Sale Terminal) license for our business.

What about the territory in which your franchisee operated? Does it give you favorable returns or is it limited?
The area is good enough for a store to make enough money for ROI to be more than 55 percent per annum.

Does the franchise offer any great competitive advantages, when we compare with the level of competition from other brands?
Yes.

How would you describe your relationship with the franchisor and other franchisees?
Good and mutually beneficial.

Is there good two-way communication with the franchisor? How does this happen?
We have a ticketing system to raise an issue; we discuss the prospects and other business-related activities.

How frequently do you hear from the franchisor's representatives? Do they assist you in operating your business?
Absolutely. The master franchisee and his team get in touch with us on a daily basis if need be else on a weekly basis for audits.

If you want to make a complaint, how do you do it, and how does the franchisor respond?
As discussed, the ticketing system helps in addressing the complaints.

What is the most negative thing you can say about the franchisor?
None.

Were the franchisor's projections correct about the amount of capital and/or borrowing you would initially require?
Yes. The initial investment was a nautch higher than expected. But the returns were close to projections.

Have you had to increase your investment since?
No. However, as and when we introduce a new equipment for better operations, there has been additional investment.

Were there any hidden fees or unexpected costs?
May be 3–5 percent, which is part and parcel of any investment modules.

What was your approximate investment?
All inclusive 23 lakhs.

What is the ROI; how much time did it take to breakeven?
17 months.

Has the return been in line with your expectations?
Yes.

How do you stay updated on industry trends?
We have weekly huddles where the discussion is at micro and macro levels to understand the industry and market.

Are there expansion opportunities for additional franchise ownership in this system?
If the franchise finds time and wants to diversify, the franchisor has no reservations.

Knowing what you know now, would you make this investment again?
Yes.

What challenges do you foresee in the future for your business?
As this is a fast moving snack segment, we don›t see a dearth of business at least in the next 5 years. Touch wood!

What is your next big goal?
To scale up to five stores and develop a concrete system to manage this scaled-up business.

What is your message for people looking to invest in franchisees?
I will once again recommend a matured decision after studying the details and nuances. Jot down all the pros and cons and take a head start. Invest time, money, and efforts judiciously backed by the franchisor support and meet SUCCESS!

1. A leader can either lead or bleed

All major success stories in entrepreneurship that I have seen primarily have one thing in common. Each enterprise has an inspiring leadership at the top. Managers can ensure efficiency in an organization, but to envision and create something out of nothing, you need great leaders with unparalleled vision and drive. These great leaders carve a path for themselves to achieve their dreams and motivate others to follow their path.

"The future belongs to those who believe in the beauty of their dreams," said Eleanor Roosevelt. An undying faith in your dream and the willingness to sweat it out without getting discouraged is the sign of a true leader. But what is important is to onboard your team with your vision. It gives them clarity and direction, creating higher chances of success to manifest. We see 95 percent of the businesses failing in the first few years of business due to lack of efficient leadership and absence of clarity in the team's understanding of the direction the business owner wants his business to grow.

Now, I have noticed that when the path to the end result is broken down into achievable targets, the process becomes easier and attainable. Goals are normally of three types:

1. Limitation Goal
2. Reaction Goal
3. Aspiration Goal.

<u>Limitation Goal</u> is set based on a past result. For example, if I have achieved INR 10 lakhs turnover last year, I will strive for 10 percent increase in revenue this year, which is INR 11 lakhs. This goal is purely based on past numbers, without giving any consideration to factors like economy, capabilities, etc.

Reaction Goal is based on benchmarks set based on others' achievements. For example, competitor achieved INR 10 crore turnover, so I should set a goal of INR 11 crores to show a competitive edge.

Aspiration Goal is also called as Inspirational Goal. These are value-added goals resulting in generating huge profit and business transformation. It is a futuristic goal, resulting in positive momentum and ultimate growth (personal and business). An aspiration goal can be created by a true leader. And he will also infuse energy and zest into the team molding an average team into a great one.

2. What money making activity will I do today?

Business is always done to make profits. And a business owner must never deviate from this primary goal of his business; else it is doomed to fail. Of the various activities that a business entails, HR, R&D, and Accounts are the backend operations or business servicing activities while the most revenue generating activity is Sales. As an entrepreneur you should focus most of your time in this activity. This activity generates revenue and leads to cash flow in business that drives business. A higher turnover also means that the customer trusts your brand. Customer acquisition and retention is the core to any successful sales strategy and needs utmost emphasis.

It is critical to focus on this activity for a sustainable business model. As the business grows, a dedicated and highly skilled sales force has to be developed to manage this process. An efficient sales management program has to be developed that can track progress, train the team regularly, and report to the senior management. Accountability to showcase results is very important. Your customers' trust is the biggest asset in your organization. Companies that are successful and experience continuous growth have a large sales force and they get trained on a regular basis and it has been said that most successful companies do role plays for the sales team every day before visiting clients.

So, in addition to sales, another money making activity is capacity building. This includes:

1. Hiring the right talent
2. Training and development of the recruits
3. Goal setting and performance appraisal
4. Appreciation.

If you follow this cycle, I can guarantee, you will develop a highly skilled workforce of intrapreneurs who will bring your dream to reality.

3. Make your business dashboard

As a business owner, it is impossible to be involved in every small detail of business. To ensure that you can monitor the progress and challenges of all seven core departments of business, it is important to get all the information in a consolidated and simple form. This can be achieved through a business dashboard that will help you read, analyze, track, and take decision effectively.

Here, I always give the analogy of a vehicle. Every car, truck, or two wheeler truck has dashboard. It has gages, speedometer, RPM meter, fuel gauge, oil gage, indicator light, main light, oil status, sidelight indicator. The entire vehicle's performance can be assimilated through this dashboard. It has display and messaging through alerts for seat belts or an open door. A complete performance assessment system in a single dashboard.

So I feel that a Business is like a six wheeler truck:

The six wheels are the six functions as below:

1. Marketing
2. Sales
3. Operation
4. Accounts
5. Research & Development
6. Human Resource.

As the business owner, you are the driver, and you need to have complete access to the dashboard to understand and monitor the performance of all functions. Based on your end goal, you maneuver the vehicle and periodically check the dashboard and other vitals to ensure a smooth ride.

To take this analogy a bit further, I want to say, if there is no clarity in your vision and goals, your vehicle might not reach its destination or take much longer and the drive might get bumpy!

With technology aiding businesses with interactive tools, you can find multiple free and paid tools that can help analyze the business performance. Using these dashboards in regular status meetings helps gage individual performance as well as strategize and build the model further. You just need to ensure that the tool you use is easy to understand and configure, else the acceptance will be poor.

4. Invest wisely in what is required

Do you remember KSTPI? What does it stand for? Yes, you're right— Knowledge, Skills Technology, People, and Infrastructure.

Knowledge is critical in all your business decisions. And one of the first decisions you need to take is about capital investment. Investment decisions can make or break a business. So make a business plan and work with your financial advisors, discuss, and negotiate with your vendors and finally arrive at a realistic estimate of investment needed to kick start your business. Decisions like investment in capital goods and infrastructure, estimation for expenses like grand launches of the store etc. can be made based on your available funds. Remember, there are operational costs like HR, R&D; Marketing cannot be ignored while estimating your capital requirement. While choosing your marketing budget, first do a pilot and test what works best for your nature of business. Don't follow the herd mentality and overspend unnecessarily.

If you are starting a franchisee, most of these expenses are provided in the form of a franchisee fee, but for a traditional business, this challenge is crucial. Advantage of being a franchisee is that the franchisor gives provisional financial statement for the next 5 years.

Good entrepreneurs invest money in hiring competent professional who can give:

1. Revenue statement
2. HR cost
3. Equipment costing
4. Setup cost
5. Income statement.

The franchisor provides readymade estimates and working to the franchisee, so you can ask the right questions to the franchisor to get clarity to avoid over capitalization and under capitalization. While starting a new business is exhilarating, taking business decisions requires a practical approach, which is based heavily on analysis. If these decisions are based on emotions or sentiments, miscalculations are more than likely resulting in over expenditure and losses.

5. Be happy and hungry

A positive mind can generate a positive environment and spread happiness. Such environment is an incubation for great ideas and growing business. It enhances team spirit and team bonding. So be happy. Be happy for who you are and be happy for who you are going to be and stay hungry for success.

We are caught in a world of win and loss. World filled with happiness and sadness, a world full of depression. But I feel that happiness is our nature least dependent on external conditions. You don't require a reason to be happy. It is human nature. The more you relate happiness as your state of mind and the less you correlate it to materialistic gains, you will always be happy. This is why young children are mostly happy. A long forgotten trait, which we need to re-embrace.

How to maintain happiness?
Did you know—a child smiles 400 times in a day and an adult smiles 20 times? Once you can isolate your mental state from the physical gains in the world, you can always remain happy. Life throws many things at you. But know that what doesn't break you makes you stronger. So they're learning lessons, not causes for depression.

You really achieve success in your personal and professional life by following this particular philosophy. To be successful as a person and a business, one must understand and imbibe the rules of social responsibility. The more you give, the more you gain. It is that simple. But yet so many people in life have failed to understand this. They want before they can give, they want higher wages, and they want more success.

I met a wise man once who made a very interesting quote that has stayed with me forever—*Knowledge decides what to say, attitude decides how to say, skill decides how much to say and wisdom decides whether to say or not.*

6. Try first with one store - taste success and set others

A franchise business offers a readymade setup with modules, schedules, strategies, and structure pre-defined by the franchisor. This gives you the opportunity to first train yourself on the processes and procedures. Once mastered, these techniques can be taught to the team so that they become self-starters in running the business for you. This way, you can venture into starting more than one outlet and maximize your gain in the franchisee business. In franchise world, sometimes a smart franchisor gives discount on opening multiple franchises.

Once the team is trained, make them responsible. It is very important to start delegating responsibility once your team starts giving results and allow them little space to grow. Don't expect perfection at this stage but expect progress. I always say, *"Perfection is a myth, progress is the key. Doing it again and again will give you perfection."*

Use technique of 10-10-10. This technique works like magic. Give feedback periodically. You can use the three magical questions technique. It creates awareness in an employee. It helps them to introspect on their action and stick to their role and goal.

Managing a single outlet is easy, managing multiple outlets require skill. It requires completely different type of mindset. Your master franchisor will help you by teaching you how to manage multiple outlets. Managing the second outlet is the most critical. Once you learn to manage the second outlet, managing multiple outlets is easy. You can then set up a chain of outlets and sign for an area franchise at this stage. Your income is now not dependent on a single outlet. When your income is more than your expenses, at this stage you can experience financial freedom. Invest wisely at this stage and don't keep all eggs in the same basket. Let your money earn more money for you.

Let us look at the story of Kuldeep Kumar, who is running nine branches of Hello Kids Franchisee.

Kuldeep Kumar –
A businessman who brings education and business together

This franchise owner was difficult to connect. He is a busy man running nine branches of Hello Kids franchisees. Starting in 2007, he has been successfully running this business for over 12 years now. He has a total of over 400 students and aims to open new new branch of Hello Kids preschool every year.

We bring to you Mr. Kuldeep Kumar. We thank him profusely for giving us is time in spite of a hectic schedule and an ailing father. His honest responses and clear vision were inspiring.

In a recession-laden industry, Kumar realized that education and healthcare were the only two sectors that would thrive. He chose Hello Kids franchise mainly because Hello Kids was the only preschool with a no-royalty model, which is very attractive financially for a franchisee.

Now a professional in setting up new franchisees, Kumar is quite hands-on with the entire process. The only challenge he finds in the preschool industries is getting good teachers and maids, finding good premises, and doing right marketing. *"Your marketing strategy can make or break your business,"* he says.

Kumar is passionate about the pre-K industry. Some 80 percent of brain development of the child happens in 0-6 years of age and it is this period when the child can be molded the most. He finds satisfaction that they are playing a very good part in imparting quality education to this future generation of the country. We couldn't help smiling when he says—*"The best part of my job is to see the smiling young faces every day in the morning."* Of course, money can be earned everywhere, but someone who appreciates these small pleasures is indeed an inspiring person.

What Kuldeep finds the most challenging is the lack of disciplined attitude in parents who feel it is their right to reach out with complaints or questions at any time during the day or night. While the parents do appreciate the efforts of the institution at the end of the school year, these every day struggles are overbearing at times. Another struggle is keeping the target number of students. Kumar's internal target is 450 students, and getting the numbers in place is another challenge, which is core to the industry he operates in.

But Kumar is very happy with the Hello Kids franchisee and highly advocates the franchisee business to everyone. The founder, Mr. Pritam is very involved and accessible for his franchisee owners to answer and attend to queries and grievances, which bring comfort to the franchisees that are new to the business. He feels it's better to learn from others mistake rather than commit your own mistake. In a franchisee, the franchiser is always there to guide you. So finally you save a lot of time and money. Business risk exists in every business. But in his opinion, for a new business owner, franchising is comparatively less risky, especially if you have chosen your franchisor with care. If your decision is wrong, someone might just take your money and run away, but a little bit research and talking to the right set of people can tell you how good your franchiser is.

His experience with Hello Kids was always pleasant. When he started off for the first time, he got all kind of support from their team. Be it monetary support or information sharing, they were always available. One thing which Kuldeep likes about Hello Kids is their training, which is a continuous process. They have trainings every year for continuous improvement with changing market trends. They have various kinds of training programs including business trainings as well. Over the years, the training programs have also evolved to keep people engaged. The changing curriculums and newer teaching patterns also create newer programs for the team.

Being a senior member of the Hello Kids family, Kumar is involved in trainings at the corporate level. This brings him in regular contact with the other franchisees as well and this has resulted in a friendly, almost family-like relationship with others.

One thing which makes Kuldeep Kumar a thorough businessman is his attitude toward marketing. *"Marketing is not an expense but an investment,"* he says and believes in using different and unique marketing strategies than the competitors.

Kumar boasts about using some of the most advanced marketing techniques in the preschool industry. From the start of his first franchise, he has invested heavily in marketing, giving him a cutting edge over competition. As in every case, competition followed his footsteps, but this marketing investment has helped him achieve the targets he has set for his franchisees.

The franchisor does not provide marketing support for each individual franchisee. The franchisee owner is expected to do it themselves. But Kumar justifies this approach by stating that the franchisor does not charge royalty from the franchisee, so this compensates and leaves enough funds with the franchisee to invest in marketing.

Kumar encourages people to think long term while entering a franchise business. *"If you have a short term vision to remain in the franchise and eventually start on your own, it would be difficult to maximize the return on investment as you're unable to do justice to either businesses,"* he says. Parents mostly take admissions based on the brand name and if you leave the franchise to start on your own, there is a high probability of losing the admissions, resulting in skewed returns and significant loss in quality. Creating a new brand takes time. So separating from the franchise to start your own setup definitely has challenges with long-term effects on the business, feels Kumar.

Kuldeep uses the franchisor's payment gateway for fees and other payments. He is very happy with the returns the franchisees are earning except the new ones which take time to setup and establish themselves. Because of the no-royalty model followed by the franchisor, the franchisees are able to maintain a competitive advantage.

The franchisor themselves have kept a transparent communication with the other franchisees. The owner, Mr. Pritam is available to talk whenever anyone needs using any common medium like email, WhatsApp, or telephone call. Escalations are also efficiently managed with emails and a record response time. This effective two-way communication builds greater confidence in the minds of the franchisees for the founders and their team. Any new trends or notifications are communicated by the franchisor's team to all franchisees over email regularly. This keeps them abreast with the news and trends effectively.

Kumar encourages people to take responsibility for their own business. In a no-royalty business model, which works in the favor of the franchisee, he urges the franchisee owners to avoid keeping unnecessary expectations and take more ownership of their business. *After all, a franchiser can give you full support, but he can't give you a business,* he quips wisely.

He was very happy with the initial financial projections made by the franchisor for his business. There are no hidden fees. Most franchisees miscalculate when they plan for their franchisees. There are two types of investments—an initial investment and market investment. Most franchisees miss considering the market investment while working on their projections. So if there is an initial franchisee fee of INR 5 lakhs, he also kept a provision of INR 2 lakhs for running the preschool. But with efficient planning, he was able to manage the expenses within INR 2 lakhs itself.

Have you had to increase your investment since you started?

No ma'am, because after the initial investment, you earn, then you invest to grow more, same amount of investment is required to open new school that's how it's going to work.

Kumar has invested around INR 70–80 lakhs in all nine branches. He hit his breakeven with a record 2 months' time, which is an amazing feat. This was beyond his own expectations.

From here, we started a rapid fire round with Mr. Kuldeep Kumar to get a general understanding of his business model.

As a franchisee what do you think is essential to make this type of a business model a success?
Trust in the franchisor is the key. It is important to follow their instructions completely. Halfhearted efforts will only generated halfhearted results. Trusting the franchisor and following their rules will help make this business model a success.

How do you stay updated on industry trends?
Attending all trainings provided by the franchisor can help you update your knowledge about the latest trends and happenings. Regularly reading the franchisor's groups and messages is also equally important.

As you train people also so you need to attend trainings a lot also right?
Yes, I am a trainer, so I attend a lot of trainings. But there are many franchisees who are not attending all trainings as it is an additional cost to them.

Are there any expansion opportunities for additional franchisee ownership in this system?
Yeah ma'am, I am running nine.

Knowing what you know now would you make this investment again? You will say yes right?
Yeah.

What challenges do you for see in the future for your business?
Other than changes in government regulations, I don't see any challenges. Sudden change in government regulations can be the only big challenge.

What is your next big goal?
I would like to increase my turnover to INR 1 crore per annum. For that, if I need to start 10 more franchisees, I will start.

What is your message to people who are looking to invest in a franchisee or a franchisee business?
I would always recommend people to start a franchisee rather than their own business. Learning from others' mistake is cheaper than making your own and learning from them.

It was a real pleasure talking to Mr. Kuldeep Kumar, one of the most successful franchisee owners with nine franchisees of Hello Kids in his name. We thank him for taking the time and answering all our questions, as we slowly close the curtains on this interview.

7. Helicopter ride

Helicopter ride is viewing your business dashboard parameter, without being a part of daily activity, conducting meetings with management, giving feedback and exploring new ideas of business growth. You should be playing the role of mentor and coach or trainer if required.

Leading silently or leading from behind is the philosophy to be followed, so that the team can take charge 100 percent.

Once you become financially free, you can start pursuing your dream and passion, whilst taking a helicopter ride to check business progress. Keep the dashboard in your control and you have to train others who are more competent and committed to you to drive your businesses.

Regularly take helicopter ride to audit and protect your asset while ensuring that the team is working toward the common goal that you have set for the business. After all, it is your baby. Through the role of a coach, mentor you are inspiring your team to work toward and achieve that team goal. Your involvement in business can be limited to reviewing high level performance metrics and exploring areas for expansion and investment.

As Donald Trump says, *"Don't get attached to your assets."* So if you have a golden opportunity to sell your business, go ahead. With the money earned, you can invest in another idea or business and move ahead.

The story of the Chinese bamboo tree

There is a parable of the Chinese Bamboo Tree that teaches us lessons about patience, faith, growth, and the potential of our business.

Like any plant, growth of the Chinese Bamboo Tree requires nurturing with water, fertile soil, and sunshine. In its first year, there are no visible signs of activity. In the second year, again there is no growth above the soil. The third, the fourth, still nothing. Our patience is tested and we begin to wonder if our efforts will ever be rewarded.

And finally in the fifth, the Chinese Bamboo Tree grows 80 feet in just six weeks. But let's be serious, does the Chinese Bamboo Tree really grow 80 feet in six weeks? Did the Chinese Bamboo Tree lie dormant for 4 years only to grow exponentially in the fifth? Or, was the little tree growing underground, developing a root system strong enough to support its potential for outward growth in the fifth year and beyond? The answer is, of course, obvious. The Chinese Bamboo Tree was growing underground, developing a root system strong enough to support its potential for the growth in the fifth year. If the tree had not developed a strong unseen foundation it could not have sustained its life as it grew. The same principle is true for people who want to start a business. People who patiently toil toward their dreams and goals, building strong character while overcoming adversity and challenges, grow a strong internal foundation to handle success.

Had the Chinese Bamboo Tree farmer dug up his little seed every year to see if it was growing, he would have stunted the Chinese Bamboo tree's growth. Starting your own business is very similar. We often water and fertilize our ideas over and over again and for months without results. However, by staying focused and working toward your goal, remarkable progress can take place in an amazing manner within a short period of time just like the Chinese bamboo tree.

Yet, all of this requires one thing, Faith. The cultivators of the Chinese Bamboo Tree have faith that if they keep watering and fertilizing the ground, the tree will break through. Well, you must have the same kind of faith in your business when planning to start it. This is the hardest part for most of us. We get so excited about the idea that's been planted inside of us that we simply can't wait for it to blossom. Therefore, within initial days or months, we become discouraged and begin to second guess ourselves, or worse, quit.

What this story teaches us is Faith can take us a long way. From a laborer at the gas station to owning the biggest industrial conglomerate in the country, Mr. Dhirubhai Ambani's journey is inspirational. And this was not possible without the power of dreams and faith in yourself.

Henry Ford had to water his Chinese Bamboo Tree through many business failures before he finally succeeded with the Ford Motor Company. So don't give up on your Chinese Bamboo Tree growing inside of you just waiting to break through. Keep watering and believe that you too will be flying high before you know it.

Scan this QR code to get the FREE additional bonus chapter on How to Lead Silently

Or visit www.sameerindia.com/leadsilently

SAMEER KUNCOLIEKAR

Sameer Kuncoliekar is an Author, Entrepreneur, and Social Activist who is on a mission to help educate aspirant entrepreneurs and corporate professionals on how to start a low investment and high profit food business. Sameer is currently running two successful businesses, as he moved from the traditional people-oriented business format to a system-oriented business. With his vast experience in the food industry for over 21 years and in-depth research of systems, strategies, and team building he has been able to decode the science behind successful businesses.

After looking at the competitions in the earlier era, where business would suffer in the fight to survive, he has understood that in today's world businesses have to collaborate and come together to serve the society as a whole. Taking the three decade old company to new heights across PAN India is the main force that drives him to work harder constantly, and the big vision behind everything he does. A visionary, he is a firm believer in creating growth opportunities for employees, customers, channel partners, and the company as a whole.

He is an ardent follower of Sri Sri Ravi Shankar and an apex member of Art of Living www.artofliving.org. He has always strived to help people and give back to the society hence in year 2013, he launched a PAN India social project SaveLife India www.savelifeindia.org (Blood Donors Network) that currently has 20,000+ donors registered, which has helped save lives of thousands of people due to timely donation of blood. He always believes in building something that will last even after he is long gone.

He is also the Editor in Chief of the E-magazine Food Experts of India; he created this platform as a dedication to his father with an aim to provide recognition to individuals who, like him, are successful and working devotedly for improving customer experience and the food industry as a whole. He aims to inspire and guide the youth who aspire to make a career in the customer- centric hospitality industry with these inspirational stories.

ABOUT OUR VENTURES

Ambica Chicken

Is a 35-year-old, leading brand in the food industry in Goa supplying best quality poultry products like chicken and eggs to a large client base through 10 outlets across the state and has been a major supplier to Resorts, Hotels, and Caterers providing excellent service backed with trusted and quality supply. Moving from the traditional way of doing business into an organized sector has been a major revolution of the company. The company also has a wide variety of ready to fry products in Chicken, Veg, and Fish Categories under the brand name Ambica that are supplied in Goa and outside, and are produced in world-class manufacturing facilities.

Visit www.ambica.ltd to know more.

Ambica Hotspot

In today's competitive food industry the QSR format has emerged as a winner. The ease and financial freedom of creating and operating a QSR outlet has been a major contributor in the growth of this new format. Currently international players have established themselves in the Indian Market.

The combination of extensive research that included conducting surveys of PAN India, working with India's best chef, along with the backing of 30 years of experience in the food industry, ensured Ambica Hotspot to be able to bring together not only the finest and healthiest ingredients into the recipes, but a caravan of flavors from corners of the world which is now associated with the brand, and infusing them in the delicious range of Hot Magic Fries, Burgers, Hots & Crispy Chicken, Wraps, Hotdogs and Beverages; the result is an experience of a hearty flavorsome meal that customers just cannot get enough of.

The company has worked with the best international coaches, to develop systems and strategies to run this model successfully. The vision is to take our food encompassing caravan of flavors of the world, to every city in India. The name Ambica Hotspot itself speaks about creating our QSR zones across India. We believe in sharing successful business opportunities, and are looking for committed and driven entrepreneurs who would like to grow with this franchisee opportunity.

Visit www.ambicahotspot.com to know more.

Food Experts of India

This is a blog site or e-magazine created by Mr. Sameer Kuncoliekar. Food experts of India is a platform, where successful personalities working tirelessly in the food industry are recognized, their stories brought forward, their journey and challenges shared with the audience to be an inspiration to the future generation. Sameer has grown up watching his father, Mr. Kanta Kuncoliekar – founder of Ambica Chicken, toil the midnight oil to ensure customer satisfaction through superior quality maintenance. Striving to build a business through effective vendor management and efficient customer servicing left little time for family. Although these unswerving efforts in the competitive food industry gained him a trusted brand name, his contribution toward building it went unrecognized by the society. This left a mark on his son.

Mr. Sameer took over the reins of the business from his father with a dream and commitment to take the business to newer heights, equipped with experience and an undying focus to succeed. He created this platform as a dedication to his father with an aim to provide recognition to individuals who, like himself, are successful and working devotedly for improving customer experience and the food industry as a whole. He plans to educate the masses about the hardships and efforts in the F&B segment with these inspirational stories. He wants to inspire and guide the youth who aspire to make a career in the customer-centric hospitality industry. These stories also aim to motivate the new generation.

Visit www.foodexpertsofindia.com to know more.

RESOURCES

Kiyosaki, Robert (2011). *Rich Dad, Poor Dad: What the Rich Teach their Kids About Money that the Poor and Middle Class Do Not!* Perseus Books Group

Art of Living
Rajiv Talreja Seminars

BONUS PAGE

Scan this QR code to get the FREE Declarations that are a powerful self-talk. The most successful people in life have an empowering way to communicate with themselves. With these declarations you can practice positive self-talk throughout your day, and you will begin to realize more favorable rewards in life.

Or visit www.sameerindia.com/declarations

Scan this QR code to get the FREE Daily Planner that will help you to focus on the most important activities, keep track of them and avoid running out of time because of poor task prioritizing.

Or visit www.sameerindia.com/dailyplanner

Scan this QR code to get the FREE additional bonus chapter on How to Lead Silently

Or visit www.sameerindia.com/leadsilently

If you are keen on starting a franchisee business, and need some help you can reach me on sameer@sameerindia.com

To learn more about financial education, join our seminars at www.sameerindia.com/seminar

If you are looking to contribute to my mission, write to us on sameer@sameerindia.com

ABOUT SUCCESS GYAN PUBLISHING

We believe that everyone has knowledge to share and lessons to teach and what better way to do so than through a book.

Success Gyan Publishing, a publishing house formed with the mission to bring out the creative genius within everyone, aims to simplify the book publishing process for those who wish to share their knowledge through books.

Earlier, if you were to write and publish a book, you needed an agent to get a publishing house to look at your manuscript and even then there was no guarantee that they will publish your book.

Now, if you're wondering if there's a better way, there most certainly is. You can now take control of your book and how it is published through the Success Gyan Publishing platform. From planning your book cover to setting a timeline, the SGP team makes this daunting journey to becoming an author.

We are on a mission to help business owners and professionals to bring out the book in them, and help them transform their business or profession, by becoming an author.

Website - www.sgpublication.com
Email - info@successgyan.com

www.ingramcontent.com/pod-product-compliance
Lightning Source LLC
Chambersburg PA
CBHW030942240526
45463CB00016B/1214